# The Heinemann
# TOEFL®
## Practice Tests

Carolyn B. Duffy and M. Kathleen Mahnke

## HEINEMANN

TOEFL® is a registered trademark of Educational Testing Service. However, there
is no connection between Heinemann International and Educational Testing Service.

from Heather to Walentyne

## The Heinemann TOEFL® Practice Tests

*The Heinemann TOEFL Practice Tests* book is designed to help students prepare for the TOEFL (Test of English as a Foreign Language). To create reliable and valid tests for this book, the authors conducted extensive research into the TOEFL. They examined TOEFL test items, characterizing them in terms of material tested and difficulty level. Following this analysis, they wrote questions with the same characteristics as those on the TOEFL and incorporated these questions into practice TOEFLs and then pilot tested these tests with international students from over twenty different countries. From these pilot tests, the authors selected only those questions that, when statistically analyzed, worked in the same way that official TOEFL questions do. Using these questions, they created the practice tests that are found in this book and its companion, *The Heinemann TOEFL Preparation Course*. These tests contain all of the question types found on the TOEFL, and they function in the same way that official TOEFLs do.

## The Heinemann TOEFL® Preparation Course Program

Additional materials accompany *The Heinemann TOEFL Practice Tests* to complete the Heinemann TOEFL course of study.

The Heinemann TOEFL Practice Tests Cassettes are a set of two cassette tapes containing recordings of the listening comprehension sections of the five practice tests.

*The Heinemann TOEFL Preparation Course* book provides a step-by-step guide to developing the language skills and test-taking strategies which can be taught and mastered to promote student success on the TOEFL. This book is accompanied by the *Heinemann TOEFL Tapescripts and Answers* book that provides a script for all listening comprehension exercises and tests, and the Heinemann TOEFL Course Cassettes that contain recordings of the listening comprehension sections of the tests and exercises used in the text.

Heinemann International
A division of Heinemann Publishers (Oxford), Ltd.
Halley Court, Jordan Hill, Oxford OX2 8EJ, U.K.

| | | | | |
|---|---|---|---|---|
| OXFORD | LONDON | EDINBURGH | | |
| MADRID | ATHENS | BOLOGNA | PARIS | |
| MELBOURNE | SYDNEY | AUCKLAND | SINGAPORE | TOKYO |
| IBADAN | NAIROBI | HARARE | GABORONE | |
| PORTSMOUTH (NH) | | | | |

Consultant: Jacqueline Flamm

Editorial Direction and Production Management by Robert Ventre Associates, Newburyport, MA
Editorial and Production by Chameleon Publishing Services
Audio Production by Phyllis Dolgin in New York

Printed and bound in the United States

ISBN 0 435 28846 6

92  93  94  95  96  97  10 9 8 7 6 5 4 3 2 1

# Contents Chart

# INTRODUCTION

## About the TOEFL

The TOEFL (Test of English as a Foreign Language) measures the level of English language proficiency of non-native speakers of English. It is written and published by the Educational Testing Service (ETS) of Princeton, New Jersey, U.S.A. The TOEFL is an admissions requirement at over 2,500 colleges and universities in the United States and other parts of the world. In addition, many scholarship and professional certification programs now require their applicants to take the TOEFL.

The TOEFL normally contains 150 questions. Sometimes, in TOEFLs given in the U.S. or Canada, there are 200 questions. When this is the case, the 50 extra TOEFL questions are experimental and do not count in your total TOEFL score. However, these experimental questions are mixed in with the real questions, so you will not know which ones they are. This means that you must do your best on all 200 questions, even those that are experimental.

The TOEFL has four sections: Listening Comprehension, Structure and Written Expression, Vocabulary and Reading Comprehension, and the Test of Written English. The first three sections contain multiple choice questions. Each multiple choice question has four answer choices. The fourth section of the test, the Test of Written English, contains only one question. This question is an essay question.

**Section One: Listening Comprehension**
This section of the test is administered by audiocassette and normally takes between 30 and 40 minutes. There are 50 questions in this section, which has three parts.

Part A: Restatements (20 questions)—In Part A, you choose the correct written restatement of a spoken sentence.

Part B: Mini-Dialogues (15 questions)—In Part B, you choose the correct written answer to a spoken question based on a short spoken dialogue.

Part C: Talks and Longer Conversations (15 questions)—In Part C, you choose the correct written answers to a series of questions about a longer spoken dialogue between two speakers or a talk given by one speaker.

**Section Two: Structure and Written Expression**
You are allowed 25 minutes to complete this section of the test. There are 40 questions in this section, which consists of two subsections.

Structure (15 questions)—In this subsection, you choose grammatically *correct* sentence completions for sentences with missing parts.

Written Expression (25 questions)—In this subsection, you choose the *incorrect* segments in complete sentences.

**Section Three: Vocabulary and Reading Comprehension**
You are allowed 45 minutes to complete this section of the test. There are 60 questions in this section, which consists of two subsections.

Vocabulary (30 questions)—In this subsection, you choose synonyms for underlined words in sentences.

Reading Comprehension (30 questions)—In this subsection, you read passages and answer questions about them.

**Section Four: Test of Written English**
You are allowed 30 minutes to complete this section of the test. You are given a topic and asked to write an essay about that topic. There are two types of essay questions asked on the Test of Written English: comparison and contrast questions, and questions which ask you to interpret charts and graphs. The Test of Written English is not included in all TOEFLs. It is included during the months of September, October, March, and May.

## ABOUT TOEFL SCORES
Each individual section of the TOEFL (not including Section Four, the Test of Written English) is reported as a converted score based on a scale of from below 30 to a high of 68 points.

Your total TOEFL score is reported on a scale of from below 300 to a high of 677 points. This scale is ten times as big as the scale for the individual sections (from below 30 to 68 points). Very few people ever receive less than 300 points on the TOEFL, because it is possible to answer one fourth of the questions correctly just by guessing. If you guess at all the questions on the TOEFL, you are likely to get a score of about 330.

You can use Score Conversion Table 1, which begins on page 185, to estimate your converted score on each of the sections of the Practice TOEFL Tests in this book. You can also use Score Conversion Table 2 to estimate your total TOEFL score for these tests.

The Test of Written English is not included in your total TOEFL score. It is scored separately on a scale of 1 to 6.

## HOW TO REGISTER TO TAKE AN OFFICIAL TOEFL
You can register to take the TOEFL in the United States or Canada by completing the registration form found in the *Bulletin of Information for TOEFL and TSE*. You can receive this free bulletin by writing to:

> TOEFL Registration Office
> P.O. Box 6151
> Princeton, NJ 08541-6151
> USA

There is a special registration bulletin for TOEFLs that are given outside the United States or Canada. If you plan to take the TOEFL in a country other than the United States or Canada, you should ask for the specially prepared *Bulletin of Information, Overseas Edition* from the above address.

## HOW TO PREPARE FOR THE TOEFL
The TOEFL is designed to test a wide variety of skills and abilities in English. For this reason, there are two important steps that you should follow to prepare for it.

1. The first thing you should do is take part in a regular program of study of English. This is best accomplished by enrolling in a course that aims at teaching general proficiency in English, not just TOEFL preparation. Many colleges and universities in the United States and elsewhere offer intensive English programs for developing general proficiency.

2. The second thing you should do is take part in a regular program of TOEFL preparation study. This study should include taking practice TOEFLs. It should also include the study and review of specific TOEFL language skills and test-taking strategies. This is best accomplished by using *The Heinemann TOEFL Preparation Course* along with *The Heinemann TOEFL Practice Tests*. The course book provides the opportunity for in-depth review of all of the language skills that are specifically tested on the TOEFL. In addition, it provides practice using test-taking strategies that are particularly useful for this test.

Students who are the most successful on the TOEFL are those who follow both of the steps listed above.

# About This Book

1. **Test-taking strategies** are presented. You should practice these strategies as you take the tests in this book.

2. **Sample questions** for each of the question types used on the TOEFL are presented and analyzed. You should familiarize yourself with sample questions before you take the tests in this book.

3. **Five practice TOEFL tests** provide you with the opportunity for extensive test-taking practice.

4. **The Listening Comprehension Tapescript** gives you a written version of the listening comprehension section of each practice test. You should use this tapescript to help you understand mistakes that you make on Section One questions.

5. **The Annotated Answer Key** allows you to check your answers to each test. This answer key provides explanations for the answers to the Section Two Structure and Written Expression questions of each practice test and for the reading comprehension questions of Section Three. In addition, next to each correct answer to these questions, you will find a checkpoint number (e.g., R✔7 or G✔22). These numbers refer you to *The Heinemann TOEFL Preparation Course* book where you will find further explanations and exercises. By studying the course book checkpoint studies and exercises for the questions you miss, you will gain a better understanding of why you missed them. You will also learn valuable language and test-taking skills for the next TOEFL test you take.

6. **Score Conversion Tables** allow you to estimate your TOEFL section and total test scores for each test.

7. **Answer Sheets** make it possible for you to practice correctly filling in TOEFL-like forms.

*The Heinemann TOEFL Practice Tests* can be used in a variety of ways, depending on the situation.
- It can be used along with *The Heinemann TOEFL Preparation Course* in a TOEFL preparation class.
- It can be used as a supplementary text for TOEFL practice in a more general English language course.
- It can be used as a self-study text by people who are not enrolled in any formal courses.

In all of these situations, the general procedures recommended for using this book are as follows:
1. Review the TOEFL question types analyzed.

2. Study the strategies presented.

3. Take the five practice TOEFL tests, practicing the strategies you have studied as you go.

4. When you take the tests, try to simulate a real TOEFL test-taking situation as much as possible.
   A. Sit at a comfortable desk in a room that is quiet. Take each test at a time when you will not be interrupted.
   B. Use the answer sheets in the back of the book to record your answers. Use one answer sheet for each test. Carefully fill in the answer circles that correspond to the answers you choose.
   C. Take the test according to the time limits set for official TOEFLs. Section One will last 30–40 minutes and will be self-timed by the audiocassette that accompanies it. Allow yourself 25 minutes to complete Section Two, 45 minutes to complete Section Three, and 30 minutes to complete Section Four. Do not work on more than one section at a time.
   D. Try to take one entire practice TOEFL test at each sitting. If this is not possible, take at least one entire section of each test at a sitting.

6. Score each test using the Answer Key which begins on page 162.

7. Estimate your TOEFL score for each test section and for the total test using the Score Conversion Tables which begin on page 185.

8. Review all of your answers carefully. Look especially carefully at your mistakes and try to understand what caused them. If you need help with this, use *The Heinemann TOEFL Preparation Course* as a guide.

# TOEFL STRATEGIES AND SAMPLE QUESTIONS

## GENERAL TOEFL TEST STRATEGIES

1. Use your time wisely. The TOEFL is a timed test. You must work very quickly and efficiently to finish all of the questions in the time you are allowed. The skill strategy practice in this book will help you learn to budget your time on each section of the TOEFL. In addition, you should bring a watch to the TOEFL so that you can keep track of your time .

2. Don't read the instructions to each TOEFL section. The test instructions used in this text are exactly the same as the ones used on the TOEFL. You should become familiar with these instructions. If you are familiar with them before you take the TOEFL, you do not have to read them when you begin the test. Instead, you can move immediately to the test questions and begin working.

3. If you don't know the answer to a question, GUESS. This is a very important strategy to use when taking the TOEFL. There is no penalty for guessing. You have a twenty-five percent chance of guessing the correct answer to each question. **Unmarked answers will be counted as wrong and will lower your score.**

4. Mark your answer sheet very carefully. To prevent marking answers in the wrong order, you should follow your place on your answer sheet with one finger. Check to see that the number next to this finger is the same as the number of the question you are looking at in your test booklet. When you choose your answer, fill in the circle completely with a Number 2 pencil. If you need to change an answer, erase it completely, and mark your new answer.

5. Do not write in your test booklet. You are not allowed to make any marks on your TOEFL test book during the test.

6. The night before the TOEFL, relax. Don't try to do any serious studying the night before the test. This will only make you nervous and tired. The night before the TOEFL, it is a good idea to relax and go to bed early. Then, you will be at your best for the test.

7. It is a good idea to eat something substantial before the TOEFL. The TOEFL is a long exam, and having something to eat beforehand can help you to focus and concentrate on the test.

8. Arrive at the test center ahead of time. **If you are late for a TOEFL, you will not be allowed to take it.**

# Section One: Listening Comprehension

The purpose of Section One of the TOEFL is to test your understanding of spoken North American English. Vocabulary, spoken structures, and English sounds and intonation are tested. For the most part, topics used in this section are informal and conversational. Some general academic topics are used in the short lecture segments of this section. Even in these topics, however, the language is not as formal as that used in written English.

Section One contains 50 questions. These questions and the information necessary to answer them are played for you on a tape. Only the answer choices for the questions are printed in the TOEFL test booklet. All Section One questions are spoken only one time. You are allowed 12 seconds to answer each question.

---

### GENERAL STRATEGIES FOR SECTION ONE

1. Be familiar with Section One instructions before you take the official TOEFL. Then, during the test, you do not have to listen to all of the instructions. Listen only long enough to familiarize yourself with the voices on the tape. Be sure you can hear the tape loudly and clearly. **DO NOT turn the page to look ahead while the instructions for Section One are being read.**
2. Listen carefully for meaning in statements, dialogues, and talks. Concentrate on trying to understand the overall meaning.
3. Use your time wisely. You have only 12 seconds to answer each question in Section One of the test.

---

## Listening Comprehension Part A: Restatements

The Part A questions in Section One of the TOEFL measure your ability to understand spoken English sentences. For each question in Part A, you hear a sentence. After you hear the sentence, read the four answer choices in the test book and choose the one that is closest in meaning to the sentence you heard.

The test uses three types of sentences: declaratives, exclamations, and questions. When written, each type of sentence uses different punctuation. A written declarative sentence is a statement followed by a period (.). A written exclamation is an emotional statement followed by an exclamation point (!). A written question is followed by a question mark (?). Most of the sentences you hear in this part are declarative sentences.

There are 20 restatement questions in Part A of the TOEFL. You hear each sentence one time. You have 12 seconds to read four answer choices and choose the one that best restates the meaning of the sentence you heard. The best restatement is the answer choice that is closest in meaning to the sentence that you heard.

---

### MODEL

You will hear:
   Larry doesn't get along with Dave.

You will read:
   (A) Larry and Dave aren't going.
   (B) The days are getting long.
   (C) Larry and Dave are good friends.
   (D) Larry disagrees with Dave.

Answer:

---

▼ **Explanation** ▲

In this question, you hear a statement containing the idiom, *to get along with*. This idiom means *to agree with* or *to cooperate with*. This question also contains the negative contraction, *doesn't*, which gives the statement a negative meaning.

The incorrect answer choices for this question contain sounds, vocabulary, and/or spoken structures which can be confusing.

Answer (A) contains the phrase *aren't going*, which could seem close in meaning to *doesn't get along with*. You might choose this answer if you do not know the meaning of the idiom *get along with*. Answer (B) contains the phrase *getting long*, which sounds very much like *get along*, and the word *days*, which sounds very much like *Dave*. You might choose this answer if you did not correctly hear and understand the sounds in the spoken sentence. Answer (C) has the opposite meaning of the spoken sentence. You might choose this answer if you did not hear and understand the negative spoken structure in the spoken sentence. Answer (D) is the correct answer to the question even though it is different in vocabulary, sound, and structure. It is the only answer choice which restates the meaning of the spoken sentence.

---

### RESTATEMENT STRATEGIES

1. Be careful of vocabulary. Words with more than one meaning will be tested in Section One of the TOEFL. Listen for idioms. Look again at answer choice (A) in the model question for an example of how vocabulary is tested in this part of the TOEFL.

2. Be careful of sounds. Look for sound-alikes in the restatement answer choices. Do not be tricked by words and expressions which sound like those in the spoken sentences but which are different in meaning. Look again at answer choice (B) in the model question for an example of how sounds are tested in this part of the TOEFL.

3. Listen carefully to the intonation and stress of each spoken sentence. Intonation and stress have meaning in English. They can be used to show strong emotion or even to change a statement into a question.

4. Be careful of spoken structures. Listen carefully for tricky spoken structures such as contractions, negatives, causative verbs, conditions, tag questions, modals, passives, and relationship signals. Look at answer choice (C) in the sample question for an example of how spoken structures are tested in this part of the TOEFL.

5. Guess if you don't know the answer to a question. Choose the answer that sounds LEAST like the spoken sentence. This answer is often the correct answer.

6. Use any extra time between questions to look ahead at the answer choices. Look for key words and key word synonyms in the answer choices. Try to understand the overall meaning of the answer choices. This will help you to match the meaning of the sentence you hear with the correct written restatement.

---

## Listening Comprehension Part B: Mini-Dialogues

The Part B questions in Section One of the TOEFL measure your ability to understand mini-dialogues between two people, as well as to understand and respond to spoken questions about each short dialogue. Each dialogue in this section is two lines long and involves a woman and a man. A third person asks a question about what was said. You hear each dialogue and the question about it just one time.

After you hear the question, you have 12 seconds to read four answer choices and decide which one is the best answer to the question you heard. There are 15 mini-dialogues and 15 questions in Part B.

---

### MODEL

You will hear:

    (Man)       M:  This view is really something else!

    (Woman)    W:  I'll say!

    (Question)   Q:  What does the woman mean?

You will read:

    (A)  She has something to say.

    (B)  She agrees with the man.

    (C)  She wants to see something else.

    (D)  She thinks it's time to review something else.

Answer:

---

### ▼ Explanation ▲

In this mini-dialogue and question, several things are being tested. The man uses the idiom *something else* to express his enthusiasm for the view. *I'll say*, the response of the woman, functions to show her agreement with the man about his opinion. Answer (A) contains a different meaning of *say*, and does not describe what the woman means. Answer (C) contains *see*, which sounds like *say*. It also contains *something else* used to mean *another thing*. This is not the idiomatic meaning of *something else*. Answer (D) contains *review*, which sounds like *view*, and again uses *something else* in its literal (non-idiomatic) meaning. Answer (B) is the correct answer to this question because it restates the function of the woman's response even though it sounds the least like the mini-dialogue.

---

### MINI-DIALOGUE STRATEGIES

1. Be careful of vocabulary, sounds, spoken structures, and intonation and stress in dialogues and questions. Review the Restatement Strategies, page 9, for more information.
2. Listen carefully to the second speaker. The second speaker always give important information. The correct answer to Part B questions is often contained in the second speaker's sentence.
3. Determine the situation in the dialogue. Try to determine *who* is speaking and *where* the speakers are having their conversation.
4. Determine the topic of the dialogue. Try to determine *what* the speakers are talking about.
5. Determine the language functions in the dialogue. Try to determine the function of the language being used by the speakers.
6. Guess if you don't know the answer to a question: choose the answer that sounds LEAST like the dialogue. This answer is often the correct answer.
7. Use extra time between questions to look ahead at the answer choices. Try to predict what the question types might be for each dialogue.

## Listening Comprehension Part C: Talks and Longer Conversations

The Part C questions in Section One of the TOEFL measure your ability to understand longer passages of spoken English. There are two types of passages in Part C. One type is a longer dialogue between a man and a woman. The other type is a lecture or talk given by one person, either a man or a woman. Part C of the TOEFL contains three passages, which always include at least one of each of the two types described above. The third passage may be of either type.

The topics in Part C passages are often about college life. The longer conversations often involve two students talking about a class, a professor, or some aspect of college life. The talks frequently discuss classroom procedures and assignments or are short lectures in a general academic area, such as science, history, psychology, or anthropology. No previous knowledge of any of the topics is necessary to answer the questions on this part of the TOEFL.

Although most of the topics for Part C are college related, some are daily life topics. These include such things as conversations in grocery stores or apartments, and talks by tour guides and sports coaches.

Each passage in Part C is between 100 and 300 words long and lasts an average of one to two minutes. You are not allowed to take notes while listening to the spoken passages. Each passage and the questions about it are spoken only one time.

> **SPECIAL NOTE:** Each passage in Part C begins with a short spoken introduction. You will hear a sentence such as, "Questions 36 to 40 refer to the following conversation." These introductions give you valuable information about the passage you are going to hear. Notice that in this short statement you find out (1) whether the selection will be a talk or a conversation; and (2) how many questions will be asked about it. Sometimes even more information is provided in the introductory statement, as in "Questions 36 to 40 refer to the following talk given by a tennis coach at a college." Notice that in this short statement you find out (1) that the selection will be a talk, not a conversation; (2) that there will be five questions about the talk; (3) who will give the talk; and (4) where the talk will take place. Because you can learn so much valuable information from the short introductory statements, it is extremely important that you listen to them carefully.

After each passage, you will hear several spoken questions about it. After each question, you will have 12 seconds to read four answer choices and choose the one that answers the spoken question. There are 15 questions in Part C.

You will hear:

Questions 1 to 6 are based on the following talk:

Last week we talked about the Declaration of Independence. Today I'd like to discuss the United States Constitution. The Constitution is the basic instrument of American government and the supreme law of the land. It was completed in September of 1787, and was officially adopted by the American people in 1789. For over two centuries, it has guided our government and provided the basis for political stability, economic growth, and social progress. It is the oldest written constitution currently being used in any nation of the world. The Constitution owes its long life and its lasting influence to its magnificent simplicity and flexibility. Originally designed to provide a framework for governing thirteen very different former colonies, its basic elements were so carefully conceived that it still serves well the needs of all Americans.

You will hear:

1.  What would be a good title for this talk?

You will read:

1.  (A)  The Founding of the Thirteen Colonies.
    (B)  The Declaration of Independence.
    (C)  The United States Constitution.
    (D)  Economic Growth.

You will hear:

2.  Where does this talk most likely take place?

You will read:

2.  (A)  In a United States history class.
    (B)  In a science class.
    (C)  In a library.
    (D)  In the school cafeteria.

You will hear:

3.  According to the speaker, what is the supreme law of the land?

You will read:

3.  (A)  The American people.
    (B)  The Constitution.
    (C)  The government.
    (D)  The Declaration of Independence.

You will hear:

4.  When was the Constitution officially adopted?

You will read:

4.  (A)  In 1787.
    (B)  In 1887.
    (C)  In 1789.
    (D)  In 1813.

You will hear:

5.  According to the speaker, why has the United States Constitution lasted so long?

You will read:

5.  (A)  Because it was designed for the thirteen colonies.
    (B)  Because it is simple and flexible.
    (C)  Because it is the basic instrument of American government.
    (D)  Because it is being used in many nations.

You will hear:

6.  How does the speaker probably feel about the Constitution?

You will read:

6.  (A)  He would like to have a copy of the Constitution.
    (B)  He is afraid that the Constitution will not last much longer.
    (C)  He is critical of the Constitution.
    (D)  He admires the Constitution.

Answers:

▼ **Explanation** ▲

The introductory statement for this passage tells you that it will be a talk, not a conversation. In addition, it tells you that you will answer six questions about this talk.

Question 1 is a main idea question. The answer to this question is given at the beginning of the talk, in the second sentence. Answer (C) is the correct answer to this question because it restates the main idea of the talk in a title. **The answers to main idea questions are often given at the beginning of the passages in Part C of the Listening Section of the TOEFL.**

Question 2 is an inference question about the situation in which the talk takes place. Although the location of the talk is not directly mentioned, it is an academic talk about an aspect of United States history. Therefore, we can assume that it would take place in an American history class. Answer (A) is the correct answer to this question because it implies *where* the talk will take place.

Question 3 is a fact question which asks about a direct statement made by the speaker. Answer (B) is the correct answer to this question.

Question 4 is another fact question which asks for a detail given by the speaker after the information mentioned in Question 3. Fact questions are always asked in the order that the information is given in the passage. To answer this question, you need to remember an important date mentioned in the passage. Answer (C) is the correct answer to this question.

Question 5 is a third fact question. It asks about a direct statement made by the speaker after the information asked for in Question 4. Answer (B) is the correct answer to this question.

Question 6 is an inference question. It asks about the feelings or the attitude of the speaker. The speaker does not tell us directly how he feels about the Constitution. However, there are clues to his feelings in the passage. *Magnificent simplicity and flexibility* and *serves well* are positive expressions which tell us that the speaker probably admires the Constitution. Answer (D) is the correct answer to this question because it implies the speaker's attitude about the topic.

---

### STRATEGIES FOR TALKS AND LONGER CONVERSATIONS

1. Listen carefully to the short introductory statement given before each passage. You can learn from this statement whether the passage will be a talk or a conversation. You can also learn how many questions you will answer about the passage. The introductory statement can also give you information about the situation and topic of the passage—who, where, and what.

2. Quickly determine the situation and the topic of the passage. This information is often at the beginning of a passage. You should listen carefully to the beginning of each passage.

3. Listen carefully for facts and details. Details such as places, dates, names, and times are tested in Part C of the TOEFL.

4. Questions about facts and details occur in the same order that you hear them in the passage. Many TOEFL test-takers find it helpful to read along with the answer choices while listening to the passage. You can practice this strategy while doing the exercises and practice tests in this book. Only use this strategy if it works for you. If it distracts you from understanding a passage, DO NOT use this strategy.

5. Guess if you don't know the answer to a question. Choose the answer that sounds the MOST like the passage. In this part of the TOEFL, this is often the correct answer to the question.
   **NOTE:** This strategy is different from the guessing strategy for Parts A and B. You will need to change your guessing approach for Part C.

6. Use extra time between questions to look ahead at the answer choices. Try to predict questions.

# Section Two: Structure and Written Expression

The purpose of Section Two of the TOEFL is to test your knowledge of the structure of standard written English. The language tested in this section is mostly formal, not conversational. Many of the sentence topics used in this section are of a general academic nature. The vocabulary used in Section Two questions is similar to the vocabulary used in TOEFL Section Three, Vocabulary and Reading Comprehension.

---

**GENERAL STRATEGIES FOR SECTION TWO**

1. Be familiar with Section Two instructions before you take the actual TOEFL. Then, during the test, you do not need to read the instructions. Move immediately to the first question and begin working.

2. Use your time wisely. You have only about 35 seconds to complete each question in this section.

3. Try to identify the grammar point being tested in each question you read. You can often discover the correct answer right away if you do this.

---

**Structure and Written Expression: Question Types**

Section Two contains 40 questions. You have 25 minutes to answer all the questions. There are two parts in this section of the TOEFL. Each part has a different type of question.

Structure (15 questions)
You choose the *correct* sentence completions.

Written Expression (25 questions)
You choose the *incorrect* sentence segments.

**Structure Questions**

The Structure questions in Section Two of the TOEFL measure your understanding of basic grammar. There are 15 incomplete sentences in this part of the test. Four possible completions are provided in the answer choices for each of the sentences. You must choose the *one correct* answer that completes the sentence.

---

**MODEL**

_____ Americans like movies is a well-known fact.

   (A) Most
   (B) That most
   (C) Some
   (D) Because

**What is needed in this sentence?**
**Answer:** The subject

---

▼ **Explanation** ▲

In this sample question, the subject is being tested. The verb is complete. However, the subject of this sentence, which is a noun clause, is incomplete. You should look for a word to complete this subject. Answer (B) is the correct answer to the question because it completes the subject.

## STRUCTURE QUESTION STRATEGIES

1. Read the whole sentence before you choose your answer. In the model, answer choices (A) and (C) sound correct if you only read the first part of the sentence. You must consider the entire sentence before choosing your answer.

2. Ask yourself, "What is needed in this sentence?" Then, look for the answer choice that completes the sentence. If you cannot immediately identify what is needed, follow the steps in strategy 3.

3. A. Locate the *subject* and the *verb* of the main clause. If the *subject* or *verb* is missing or incomplete, look for it in the answer choices. If the two sentence parts are not missing or incomplete, proceed to Step B.
   B. Look for the *object* or the *complement* of the sentence. If the *object* or *complement* is needed but is missing or incomplete, look for it in the answer choices. If one of these parts is not needed or is not missing, proceed to Step C.
   C. Look for a *subordinate clause*. If the *subordinate clause* is needed and if it is missing a *subject*, a *verb*, or a *clause marker*, look for the missing part in the answer choices. If none of these sentence parts is missing, proceed to Step D.
   D. Look for a *phrase*. If there is a modifying phrase, and if any part of the phrase is missing, look for it in the answer choices.

4. Do not look for ungrammatical segments in the answer choices. Most of the answer choices are grammatically correct by themselves. They only become incorrect when they are put into the sentence.

### Written Expression Questions

The Written Expression questions in Section Two of the TOEFL measure your understanding of the grammar of written English. There are 25 sentences in this part of the test. Each sentence has four underlined segments. You must choose the *one incorrect* segment.

---

### MODEL

Mining <u>is</u> the most <u>importantest</u> industry <u>in</u> <u>this</u> state.
      A              B                      C  D

**What is wrong with this sentence?**
**Answer:** The form of the adjective

---

▼ Explanation ▲
In this question, the correct formation of superlative adjectives is being tested. *Importantest* is not a word in English. Answer (B) is the correct answer to the question because *importantest* is incorrect.
**Correction:** *important*

---

### MODEL

Tomorrow we <u>went</u> to <u>the store</u> to buy <u>some</u> new <u>furniture</u>.
                A      B              C         D

**What is wrong with this sentence?**
**Answer:** The verb tense

---

▼ Explanation ▲
In this sentence, the tense of the verb is being tested. The past tense *went* does not agree with the time marker *tomorrow*. Answer (A) is the correct answer to the question because *went* is incorrect.
**Correction:** *are going/will go/are going to*

## WRITTEN EXPRESSION QUESTION STRATEGIES

1. Ask yourself, "What is wrong with this sentence?" In this part of the test, you are looking for the *incorrect* part of a sentence. This is a very different task from the task in the Structure questions. You must remember to quickly change your approach when you begin the Written Expression part of the test.

2. QUICKLY scan the four underlined segments to find what is wrong. One of these segments may be incorrect on its own, as in the first model above. If none of the choices is incorrect on its own, proceed to strategy 3.

3. Read the entire sentence. Compare the underlined segments to other parts of the sentence. Most of the incorrect segments in this section are wrong because of their relationship to other parts of the sentence, as in the second model above.

4. Do not waste time looking for errors that are not underlined. All errors occur in the underlined segments of the sentences.

5. Do not waste time thinking about how to correct the incorrect segment of the sentence. Once you locate the incorrect segment, mark it in your answer sheet and move on.

## Section Three: Vocabulary and Reading Comprehension

The purpose of Section Three of the TOEFL is to test your knowledge of the meanings and uses of words in written English and your ability to understand a variety of reading materials. The vocabulary and reading topics in Section Three are taken from general and formal English. For the most part, informal and conversational language is not tested in this section. The questions based on the reading passages will not require you to have outside knowledge of the topics.

## GENERAL STRATEGIES FOR SECTION THREE

1. Be familiar with Section Three instructions before you take the actual TOEFL test. Then, during the test, do not read the instructions. Move immediately to the first question and begin working.

2. Use your time wisely. You should spend 10 to 12 minutes on the complete vocabulary section. Plan to spend more time on the reading passages, where thinking about the questions will help you choose the correct answers.

3. Remember to change your overall approach. In Section Three Vocabulary you must select the correct word from the choices. This is different from the Written Expression questions, where you are asked to identify the mistake. Work quickly through this section. In most cases, you either know the answer or you don't.

### Vocabulary and Reading Comprehension: Question Types

Section Three contains 60 questions which must be completed in 45 minutes. There are two parts to this section of the TOEFL.

Vocabulary (30 questions)
You read a sentence that has an underlined word or phrase. Then, you choose the word or phrase that is closest in meaning to the part underlined.

Reading (5 or 6 passages with a total of 30 questions)
You read a written passage followed by several questions, and choose the correct written answers to those questions.

# Vocabulary

The vocabulary tested in the Vocabulary and Reading Comprehension Section of the TOEFL is general and formal. The words are often taken from academic topics. You will NOT be tested on idioms, technical words, or proper names.

All choices in the vocabulary questions are grammatically correct, so grammatical clues will not help you to choose the best word. The sentences in this section will not provide you with contextual clues to meaning. You need to know the vocabulary item being tested and make automatic responses to the choices.

In the Vocabulary Section of the TOEFL there are 30 sentences with an underlined word or phrase. You have between 20 and 30 seconds to read each sentence and the four answer choices, and choose the word or phase that is closest in meaning to the underlined part.

You should complete the vocabulary questions in 10 to 12 minutes to allow more time for the reading comprehension questions, where context will help you to decide on the correct answer.

Read the following question for an example of items in the vocabulary part of Section Three of the TOEFL.

---

**MODEL**

Circle the letter of the word that is closest in meaning to the underlined word or phrase.

Though whistling swans live mainly in the tundra regions of the north, they winter in large <u>flocks</u> on the Chesapeake Bay.

    (A)  islands
    (B)  ice floes
    (C)  numbers
    (D)  preserves

Answer:

---

## ▼ Explanation ▲

In order to answer this question correctly, you need to know that *flocks* is a term used to refer to large *numbers* of birds. Grammatical clues don't help since all choices are nouns, which is the grammatical form needed. Contextual clues are not helpful in this type of question either. The relation of *islands* to *the Chesapeake Bay* is possible, as is the relation of ice floes to both the *Bay* and *northern tundra regions*. *Preserves* could also be possible, since many birds are protected in certain areas of the country. Answer (C) is the correct answer to the question because *numbers* is closest in meaning to *flocks*.

In this section of the TOEFL an extensive knowledge of English vocabulary is important. You need to know what the underlined words and phrases and choices mean and make a quick match.

---

**VOCABULARY QUESTION STRATEGIES**

1. Read the underlined word and scan the choices. Match the word with the choice which is closest in meaning. QUICKLY read the sentence to be sure that the word or phrase fits the meaning of the sentence.
2. Complete your word and choice matches first.
3. If you cannot make a match, go back and re-read the sentence. Try to determine the general meaning of the sentence. If you do not know the underlined word or phase, you can sometimes predict which of the choices is correct from the general meaning of the sentence by using logical reasoning.
4. Do not spend time trying to find grammatical or contextual clues in the sentence. Remember that in this section of the TOEFL, grammatical and contextual clues will not help you much.
5. Use your time wisely. You should only spend 20 seconds on each vocabulary question.
6. Guess if you don't know the answer to a question. **Unanswered questions on the TOEFL are marked wrong.** Choose the word that you feel might be correct, but beware of TOEFL tricks—words that have the same form or the same root, but have a different meaning from the word underlined.

---

# Reading Comprehension

The purpose of the Reading Comprehension Section of the TOEFL is to measure your ability to quickly read and understand a variety of short reading passages. You have approximately 30 minutes to read five or six passages and answer 30 multiple choice questions about their meaning.

The topics of the reading passages in Section Three of the TOEFL are often academic in nature. Popular topics are the physical sciences (biology, physics, geology), American history (events and people), business, art and dance, literature, medicine, and the social sciences (sociology and psychology). Other topics for reading passages are general information about people and places in the United States. Whatever the topic, the style of the reading passages is formal English and they are written to give information appropriate for a first-year college student.

The questions about the reading passages can all be answered using information in the passages themselves. Outside knowledge of the subject matter is not necessary.

The biggest factor in the Reading Comprehension Section of the TOEFL is time. You should spend no more than 6 minutes on each passage and its questions.

Success in the Reading Comprehension Section will also depend on your knowledge of English vocabulary. In this section of the TOEFL, knowing the meaning of formal and academic words in English will help you to understand better the meaning of the reading passages.

Remember:
- Reading passages on the TOEFL are written in formal English and are general and academic in nature.
- Reading quickly with comprehension is the key to being successful on the Reading Comprehension Section of the TOEFL.
- A large vocabulary in English is very important for success on the Reading Comprehension Section of the TOEFL.

---

## GENERAL STRATEGIES FOR SECTION THREE

1. Use your time wisely. You have only 30 to 35 minutes to read all the passages and answer 30 questions. This means you should spend only 6 minutes on each passage and its questions. Concentrate and work QUICKLY.

2. Acquire a large vocabulary of formal and academic English to help you to understand better the meaning of the reading passages.

3. Read actively and concentrate on reading for information. Active reading is the most important strategy you can develop for this part of the TOEFL.

4. Identify the types of questions you will need to answer before you read the passage. Knowing what the questions are will help you to read more effectively and with a purpose.

---

**Reading Comprehension: Question Types**

In the Reading Comprehension Section there are five or six passages that have 200 to 400 words. Each passage is followed by three to seven questions. There are 30 questions in the Reading Comprehension Section, and the most difficult passages are those at the end of this section.

The following is a model reading comprehension passage and questions. Read the passage and answer the questions. Then read the explanation.

The dingo, Australia's wild dog, was first spotted on the northwest shores of the subcontinent in the late seventeenth century. The arrival of the dingo brought about substantial changes in the continent's ecosystem. It is noted that with the establishment of dingoes, native predators declined. Among the animals probably displaced from the mainland by the dingo was the Tasmanian tiger, a recently extinct wolf-like marsupial.

1. What is the main point the author makes in this passage?
   (A) The dingo caused changes in Australia's balance of nature.
   (B) The dingo is not native to Australia.
   (C) The dingo is similar to a dog.
   (D) The dingo came to Australia in the 1600s.

2. According to the passage, after the dingoes arrived in Australia the Tasmanian tiger
   (A) took on the characteristics of a wolf
   (B) began hunting the dingo
   (C) began to die out
   (D) moved to the south of the continent

3. It can be inferred from the passage that the dingo
   (A) is becoming extinct
   (B) was not domesticated in large numbers
   (C) lived in a particular part of Australia
   (D) befriended many native animals

Answers:

▼ **Explanation** ▲

The correct answer to Question 1 is (A). Although all four choices are true, the main point of the passage is (A) *The dingo caused changes in Australia's balance of nature*. The passage states *The arrival of the dingo brought about substantial changes in the continent's ecosystem*. This point is then supported by information in the next two sentences.

The correct answer to Question 2 is (C). None of the choices is true from the information in the passage except (C) *began to die out*. The last sentence in the passage states: *Among the animals that the dingo probably displaced was the Tasmanian tiger, a recently extinct wolf-like marsupial*. The words *displaced* and *recently extinct* are similar in meaning to the choice *began to die out*, which is the correct answer.
The correct answer to Question 3 is (B). We do not have enough information in the passage to infer any of the choices except (B) *was not domesticated in large numbers*. This can be inferred because in the first sentence of the passage the dingo was described as *Australia's wild dog*. We know that *wild* is similar in meaning to *not domesticated*, which makes (B) the best answer.

The TOEFL will test your ability to read a passage quickly for information and to answer questions about the meaning of the passage. This is the same type of reading that you will be asked to do in an academic course or in job-related tasks. In order to develop your ability to read well in English, you need to develop effective reading skills and strategies. The following strategies will help you with the questions in the Reading Comprehension Section of the TOEFL.

## READING COMPREHENSION QUESTION STRATEGIES

1. Read the first and last sentences of the passage to establish the topic and main idea. Skim the passage for the key concepts and vocabulary.

2. Read the questions following the passage to find out what information you are looking for. DO NOT read the answer choices at this time; just read the questions.

3. Read the passage carefully, keeping in mind the questions you will have to answer.

4. Answer the questions. Use key words and phrases in the questions to scan the passage for the correct answer. When you find the answer in the passage, match it with one of the answer choices.

5. **Guess if you do not know the correct answer.** Use any clues in the question and passage to make your best guess. If you finish the Reading Comprehension Section before the time is up, you can go back to questions that you were not sure about.

## Section Four: Test of Written English

The purpose of the Test of Written English (TWE) is to test your ability to write in standard written English. The writing tasks you are asked to perform on the TWE are similar to those required of students in academic courses in universities in North America. In your TWE essay you will be evaluated on your ability to:

> Generate and organize ideas on paper.
> Support those ideas with evidence or examples.
> Use the conventions of standard written English.

The Test of Written English requires that you write for 30 minutes on one topic. Your essay is read by at least two readers and assigned a score based on a six-point, criterion-referenced scoring guide. Your score on the TWE is not included in your total TOEFL score, but is reported separately on the TOEFL score report. Colleges and universities that require the TWE will expect a score of 4, 5, or 6 on the essay. The TWE is not given on every TOEFL testing date. Check the *Bulletin of Information for TOEFL and TSE* for the dates that the TWE will be administered.

## GENERAL STRATEGIES FOR SECTION FOUR

1. Understand the question. Know what the question is asking you to do.

2. Spend about five minutes thinking and organizing your ideas. Write your notes on the TOEFL question sheet. You will write your essay on the lined pages provided in the test book.

3. Be sure that you give adequate support for the major points that you make. Write only on the points in the question. DO NOT include irrelevant or unnecessary information.

4. Use vocabulary and structures with which you are familiar. Try to express yourself simply and clearly. Use vocabulary and structures of organization to introduce and to connect your ideas.

5. Write legibly and concisely. You have only two pages on which to write a 200–300 word essay. Extra pages are not provided.

6. Spend three to five minutes at the end reading your essay for careless mistakes of spelling, grammar, and punctuation.

# PRACTICE TEST ONE

## SECTION 1
## LISTENING COMPREHENSION

In this section of the test, you will have an opportunity to demonstrate your ability to understand spoken English. There are three parts to this section, with special directions for each part.

### Part A

Directions:   For each question in Part A, you will hear a short sentence. Each sentence will be spoken just one time. The sentences you hear will not be written out for you. Therefore, you must listen carefully to understand what the speaker says.

After you hear a sentence, read the four choices in your test book, marked (A), (B), (C), and (D), and decide which <u>one</u> is closest in meaning to the sentence you heard. Then, on your answer sheet, find the number of the question and fill in the space that corresponds to the letter of the answer you have chosen. Fill in the space so that the letter inside the oval cannot be seen.

Example I                                                   Sample Answer
                                                            (A) (B) ● (D)

You will hear:

You will read:      (A)  Greg didn't bother to leave a tip.
                    (B)  Greg thought about typing a
                         letter to his brother.
                    (C)  Greg didn't like to type.
                    (D)  My typing bothered Greg.

The speaker said, "Greg thought typing was a bother." Sentence (C), "Greg didn't like to type," is closest in meaning to the sentence you heard. Therefore, you should choose answer (C).

Example II                                                  Sample Answer
                                                            (A) ● (C) (D)

You will hear:

You will read:      (A)  Everyone will be able to take this
                         exam later.
                    (B)  Students should bring a calculator
                         to this exam.
                    (C)  This test will be part of every
                         student's final grade.
                    (D)  No one can calculate the grades
                         for this test.

The speaker said, "Everyone needs a calculator for this test." Sentence (B), "Students should bring a calculator to this exam," is closest in meaning to the sentence you heard. Therefore, you should choose answer (B).

**GO ON TO THE NEXT PAGE**

1. (A) May I help you?
   (B) I can do that for you.
   (C) Are you done with that can?
   (D) What did you do with that can?

2. (A) Sarah bought a bicycle on her tour.
   (B) Sarah toured the state on her bicycle.
   (C) Sarah and Michael toured the estate.
   (D) Sarah brought her bicycle to the estate.

3. (A) He doesn't hear very well.
   (B) He isn't writing at the moment.
   (C) He is gone.
   (D) This time he isn't right.

4. (A) Don't they have a nice view from their apartment?
   (B) Doesn't their department write good reviews?
   (C) There are a dozen apartments with a view like theirs.
   (D) The departmental review went very well.

5. (A) Frank will be my waiter.
   (B) Tell Frank not to leave.
   (C) I will wait for Frank here.
   (D) Ask Frank to call the waiter.

6. (A) Only Mary was worried about the test.
   (B) Mary tried not to be anxious about the exam.
   (C) She knew that Mary was worried about the exam.
   (D) Mary told her not to be anxious about the test.

7. (A) Jack's whole head aches.
   (B) Jack hasn't become too proud.
   (C) For the most part, Jack has not succeeded.
   (D) Jack is ahead of the whole class.

8. (A) Craig finally went back to bed.
   (B) Craig's final bet was the best one.
   (C) Craig finally found one bat.
   (D) Craig was the one to finally win.

9. (A) She expects to be done with her work on Tuesday.
   (B) She has two days to think about her paper.
   (C) I believe she'll be able to finish her paper today.
   (D) She's thinking about how to finish her paper.

10. (A) Would you like to listen to some different music?
    (B) I know that you like only jazz music.
    (C) I certainly am glad you like jazz.
    (D) I thought you would dislike this jazz music.

11. (A) They don't believe in things they can't see.
    (B) I don't think I saw them shopping.
    (C) They didn't stop at the sign.
    (D) I think that should stop right now.

12. (A) He couldn't hear us.
    (B) He ignored us.
    (C) He didn't believe us.
    (D) He turned over.

13. (A) They didn't read the book.
    (B) They understood the movie better than the book.
    (C) The book was better than the movie.
    (D) After they read the book, they understood the movie better.

14. (A) She stopped by the doctor's office for more medicine.
    (B) The doctor has stopped taking new patients.
    (C) She was supposed to stop and take her medicine.
    (D) She doesn't take her medicine anymore.

**GO ON TO THE NEXT PAGE**

15. (A) She would rather not use a microphone during her presentation.
(B) Her presentation was interrupted by
my phone call.
(C) She will begin her presentation as
soon as the microphone is fixed.
(D) The microphone broke just as she
began her presentation.

16. (A) They talk on the phone once a day.
(B) They keep each other up late
every evening.
(C) They try not to phone one another
during the news broadcast.
(D) They watch the news every night.

17. (A) Geology was one of the most
informative courses I took.
(B) Of course I will remember most of
what I studied in geology.
(C) I've forgotten most of the information
presented in my geology class.
(D) I didn't return the material I
borrowed for my geology class.

18. (A) Judy never used to get worried about
her shows.
(B) Judy seemed to enjoy the show.
(C) Judy doesn't like the snow
very much.
(D) Judy is used to going very slowly.

19. (A) Kathy lives too far to ride her bike
to school.
(B) Kathy doesn't need to drive to
school anymore.
(C) Kathy drives better than she used to.
(D) Kathy isn't accustomed to driving a car.

20. (A) Paula can see the trail.
(B) Paula can't find her way.
(C) Paula has a problem with her eyes.
(D) Paula really notices the little things.

GO ON TO THE NEXT PAGE

## Part B

<u>Directions:</u>    In Part B you will hear short conversations between two speakers. At the end of each conversation, a third person will ask a question about what was said. You will hear each conversation and question about it just one time. Therefore, you must listen carefully to understand what each speaker says. After you hear a conversation and the question about it, read the four possible answers in your test book and decide which <u>one</u> is the best answer to the question you heard. Then, on your answer sheet, find the number of the question and fill in the space that corresponds to the letter of the answer you have chosen.

Look at the following example.

You will hear:

You will read:      (A)   At last winter is almost over.
                    (B)   She doesn't like winter weather
                          very much.
                    (C)   This winter's weather is similar to
                          last winter's weather.
                    (D)   Winter won't last as long this year as
                          it did last year.

Sample Answer
Ⓐ  Ⓑ  ●  Ⓓ

From the conversation you learn that the woman thinks the weather this winter is almost the same as the weather last winter. The best answer to the question "What does the woman mean?" is (C), "This winter's weather is similar to last winter's weather." Therefore, you should choose answer (C).

21. (A)  She'll stay for a little while.
    (B)  She'll talk to him about his raise.
    (C)  She prefers to continue working.
    (D)  She'd like a short vacation.

22. (A)  The food doesn't have enough
         seasonings in it.
    (B)  The man isn't very funny.
    (C)  She agrees with the man.
    (D)  She isn't sure about the rice.

23. (A)  He's feeling better.
    (B)  The picture wasn't very good.
    (C)  He didn't enjoy the talk very much.
    (D)  He will see the woman later.

24. (A)  It cost more than he thought it would.
    (B)  He would like to sell it.
    (C)  It isn't a very good one.
    (D)  He got it for a good price.

25. (A)  She felt different last week.
    (B)  She hired someone to cut her hair.
    (C)  She hasn't been the same all week.
    (D)  She cut her own hair.

26. (A)  He'll bring the food quickly.
    (B)  He needs to write down the woman's
         order.
    (C)  He'll send a waiter to the woman's
         table.
    (D)  He'll take the food away now.

27. (A)  She'll work part-time at the banquet.
    (B)  She'll try to find a blanket for
         her guest.
    (C)  She is still looking for a guest speaker.
    (D)  She lives too far away to come to
         the dinner.

28. (A)  Who is waiting to see her.
    (B)  How many people can hear her.
    (C)  When she can see someone.
    (D)  What the man said.

GO ON TO THE NEXT PAGE

29. (A) Give the woman instructions about the phone.
    (B) Read the instructions next to the phone.
    (C) Pay for his telephone.
    (D) Call the woman on the phone.

30. (A) The scholar will arrive shortly.
    (B) They didn't get as much money as they needed.
    (C) They collected two hundred dollars.
    (D) He doesn't know how to do the calculation.

31. (A) He doesn't like to walk late at night.
    (B) He has two jobs.
    (C) He can't go to the game.
    (D) He'll come to the game late.

32. (A) Tony put it together.
    (B) He is going to pick it up now.
    (C) He will bring it to the picnic.
    (D) Tony got it for them.

33. (A) He doesn't know when he'll take a vacation.
    (B) He doesn't want to move right away.
    (C) He's waiting for the woman to move out of the dorm.
    (D) He needs to move before summer vacation.

34. (A) It isn't ready to use yet.
    (B) It can't be fixed.
    (C) It needs new legs.
    (D) He'll put it in the stable to dry.

35. (A) Work on the assignment a little bit at a time.
    (B) Finish the assignment on time.
    (C) Take the assignment to someone else this time.
    (D) Stop working on the assignment.

GO ON TO THE NEXT PAGE

Part C

<u>Directions:</u>    In this part of the test, you will hear short talks and conversations. After each of them, you will be asked some questions. You will hear the talks and conversations and the questions about them just one time. They will not be written out for you. Therefore, you must listen carefully to understand what each speaker says.

After you hear a question, read the four possible answers in your test book and decide which <u>one</u> is the best answer to the question you heard. Then, on your answer sheet, find the number of the question and fill in the space that corresponds to the letter of the answer you have chosen.

Answer all questions on the basis of what is <u>stated</u> or <u>implied</u> in the talk or conversation.

Listen to this sample talk.

You will hear:

Now look at the following example.

You will hear:

You will read:    (A)  Only bumblebees can fertilize red
                        clover plants.
              (B)  Bumblebees protect red clover from
                        plant eating insects.
              (C)  Bumblebees bring water to red clover
                        plants on their tongues.
              (D)  Bumblebees keep mice and other animals
                        away from red clover plants.

Sample Answer

● Ⓑ Ⓒ Ⓓ

The best answer to the question "Why is it impossible to raise red clover where there are no bumblebees?" is (A), "Only bumblebees can fertilize red clover plants." Therefore, you should choose answer (A).

Now look at the next example.

You will hear:

You will read:    (A)  They both make honey.
              (B)  They both build combs.
              (C)  Both of them are found in
                        underground nests.
              (D)  They both live through the winter.

Sample Answer

Ⓐ Ⓑ Ⓒ ●

The best answer to the question "According to the speaker, in what way are the queen wasp and the queen bee similar?" is (D), "They both live through the winter." Therefore, you should choose answer (D).

36. (A)  A student.
    (B)  A psychology professor.
    (C)  Professor Densmore.
    (D)  A geologist.

37. (A)  He overslept.
    (B)  His alarm clock didn't work.
    (C)  He needed to stay at home and finish
            his paper.
    (D)  He had some alarming news.

**GO ON TO THE NEXT PAGE** →

38. (A) Sleeping.
    (B) Studying computer science.
    (C) Finishing a lab.
    (D) Writing a paper.

39. (A) Psychology.
    (B) Geology.
    (C) Computer science.
    (D) Writing.

40. (A) He studies too much.
    (B) He is to be admired.
    (C) He doesn't budget his time well.
    (D) He writes very well.

41. (A) In a sports center.
    (B) In a restaurant.
    (C) At a health spa.
    (D) In a doctor's office.

42. (A) To advise athletes on how to exercise.
    (B) To suggest that athletes need vitamin supplements.
    (C) To suggest that athletes cut back on certain foods.
    (D) To discuss diet and body building for strength.

43. A) An adequate diet.
    (B) A proper weight-training program.
    (C) Large amounts of protein to build muscle mass.
    (D) Sufficient vitamins and minerals.

44. (A) It should be accompanied by vitamin and mineral supplements.
    (B) It increases endurance.
    (C) It is hard to maintain strength and lose weight.
    (D) Cutting back on food is the best way to lose weight.

45. (A) It replaces carbohydrates and vitamins.
    (B) It is necessary in large amounts to build muscle mass.
    (C) It can take the place of calories.
    (D) It should be cut back for weight loss.

46. (A) The life of a tree surgeon.
    (B) A new sport.
    (C) Using a throwball.
    (D) Trees and their uses.

47. (A) He lost his job as a tree surgeon.
    (B) He thinks trees are very easy to climb.
    (C) He believes climbing trees is less dangerous and more accessible than rock climbing.
    (D) He thinks that the equipment for tree climbing is less expensive and more comfortable.

48. (A) Because Sam was heading toward the mountains.
    (B) Because Sam was carrying equipment often used by mountain climbers.
    (C) Because Sam was well know as a mountain climber.
    (D) Because they both were interested in mountain climbing.

49. (A) Pulling yourself into the tree.
    (B) Making a bed in the tree.
    (C) Fashioning a seat in the tree top.
    (D) Securing the rope over a tree branch.

50. (A) That he climbed a redwood.
    (B) That he went all the way to California to climb the tree.
    (C) That he spent the night sleeping in the tree top.
    (D) That he climbed in the rain.

**THIS IS THE END OF THE LISTENING COMPREHENSION SECTION OF THE TEST**

THE NEXT PART OF THE TEST IS SECTION 2. TURN TO THE
DIRECTIONS FOR SECTION 2 IN YOUR TEST BOOK.
READ THEM, AND BEGIN WORK.
DO NOT READ OR WORK ON ANY OTHER SECTION OF THE TEST.

  STOP STOP **STOP** STOP STOP STOP

SECTION 2
STRUCTURE AND WRITTEN EXPRESSION

Time—25 minutes

This section is designed to measure your ability to recognize language that is appropriate for standard written English. There are two types of questions in this section, with special directions for each type.

<u>Directions:</u>   Questions 1–15 are incomplete sentences. Beneath each sentence you will see four words or phrases, marked (A), (B), (C), and (D). Choose the <u>one</u> word or phrase that best completes the sentence. Then, on your answer sheet, find the number of the question and fill in the space that corresponds to the letter of the answer you have chosen. Fill in the space so that the letter inside the oval cannot be seen.

Example I

Most American families _____ at least one automobile.

    (A)  have
    (B)  in
    (C)  that
    (D)  has

<u>Sample Answer</u>

● Ⓑ Ⓒ Ⓓ

The sentence should read, "Most American families have at least one automobile." Therefore, you should choose answer (A).

Example II

_____ recent times, the discipline of biology has expanded rapidly into a variety of subdisciplines.

    (A)  It is since
    (B)  When
    (C)  Since it is
    (D)  In

<u>Sample Answer</u>

Ⓐ Ⓑ Ⓒ ●

The sentence should read, "In recent times, the discipline of biology has expanded into a variety of subdisciplines." Therefore, you should choose answer (D).

Now begin work on the questions.

1. The human brain _____ only two percent of an adult's body weight.

    (A)  which makes up
    (B)  it makes up
    (C)  makes it up
    (D)  makes up

2. The foreign policies _____ the Hoover administration undertook in 1929 were marked by good will and peaceful purpose.

    (A)  that
    (B)  where
    (C)  on which
    (D)  of

**GO ON TO THE NEXT PAGE** ➤

3. Children usually turn to their parents rather than _____ for protection from threats in the environment.

    (A) they turn to other figures of authority
    (B) authority figures to other
    (C) to other figures of authority
    (D) their turning to other figures of authority

4. _____ cause extensive damage to Pacific Island nations each year.

    (A) Because of the high tides and winds during hurricanes
    (B) The high tides and winds of hurricanes
    (C) The high hurricane tides and winds which
    (D) That the high tides and winds of hurricanes

5. Anthropologists _____ within their environments and evaluate the adaptations they have made.

    (A) societies are studied
    (B) study societies
    (C) who study societies are
    (D) their societies are studied

6. Malaria, which can be fatal if left untreated, is transmitted by the female, _____ by the male, mosquito.

    (A) not
    (B) however
    (C) despite
    (D) instead

7. _____, Henry David Thoreau is known for his transcendental views.

    (A) He was like his predecessor, Ralph Waldo Emerson
    (B) His predecessor, Ralph Waldo Emerson, was like him
    (C) Like his predecessor, Ralph Waldo Emerson
    (D) That he was like his predecessor, Ralph Waldo Emerson

8. The tallest bird on the North American continent, the white whooping crane, _____ four and a half feet tall.

    (A) stands
    (B) which stands
    (C) it stands
    (D) standing

9. For thousands of years, people have used vast amounts of wood for building and _____ their homes.

    (A) they heat
    (B) to heat
    (C) heating
    (D) heat

10. Past experience has shown that even well-trained _____ overwhelming success in forecasting interest rates.

    (A) experts do not always have
    (B) do not always have experts
    (C) there are experts who do not always have
    (D) always do not have experts

11. _____ gene in the human genome were more completely understood, many human diseases could be cured or prevented.

    (A) Each
    (B) Since each
    (C) If each
    (D) Were each

12. _____ of the United States grown during a Republican administration.

    (A) Rarely the federal government has
    (B) Rarely has the federal government
    (C) Has the federal government rarely
    (D) The federal government has rarely

GO ON TO THE NEXT PAGE

13. Water, _____ , is also one of the most
abundant compounds on earth.

   (A)  is one of the most critical elements for
        human survival
   (B)  one of the most critical elements for
        human survival
   (C)  of which one of the most critical
        elements for human survival
   (D)  one of the most critical elements for
        human survival which

14. _____ extensively by persons who
cannot speak or hear, American Sign
Language ranks as the fourth most widely
used language in the U.S. today.

   (A)  Relied on
   (B)  It is relied on
   (C)  Relying on it
   (D)  To rely on it

15. Efforts to provide equal opportunity for
minorities in the United States _____
from the Civil Rights Act of 1964.

   (A)  may be said to date
   (B)  dating
   (C)  may say to date
   (D)  to date may be said

---

Directions:   In questions 16–40 each sentence has four underlined words or phrases. The four
underlined parts of the sentence are marked (A), (B), (C), and (D). Identify the one underlined word
or phrase that must be changed in order for the sentence to be correct. Then, on your answer sheet,
find the number of the question and fill in the space that corresponds to the letter of the answer you
have chosen.

Example I

The octopus is a unique animal because they
             A                      B        C
has three functioning hearts.
              D

Sample Answer

(A) (B) ● (D)

The sentence should read, "The octopus is a unique animal because it has three functioning hearts."
Therefore, you should choose answer (C).

Example II

The beagle, one of the most ancient breeds of
            A              B
dog known, originating in England.
    C            D

Sample Answer

(A) (B) (C) ●

The sentence should read, "The beagle, one of the most ancient breeds of dog known, originated in
England." Therefore, you should choose answer (D).

Now begin work on the questions.

**GO ON TO THE NEXT PAGE** ➤

16. Chicago's Sears Tower, <u>now</u> the <u>taller</u> building in the world, <u>rises</u> 1,522 feet from the ground
    <u>to the top of</u> its antenna.

17. Vitamin E, <u>which is found</u> in <u>nutritious</u> foods such as green vegetables and whole grains, <u>action</u>
    as an antioxidant in cell <u>membranes</u>.

18. Scientists <u>is</u> <u>currently</u> trying <u>to map</u> the human genome, the blueprint <u>of human heredity</u>.

19. A snowflake is a <u>frailly</u> crystalline structure <u>which</u> maintains its delicate shape only <u>as long as</u> it
    <u>is</u> airborne.

20. James Dickey's first poem <u>was published</u> <u>during</u> he was <u>still</u> a senior <u>in</u> college.

21. <u>Most fatty</u> acids have been <u>find</u> as <u>essential</u> components of lipid <u>molecules</u>.

22. Social stratification <u>can based</u> on <u>many</u> criteria, <u>such as</u> wealth, cultural level, legal status, birth,
    personal <u>qualities</u>, and ideology.

23. In his famous domes, <u>architecture</u> Buckminster Fuller <u>utilized</u> thousands of <u>simple</u> equilateral
    triangles <u>linked</u> together.

24. <u>Early in</u> United States history, the rights of <u>woman</u> were championed in Wyoming, the state
    <u>where</u> they <u>were first guaranteed</u> the right to vote.

25. The <u>most aggressive</u> <u>bees</u> known, the African honeybee is <u>currently swarming</u> <u>into</u>
    North America.

26. <u>Only after</u> Theodore Roosevelt became president did conservation <u>developed</u> <u>into</u> a major
    <u>environmental</u> issue in the United States.

27. If he <u>were</u> alive today, F. Scott Fitzgerald <u>might be surprised</u> to learn that his novel *The Great
    Gatsby* <u>having transcended</u> <u>its own age</u> and turned into a timeless classic.

28. The world's <u>rain</u> forests <u>are being</u> cut down at the rate <u>on</u> 3,000 acres <u>per hour</u>.

29. <u>In all</u> human communities, power yields <u>certain</u> advantages and privileges, such as honor,
    <u>material</u> benefits, and <u>prestigious</u>.

30. Scientists <u>used</u> line spectra <u>identifying</u> <u>the</u> element helium <u>in</u> the sun.

31. The <u>compute</u> of the passage of time <u>has always been</u> associated with the <u>movements</u> of
    <u>celestial</u> bodies.

32. <u>Many</u> environmentalists fear <u>that</u> the earth will run <u>out essential</u> natural resources <u>before</u> the end
    of the twentieth century.

33. The <u>discovered</u> of gold <u>in</u> California in 1848 <u>led to</u> the Gold Rush <u>of</u> 1849.

34. The personality traits of children are <u>often similar to</u> those <u>that</u> of their parents, <u>but</u> these traits
    are not always genetically <u>conditioned</u>.

**GO ON TO THE NEXT PAGE**

35. Lecithins <u>and</u> other phospholipids <u>play</u> key <u>roles the</u> structure of cell <u>membranes</u>.
              A                    B        C                              D

36. Wages and salaries <u>account for</u> nearly three fourths of the total <u>nationally</u> income <u>generated</u> in
                        A                                         B             C
the United States <u>annually</u>.
                        D

37. <u>Farther</u> evidence is needed <u>to support</u> recent research which <u>suggests</u> that certain chemicals
   A                        B                        C
found in broccoli <u>may act</u> as cancer preventatives.
                      D

38. Contemporary <u>newspaper columnist</u> Russell Baker is noted for his <u>commentaries humorous</u>
                            A                                                 B
<u>written</u> in the tradition <u>of</u> Benjamin Franklin.
   C                           D

39. <u>Nutritional</u> adequacy is hard <u>to achieve</u> on a low-calorie diet; even a small person should not try
   A                      B
to <u>get by on</u> less than twelve <u>hundreds</u> calories per day.
     C                          D

40. In <u>reality</u>, all biological <u>reproductive</u> <u>begins</u> at the <u>cellular</u> level.
     A                        B           C         D

---

**THIS IS THE END OF SECTION 2**

IF YOU FINISH BEFORE TIME IS CALLED, CHECK YOUR WORK
ON SECTION 2 ONLY.
DO NOT READ OR WORK ON ANY OTHER SECTION OF THE TEST.
THE SUPERVISOR WILL TELL YOU WHEN TO BEGIN
WORK ON SECTION 3.

## SECTION 3
## VOCABULARY AND READING COMPREHENSION
### Time—45 minutes

This section is designed to measure your comprehension of standard written English. There are two types of questions in this section, with special directions for each type.

<u>Directions:</u>   In questions 1–30 each sentence has an underlined word or phrase. Below each sentence are four other words or phrases, marked (A), (B), (C), (D). You are to choose the <u>one</u> word or phrase that <u>best keeps the meaning</u> of the original sentence if it is substituted for the underlined word or phrase. Then, on your answer sheet, find the number of the question and fill in the space that corresponds to the letter you have chosen. Fill in the space so that the letter inside the oval cannot be seen.

Example                                                          <u>Sample Answer</u>

Ladybugs, small brightly colored beetles, feed on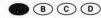
plant aphids and have considerable economic value
in <u>controlling</u> pest populations.

(A)  limiting
(B)  finding
(C)  increasing
(D)  ruling

The best answer is (A) because "Ladybugs, small brightly colored beetles, feed on plant aphids and have considerable economic value in limiting pest populations" is closest in meaning to the original sentence. Therefore, you should choose answer (A).

Now begin work on the questions.

1. Chicago's position at the <u>foot</u> of Lake Michigan makes it an important port.

   (A)  coast
   (B)  side
   (C)  mouth
   (D)  bottom

2. All vipers have a <u>poisonous</u> bite, and all are dangerous to man.

   (A)  painful
   (B)  penetrating
   (C)  venomous
   (D)  long

3. As conditions change over long periods of time, life forms change, too, <u>evolving</u> new characteristics that enable them to survive in a different environment.

   (A)  adopting
   (B)  developing
   (C)  finding
   (D)  reserving

4. A clock is an instrument used for dividing the day and night into regular <u>periods</u> of time.

   (A)  intervals
   (B)  areas
   (C)  punctuation
   (D)  eras

GO ON TO THE NEXT PAGE

5. Henry Ford's belief that every man, <u>no matter</u> what his income is, should own an automobile led to the production of the inexpensive Model T.

  (A) realizing
  (B) in addition to
  (C) regardless of
  (D) accommodating

6. A skewed stretch of railroad track in south-central Alaska <u>testifies to</u> the violence of the 1964 Good Friday earthquake.

  (A) resembles
  (B) is evidence of
  (C) reviews
  (D) overlooks

7. Before standardization, the foot as an English unit of measurement varied from about 12 inches to <u>nearly</u> twice that length.

  (A) about
  (B) less than
  (C) usually
  (D) effectively

8. <u>Viewed</u> from the perspective of plate tectonics, mountains seem more awesome than ever.

  (A) Portrayed
  (B) Situated
  (C) Understood
  (D) Applied

9. Emily Dickinson, an important 19th-century American poet, spent most of her life <u>secluded</u> in her father's home in Amherst, Massachusetts.

  (A) residing
  (B) isolated
  (C) writing
  (D) maintained

10. In his paintings of the Grand Canyon completed in the late 1800s, Thomas Moran tried to <u>convey</u> the awe he thought was lacking in geological descriptions of the time.

  (A) understate
  (B) communicate
  (C) comprehend
  (D) disregard

11. The first step in making leather is to <u>soak</u> the animal hides in an enzyme solution to make them ready for tanning.

  (A) hang
  (B) wipe
  (C) immerse
  (D) dip

12. Prefabricated, welded steel frames form <u>a vertical core</u> for the 110 floors of the Sears Tower, the tallest inhabited building in the world.

  (A) an exterior framework
  (B) a stairwell
  (C) a fire escape
  (D) a central support

13. The airplane has reached its present state of perfection <u>due to</u> a great many ideas contributed through the years.

  (A) in addition to
  (B) as a result of
  (C) notwithstanding
  (D) in spite of

14. Chicago is the country's <u>leading</u> manufacturer of machinery.

  (A) rival
  (B) progressive
  (C) major
  (D) central

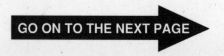

GO ON TO THE NEXT PAGE

15. Killer whales are voracious predators who hunt in small groups or form packs of 40 or more, driving their prey into shallow water where escape is impossible.

    (A) companions
    (B) coinhabitants
    (C) young
    (D) victims

16. Biologists have long understood that living creatures exist in a complex and delicate balance with one another and their surroundings.

    (A) desirable
    (B) sensuous
    (C) demanding
    (D) fragile

17. After witnessing the night bombardment of Fort McHenry by the British, Francis Scott Key wrote the words to the "Star Spangled Banner," our national anthem.

    (A) joining
    (B) hearing
    (C) viewing
    (D) avoiding

18. The flying fish hurls itself from the water with the motion of its strong tail and, once aloft, spreads out its large fins, which act like the wings of a glider.

    (A) afloat
    (B) in the air
    (C) inverted
    (D) in motion

19. The process of learning to walk is a very good illustration of the orderly, step-by-step progress marking the growth of a child.

    (A) picture
    (B) lesson
    (C) routine
    (D) example

20. Canada has the longest coastline of any country in the world; it extends about 60,000 miles along the Atlantic, Arctic, and Pacific oceans and includes the Hudson Bay area.

    (A) continues
    (B) marks
    (C) touches
    (D) limits

21. Scorpions, restricted to dry, warm regions of the world, are characterized by a strong tail curled forward over the back.

    (A) inclined
    (B) coiled
    (C) turned
    (D) pushed

22. Circulation is the means by which food is carried to the tissues of plants and animals and wastes are carried away.

    (A) process
    (B) tube
    (C) circuit
    (D) reason

23. The citizens of a country guide the destiny of the nation.

    (A) future
    (B) government
    (C) documentation
    (D) youth

24. The "safety bicycle," developed in 1885, used wheels of equal size and positioned the rider's seat slightly forward of the rear wheel.

    (A) increasingly
    (B) somewhat
    (C) merely
    (D) approximately

**GO ON TO THE NEXT PAGE**

25. Teaching evolution in state-supported schools was <u>prohibited</u> in Tennessee until the old law was repealed in 1967.

    (A) enjoyed
    (B) upheld
    (C) forbidden
    (D) carried on

26. Chiffon is a soft, <u>sheer</u> fabric made of silk, nylon, or rayon.

    (A) expensive
    (B) bright
    (C) transparent
    (D) smart

27. Mountains, the most spectacular result of the geologic processes that <u>shape</u> the earth's crust, defied comprehension for centuries.

    (A) span
    (B) form
    (C) underlie
    (D) occupy

28. It is only natural that children of tall, thin parents should be tall and thin themselves, rather than <u>plump</u> like many children.

    (A) healthy
    (B) short
    (C) chubby
    (D) small

29. Almost all the living things that populate the world's oceans are found within 700 feet of the surface; below that level, life-sustaining sunlight <u>gives way to</u> cold and darkness.

    (A) is replaced by
    (B) takes over
    (C) monitors
    (D) sustains

30. Chicle is a gumlike, milky juice obtained from <u>certain</u> tropical trees.

    (A) mature
    (B) sure
    (C) particular
    (D) harvested

**GO ON TO THE NEXT PAGE**

<u>Directions:</u>   In the rest of this section you will read several passages. Each one is followed by several questions about it. For questions 31–60, you are to choose the <u>one</u> best answer, (A), (B), (C), or (D), to each question. Then, on your answer sheet, find the number of the question and fill in the space that corresponds to the letter of the answer you have chosen.

Answer all questions following a passage on the basis of what is <u>stated</u> or <u>implied</u> in that passage.

Read the following passage:

> The flamingo is a beautiful water bird with long legs, and a curving neck like a swan's. Most flamingos have deep red or flame-colored feathers with black quills. Some have pink or white feathers. The long legs and webbed feet are well suited
> *Line* for wading. The flamingo eats in a peculiar manner. It plunges its head
> *(5)* underwater and sifts the mud with a fine hairlike "comb" along the edge of its bent bill. In this way, it strains out small shellfish and other animals. The bird nests on a mound of mud with a hollow on top to hold its single egg. Flamingos are timid and often live together in large colonies. The birds once lived in the southern United States, but plume hunters killed them faster than they could breed, and the
> *(10)* flamingo no longer lives wild in the United States.

Example I                                                      Sample Answer

The flamingo can eat shellfish and other        Ⓐ ● Ⓒ Ⓓ
animals because of its

(A)  curved neck
(B)  especially formed bill
(C)  long legs
(D)  brightly colored feathers

According to the passage, the flamingo sifts mud for food with "a fine hairlike 'comb' along the edge of its bent bill." Therefore, you should choose answer (B).

Example II                                                      Sample Answer

How many young would you expect the          Ⓐ Ⓑ ● Ⓓ
flamingo to raise at one time?

(A)  Several
(B)  Two
(C)  One
(D)  Four

The passage states that the flamingo nests on a mound of mud with a "single" egg. Therefore, you should choose answer (C).

Now begin work on the questions.

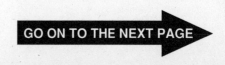

GO ON TO THE NEXT PAGE

Questions 31–36

It takes a long time to raise a family of owlets, so the great horned owl begins
early in the year. In January and February, or as late as March in the North, the
male calls to the female with a resonant hoot. The female is larger than the male.
*Line* She sometimes reaches a body length of twenty-two to twenty-four inches, with a
(5) wingspread up to fifty inches. To impress her, the male does a strange courtship
dance. He bobs. He bows. He ruffles his feathers and hops around with an
important air. He flutters from limb to limb and makes flying sorties into the air.
Sometimes he returns with an offering of food. They share the repast, after which
she joins the dance, hopping and bobbing about as though keeping time to the
(10) beat of an inner drum.

Owls are poor home builders. They prefer to nest in a large hollow in a tree or
even to occupy the deserted nest of a hawk or crow. These structures are large and
rough, built of sticks and bark and lined with leaves and feathers. Sometimes owls
nest on a rocky ledge, or even on the bare ground.

(15) The mother lays two or three round, dull white eggs. Then she stoically settles
herself on the nest and spreads her feather skirts about her to protect her precious
charges from snow and cold.

It is five weeks before the first downy white owlet pecks its way out of the shell.
As the young birds feather out, they look like wise old men with their wide eyes
(20) and quizzical expressions. They clamor for food and keep the parents busy
supplying mice, squirrels, rabbits, crayfish, and beetles. Later in the season baby
crows are taken. Migrating songsters, waterfowl, and game birds all fall prey to
the hungry family. It is nearly ten weeks before fledglings leave the nest to search
for their own food. The parent birds weary of family life by November and drive
(25) the young owls away to establish hunting ranges of their own.

GO ON TO THE NEXT PAGE

31. What is the topic of this passage?

    (A) Raising a family of great horned owls
    (B) Mating rituals of great horned owls
    (C) Nest building of great horned owls
    (D) Habits of young great horned owls

32. It can be inferred from the passage that the courtship of great horned owls

    (A) takes place on the ground
    (B) is an active process
    (C) happens in the fall
    (D) involves the male alone

33. According to the passage, great horned owls

    (A) are discriminate nest builders
    (B) need big nests for their numerous eggs
    (C) may inhabit a previously used nest
    (D) build nests on tree limbs

34. According to the passage, which of the following is the mother owl's job?

    (A) To initiate the courtship ritual
    (B) To feed the young
    (C) To sit on the nest
    (D) To build the nest

35. According to the passage, young owlets eat everything EXCEPT

    (A) other small birds
    (B) insects
    (C) small mammals
    (D) nuts and seeds

36. What can be inferred from the passage about the adult parents of the young great horned owls?

    (A) They are sorry to see their young leave home.
    (B) They are lazy and careless about feeding the small owlets.
    (C) They probably don't see their young after November.
    (D) They don't eat while they are feeding their young.

GO ON TO THE NEXT PAGE

Questions 37–42

There are many theories of aging, but virtually all fall into the category of being hypotheses with a minimum of supporting evidence. One viewpoint is that aging occurs as the body's organ systems become less efficient. Thus failures in the
*Line* immune system, hormonal system, and nervous system could all produce
(5) characteristics that we associate with aging. Following a different vein, many current researchers are looking for evidence at the cellular and subcellular level. It has been shown that cells such as human fibroblasts (generalized tissue cells) grown in culture divide only a limited number of times and then die. (Only cancer cells seem immortal in this respect.) Fibroblast cells from an embryo divide more
(10) times than those taken from an adult. Thus some researchers believe that aging occurs at the cellular level and is part of the cell's genetic makeup. Any event that disturbs the cell's genetic machinery, such as mutation, damaging chemicals in the cell's environment, or loss of genetic material, could cause cells to lose their ability to divide and thus bring on aging. Other theories of aging look at different processes.

37. The author believes the theories of aging are

(A) well-supported hypotheses
(B) poorly supported hypotheses
(C) proven theories
(D) interesting ideas

38. How many theories of aging does this passage present?

(A) One
(B) Two
(C) Four
(D) Three

39. The author of the article points out that cancer cells

(A) divide infinitely
(B) divide and then die
(C) divide more in adults than in embryos
(D) bring on aging

40. It can be inferred from the passage that fibroblast cells

(A) divide fewer times at later stages in human life
(B) are not a focus in cellular research on aging
(C) are similar to cancer cells in rate of division
(D) disfunction in the aging process of the body's immune system

41. As explained in this passage, the theory of aging which examines the cellular level would NOT assign which of the following as a cause of aging?

(A) Mutation
(B) Failure of the body's organ system
(C) Loss of genetic material
(D) Chemical damage from the environment

42. The topic of the next paragraph is probably

(A) a discussion of the creation of life
(B) more hypotheses on aging
(C) further discussion of cancer
(D) a specific description of cell division

**GO ON TO THE NEXT PAGE**

Questions 43–49

To reach the jump-off point for the West, a family from the East could either buy steamboat passage to Missouri for themselves, their wagons, and their livestock or—as happened more often—simply pile everything into a wagon, hitch up a team, and begin their overland trek right in their front yard.

*Line*
*(5)*

Along the macadamized roads and turnpikes east of the Missouri River, travel was comparatively fast, camping easy, and supplies plentiful. Then, in one river town or another, the neophyte emigrants would pause to lay in provisions. For outfitting purposes, the town of Independence had been preeminent ever since 1827, but the rising momentum of pioneer emigration had produced some rival jump-off points. Westport and Fort Leavenworth flourished a few miles upriver. St. Joseph had sprung up 55 miles to the northwest; in fact, emigrants who went to Missouri by riverboat could save four days on the trail by staying on the paddle-wheelers to St. Joe before striking overland.

*(10)*

At whatever jump-off point they chose, the emigrants studied guidebooks and directions, asked questions of others as green as themselves, and made their final decisions about outfitting. They had various, sometimes conflicting, options. For example, either pack animals or two-wheel carts or wagons could be used for the overland crossing. A family man usually chose the wagon. It was the costliest and slowest of the three, but it provided space and shelter for children and for a wife who likely as not was pregnant. Everybody knew that a top-heavy covered wagon might blow over in a prairie wind or be overturned by mountain rocks, that it might mire in river mud, or sink to its hubs in desert sand—but maybe if those things happened on this trip, they would happen to someone else. Anyway, most pioneers, with their farm background, were used to wagons.

*(15)*

*(20)*

43. What is the topic of this passage?

(A) Important river towns
(B) Getting started on the trip West
(C) The advantages of traveling
   by wagon
(D) Choosing a point of departure

44. All of the following can be inferred from the passage about travel east of the Missouri EXCEPT that it

(A) was faster than in the West
(B) was easier than in the West
(C) took place on good roads
(D) was usually by steamboat

45. Which of the cities that served as a jump-off point can be inferred from the passage to be farthest west?

(A) Independence
(B) St. Joseph
(C) Westport
(D) Fort Leavenworth

46. The author implies in the passage that the early emigrants

(A) knew a lot about travel
(B) were well stocked with provisions
   when they left their homes
(C) left from the same place in Missouri
(D) preferred wagon travel to other types
   of travel

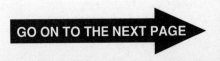
GO ON TO THE NEXT PAGE

47. All of the following were mentioned in the passage as options for modes of transportation from the Missouri River to the West EXCEPT

    (A) a wagon
    (B) a riverboat
    (C) a pack animal
    (D) a two-wheel cart

48. The word *green* in line 15 could best be replaced by which of the following?

    (A) frightened
    (B) optimistic
    (C) inexperienced
    (D) weary

49. All of the following features of the covered wagon made it unattractive to the emigrants EXCEPT

    (A) the speed at which it could travel
    (B) its bulk
    (C) its familiarity and size
    (D) its cost

**GO ON TO THE NEXT PAGE**

Questions 50–54

Our excellent natural resources paved the way for the development of abundant capital to increase our growth. Capital includes the tools—such as machines, vehicles, and buildings—that make the outputs of labor and resources more
*Line* valuable. But it also includes the funds necessary to buy those tools. If a society
(5) had to consume everything it produced just to stay alive, nothing could be put aside to increase future productions. But if a farmer can grow more corn than his family needs to eat, he can use the surplus as seed to increase the next crop, or to feed workers who build tractors. This process of capital accumulation was aided in the American economy by our cultural heritage. Saving played an important
(10) role in the European tradition; it contributed to Americans' motivation to put something aside today, for the tools to buy tomorrow.

50. With what subject is this passage mainly concerned?

(A) History
(B) Finance
(C) Economics
(D) Culture

51. The previous passage most probably discussed

(A) earlier settling of the country by Europeans
(B) our natural resources
(C) the economics of agriculture
(D) savings and loan banks

52. According to the passage, capitol includes all of the following EXCEPT

(A) factories
(B) tractors
(C) money
(D) workers

53. According to the passage, which of the following would lead to accumulating capital?

(A) Training workers who produce goods
(B) Studying the cultural history of the country
(C) Consuming what is produced
(D) Planting more of a crop than is needed

54. It can be inferred from the passage that the European ancestors of early Americans

(A) sent many tools to America
(B) taught their skills to their offspring
(C) were accustomed to saving
(D) were good farmers

GO ON TO THE NEXT PAGE

Questions 55–60

Sometimes it's hard to figure out if you have a food allergy, since it can show up so many different ways. Your symptoms could be caused by many other problems. You may have rashes, hives, joint pains mimicking arthritis, headaches, irritability, or depression.

*Line*
*(5)*      The most common food allergies are to milk, eggs, seafood, wheat, nuts, seeds, chocolate, oranges, and tomatoes. Many of these allergies will not develop if these foods are not fed to an infant until her or his intestines mature at around seven months. Breast milk also tends to be protective.    Migraines can be set off by foods containing tyramine, phenathylamine, monosodium glutamate, or sodium
*(10)*    nitrate. Common foods which contain these are chocolate, aged cheeses, sour cream, red wine, pickled herring, chicken livers, avocados, ripe bananas, cured meats, many Oriental and prepared foods (read the labels!). Some people have been successful in treating their migraines with supplements of B vitamins, particularly $B_6$ and niacin.
*(15)*    Children who are hyperactive may benefit from eliminating food additives, especially colorings, and foods high in salicylates from their diets. A few of these are almonds, green peppers, peaches, tea, grapes. This is the diet made popular by Benjamin Feingold, who has written the book *Why Your Child Is Hyperactive*. Other researchers have had mixed results when testing whether the diet is effective.

55. The topic of this passage is

   (A) reactions to foods
   (B) food and nutrition
   (C) infants and allergies
   (D) a good diet

56. According to the passage, the difficulty in diagnosing allergies to foods is due to

   (A) the vast number of different foods we eat
   (B) lack of a proper treatment plan
   (C) the similarity of symptoms of the allergy to other problems
   (D) using prepared formula to feed babies

57. What can be inferred about babies from this passage?

   (A) They can eat almost anything.
   (B) They should have a carefully restricted diet as infants.
   (C) They gain little benefit from being breast fed.
   (D) They may become hyperactive if fed solid food too early.

58. The author states that the reason that infants need to avoid certain foods related to allergies has to do with the infant's

   (A) lack of teeth
   (B) poor metabolism
   (C) underdeveloped intestinal tract
   (D) inability to swallow solid foods

GO ON TO THE NEXT PAGE

59. Which of the following was a suggested treatment for migraines in the passage?

   (A) Eating more ripe bananas
   (B) Avoiding all Oriental foods
   (C) Getting plenty of sodium nitrate
   (D) Using vitamin B in addition to a good diet

60. According to the passage, the Feingold diet is NOT

   (A) verified by researchers as being consistently effective
   (B) available in book form
   (C) beneficial for hyperactive children
   (D) designed to eliminate foods containing certain food additives

**THIS IS THE END OF SECTION 3**

IF YOU FINISH BEFORE TIME IS CALLED, CHECK YOUR WORK
ON SECTION 3 ONLY.
DO NOT READ OR WORK ON ANY OTHER SECTION OF THE TEST.

# TEST OF WRITTEN ENGLISH

## PRACTICE TEST ONE

Time—30 minutes

Some people feel that competition is an important part of adult life and that children should be exposed to competitive activities at an early age. Others feel that children should not be involved in competition. Discuss these two positions. Indicate which position you agree with and why.

### NOTES

Use this space to make your notes. Write the final version of your essay on lined paper. The Sample TWE Answer Sheet on page 192 is an example of the amount of writing space provided in the TOEFL Test.

# PRACTICE TEST TWO

SECTION 1
LISTENING COMPREHENSION

In this section of the test, you will have an opportunity to demonstrate your ability to understand spoken English. There are three parts to this section, with special directions for each part.

Part A

Directions:  For each question in Part A, you will hear a short sentence. Each sentence will be spoken just one time. The sentences you hear will not be written out for you. Therefore, you must listen carefully to understand what the speaker says.

After you hear a sentence, read the four choices in your test book, marked (A), (B), (C), and (D), and decide which one is closest in meaning to the sentence you heard. Then, on your answer sheet, find the number of the question and fill in the space that corresponds to the letter of the answer you have chosen. Fill in the space so that the letter inside the oval cannot be seen.

Example I

You will hear:

You will read:

Sample Answer

(A) (B) ● (D)

(A)  Greg didn't bother to leave a tip.
(B)  Greg thought about typing a
       letter to his brother.
(C)  Greg didn't like to type.
(D)  My typing bothered Greg.

The speaker said, "Greg thought typing was a bother." Sentence (C), "Greg didn't like to type," is closest in meaning to the sentence you heard. Therefore, you should choose answer (C).

Example II

You will hear:

You will read:

Sample Answer

(A) ● (C) (D)

(A)  Everyone will be able to take this
       exam later.
(B)  Students should bring a calculator
       to this exam.
(C)  This test will be part of every
       student's final grade.
(D)  No one can calculate the grades
       for this test.

The speaker said, "Everyone needs a calculator for this test." Sentence (B), "Students should bring a calculator to this exam," is closest in meaning to the sentence you heard. Therefore, you should choose answer (B).

**GO ON TO THE NEXT PAGE** ▶

1. (A) Frank was not able to continue
       working.
   (B) Everyone who worked with Frank
       liked him.
   (C) Frank had quite a few jobs that he liked.
   (D) Frank didn't enjoy his job, so he quit.

2. (A) He found her studying in the library.
   (B) He went to see her at the library.
   (C) She helped him find a place to study
       in the library.
   (D) He was studying in the library when
       she located him.

3. (A) He handed out his packed suitcase.
   (B) The handouts are in his suitcase.
   (C) His suit was packed in the case.
   (D) This case has gotten out of hand.

4. (A) Karen needs to know how to get from
       the theater to the dentist's office.
   (B) Dennis and Karen can go to the
       theater together.
   (C) Karen won't go to the theater
       today because she has a dental
       appointment.
   (D) Karen is afraid the dentist won't see her.

5. (A) I cleaned my office once after I started
       my new job.
   (B) I can begin working at once.
   (C) I will begin cleaning my office at
       one o'clock.
   (D) I must clean my office before I
       begin working.

6. (A) I think Tom always travels first class.
   (B) How far does Tom have to go to get to
       his first class?
   (C) Doesn't Tom usually travel in the
       most economical way possible?
   (D) Tom doesn't always travel first class.

7. (A) Does Jane know more than one
       language?
   (B) Jane has a special talent for languages.
   (C) Have you talked about what to give
       Jane yet?
   (D) Jane gave as much as you did to the
       language club.

8. (A) We weren't able to finish our work
       before it was time to go home.
   (B) We weren't allowed to work on our
       experiments outside of class.
   (C) We didn't have enough experience to
       work alone.
   (D) The physics professor finished our
       experiments for us.

9. (A) Sandy was touched by her
       family's feelings.
   (B) Sandy's family was out for
       the evening.
   (C) Sandy feels isolated from her family.
   (D) Sandy doesn't want to be in contact
       with her family.

10. (A) Professor Hartwick doesn't mind
        having people stop to see him.
    (B) Parents can take Professor Hartwick's
        classes for free.
    (C) Students are not afraid to arrive late
        for Professor Hartwick's classes.
    (D) Professor Hartwick wants students
        and parents to take his classes
        together.

11. (A) I am moving ahead as we agreed.
    (B) I look forward to hearing from
        you soon.
    (C) I will contact you as soon as possible.
    (D) A copy of the contract is being sent
        to you.

12. (A) Did someone lead her to the wrong
        classroom?
    (B) The difficult directions for this class
        are misleading.
    (C) This course seems to be more difficult
        than she thought it would be.
    (D) She is having a difficult time finding
        the class.

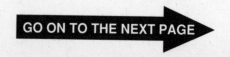

GO ON TO THE NEXT PAGE

13. (A) Don't think about a second gift.
    (B) Think about it for a second.
    (C) Don't worry about it.
    (D) Don't give it away without thinking about it.

14. (A) It doesn't matter how often my brother and I see one another.
    (B) My brother and I always manage to see each other once a year.
    (C) I will get the matter with my brother settled this year.
    (D) My brother and I will discuss the matter together.

15. (A) I would like to hear the other piano.
    (B) Arthur can not hear well any more.
    (C) Arthur has never played the piano for me.
    (D) I don't play the piano anymore.

16. (A) Professor Clark would like us to put covers on our books this semester.
    (B) Professor Clark will try to discuss the entire book during one semester.
    (C) The cover of Professor Clark's book has a hole in it.
    (D) We should attend Professor Clark's discussion of the book this semester.

17. (A) Andrew has asked for a locker.
    (B) I hope that Andrew will let me use his locker.
    (C) Andrew put his things on my rocker.
    (D) Andrew would like to use my locker.

18. (A) She seldom asks me anything.
    (B) Her class is very hard for me.
    (C) She almost never calls me at home.
    (D) I often stop to see her after class.

19. (A) I feel sorry for the librarians who have to work on Saturdays.
    (B) I wish the library didn't close early on Saturdays.
    (C) Fortunately, the library is open on Saturdays.
    (D) In this city the library is closed on Saturdays.

20. (A) Only some of the children had fun on the playground.
    (B) Some of the children went home because the playground was too noisy.
    (C) All of the children enjoyed the playground.
    (D) The playground wasn't large enough for all of the children.

**GO ON TO THE NEXT PAGE**

## Part B

<u>Directions:</u>   In Part B you will hear short conversations between two speakers. At the end of each conversation, a third person will ask a question about what was said. You will hear each conversation and question about it just one time. Therefore, you must listen carefully to understand what each speaker says. After you hear a conversation and the question about it, read the four possible answers in your test book and decide which <u>one</u> is the best answer to the question you heard. Then, on your answer sheet, find the number of the question and fill in the space that corresponds to the letter of the answer you have chosen.

Look at the following example.

You will hear:

You will read:
(A)  At last winter is almost over.
(B)  She doesn't like winter weather
     very much.
(C)  This winter's weather is similar to
     last winter's weather.
(D)  Winter won't last as long this year as
     it did last year.

<u>Sample Answer</u>
(A) (B) ● (D)

From the conversation you learn that the woman thinks the weather this winter is almost the same as the weather last winter. The best answer to the question "What does the woman mean?" is (C), "This winter's weather is similar to last winter's weather." Therefore, you should choose answer (C).

21. (A)  They are enjoying a visit after a long
         separation.
    (B)  They don't see each other unless they
         have to.
    (C)  They will not see each other again for
         a long time.
    (D)  They aren't speaking to each other.

22. (A)  Let's go to a movie.
    (B)  Let's stay home.
    (C)  Why should we go to a movie?
    (D)  Why don't we go home?

23. (A)  She could not afford to fly to Chicago.
    (B)  She has taken the bus to Chicago
         only twice.
    (C)  Taking a plane costs more but
         saves time.
    (D)  It is better to go to Chicago on the bus.

24. (A)  At an art exhibit.
    (B)  In a supermarket.
    (C)  In a shoe store.
    (D)  In a clothing store.

25. (A)  Ted didn't observe the speed limit.
    (B)  Ted should go to the hospital.
    (C)  More time is needed to evaluate
         Ted's condition.
    (D)  Ted will soon end his emergency
         training.

26. (A)  She doesn't want to practice
         any more.
    (B)  They've been dancing since
         six o'clock.
    (C)  The dance routine needs more
         right turns.
    (D)  She will be ready to practice at
         six o'clock.

27. (A)  It doesn't serve very good fish.
    (B)  It is an excellent restaurant.
    (C)  It has slow service.
    (D)  He'd like to see it again.

**GO ON TO THE NEXT PAGE**

28. (A) He ate too much and needs to go to sleep.
    (B) He can't wait to see his friends tomorrow.
    (C) The woman should wait until tomorrow to have her party.
    (D) He doesn't want to go to the party because it starts late.

29. (A) She didn't need a ride from the airport.
    (B) She might have missed her flight from Boston.
    (C) She was taking a trip to Boston.
    (D) She had decided not to make the trip.

30. (A) She knew the doctor was fifty years old.
    (B) She is not surprised by the man's statement.
    (C) The man should wait to see a doctor.
    (D) She is shocked by the man's statement.

31. (A) Be understanding toward the woman.
    (B) Lower the woman's final grade.
    (C) Work hard to get an extension.
    (D) Expect the woman to finish her paper first.

32. (A) It hasn't rained much lately.
    (B) The woman doesn't like Ray.
    (C) Ray is behaving differently than usual.
    (D) The class started late because of the rain.

33. (A) The woman doesn't need to type her English paper.
    (B) He doesn't want to type any papers.
    (C) Both of the woman's papers should be typed.
    (D) There are two papers this term.

34. (A) John's mother can't hear him very well right now.
    (B) John's mother isn't here right now.
    (C) The telephone belongs to John's mother.
    (D) The telephone is not available right now.

35. (A) She lives too far away to go to Jane's presentation.
    (B) Jane didn't appear nervous at all during her presentation.
    (C) Jane needs to take lessons in public speaking.
    (D) She didn't understand Jane's presentation.

GO ON TO THE NEXT PAGE

Part C

Directions: In this part of the test, you will hear short talks and conversations. After each of them, you will be asked some questions. You will hear the talks and conversations and the questions about them just one time. They will not be written out for you. Therefore, you must listen carefully to understand what each speaker says.

After you hear a question, read the four possible answers in your test book and decide which <u>one</u> is the best answer to the question you heard. Then, on your answer sheet, find the number of the question and fill in the space that corresponds to the letter of the answer you have chosen.

Answer all questions on the basis of what is <u>stated</u> or <u>implied</u> in the talk or conversation.

Listen to this sample talk.

You will hear:

Now look at the following example.

You will hear:

You will read:

(A)  Only bumblebees can fertilize red
        clover plants.
(B)  Bumblebees protect red clover from
        plant eating insects.
(C)  Bumblebees bring water to red clover
        plants on their tongues.
(D)  Bumblebees keep mice and other animals
        away from red clover plants.

Sample Answer
● Ⓑ Ⓒ Ⓓ

The best answer to the question "Why is it impossible to raise red clover where there are no bumblebees?" is (A), "Only bumblebees can fertilize red clover plants." Therefore, you should choose answer (A).

Now look at the next example.

You will hear:

You will read:

(A)  They both make honey.
(B)  They both build combs.
(C)  Both of them are found in
        underground nests.
(D)  They both live through the winter.

Sample Answer
Ⓐ Ⓑ Ⓒ ●

The best answer to the question "According to the speaker, in what way are the queen wasp and the queen bee similar?" is (D), "They both live through the winter." Therefore, you should choose answer (D).

36. (A)  At a public lecture.
    (B)  In an alley.
    (C)  In a pet store.
    (D)  In a zoology class.

37. (A)  Someone who is trying to find a home
        for a cat.
    (B)  Someone who has lost a cat.
    (C)  Someone who might be interested in
        buying a cat.
    (D)  Someone who wants to breed their cat.

**GO ON TO THE NEXT PAGE**

38. (A) A common cat
    (B) A hungry cat.
    (C) A pure-bred cat.
    (D) An expensive cat.

39. (A) Loss of blood.
    (B) Ancestry.
    (C) Training.
    (D) Reproducing.

40. (A) They are both very expensive.
    (B) They both make good pets.
    (C) The history of both can be traced.
    (D) They both often go homeless.

41. (A) He is indifferent.
    (B) He is angry.
    (C) He thinks it's a joke.
    (D) He is surprised.

42. (A) The man told her about it.
    (B) She received a letter about it.
    (C) She spoke to the teacher.
    (D) She was notified at preregistration.

43. (A) He will call the registrar.
    (B) The woman will explain it to him.
    (C) He will get a copy of the woman's list.
    (D) The library has extra copies.

44. (A) He is interested.
    (B) He is overwhelmed.
    (C) He is bothered.
    (D) He is unhappy.

45. (A) Go home.
    (B) Go to the registrar's office.
    (C) Go to the lecture series.
    (D) Go to the library.

46. (A) Life in Norway during Viking times.
    (B) Different ocean routes taken by the Vikings.
    (C) Methods used in Viking navigation.
    (D) The importance of migrating geese in Viking navigation.

47. (A) The construction of Viking ships.
    (B) Viking use of the stars in navigation.
    (C) Ingenuity and technology in 900 A.D.
    (D) Landmarks.

48. (A) They followed the route of migrating birds instead.
    (B) They wanted to avoid pack-ice.
    (C) Along the longer route, they could stop at islands.
    (D) They followed the path of the stars instead.

49. (A) Their feeding ground could be used by the Vikings as a landmark.
    (B) They were a good source of food for the Vikings.
    (C) The Vikings could follow their migratory route to find land.
    (D) They helped the Vikings find routes through the ice.

50. (A) They weren't able to travel very far from their homeland.
    (B) They migrated south.
    (C) They developed an advanced technology.
    (D) They were expert sailors.

**THIS IS THE END OF THE LISTENING COMPREHENSION SECTION OF THE TEST**

THE NEXT PART OF THE TEST IS SECTION 2. TURN TO THE
DIRECTIONS FOR SECTION 2 IN YOUR TEST BOOK.
READ THEM, AND BEGIN WORK.
DO NOT READ OR WORK ON ANY OTHER SECTION OF THE TEST.

SECTION 2
STRUCTURE AND WRITTEN EXPRESSION

Time—25 minutes

This section is designed to measure your ability to recognize language that is appropriate for standard written English. There are two types of questions in this section, with special directions for each type.

Directions:   Questions 1–15 are incomplete sentences. Beneath each sentence you will see four words or phrases, marked (A), (B), (C), and (D). Choose the one word or phrase that best completes the sentence. Then, on your answer sheet, find the number of the question and fill in the space that corresponds to the letter of the answer you have chosen. Fill in the space so that the letter inside the oval cannot be seen.

Example I

Most American families _____ at least one automobile.

Sample Answer

● Ⓑ Ⓒ Ⓓ

    (A)  have
    (B)  in
    (C)  that
    (D)  has

The sentence should read, "Most American families have at least one automobile." Therefore, you should choose answer (A).

Example II

_____ recent times, the discipline of biology has expanded rapidly into a variety of subdisciplines.

Sample Answer

Ⓐ Ⓑ Ⓒ ●

    (A)  It is since
    (B)  When
    (C)  Since it is
    (D)  In

The sentence should read, "In recent times, the discipline of biology has expanded into a variety of subdisciplines." Therefore, you should choose answer (D).

Now begin work on the questions.

1. The life of Benjamin Franklin, a practical man _____ many stories have been told, was unusually productive.

    (A)  of
    (B)  about whom
    (C)  about
    (D)  of which

2. Indiana University, one of the largest in the nation, is located _____ town.

    (A)  a small midwestern
    (B)  in a small midwestern
    (C)  small midwestern
    (D)  in small midwestern

**GO ON TO THE NEXT PAGE** ▶

3. _____ his life, Eugene O'Neill was regarded as the foremost American dramatist.

   (A) It was the time of
   (B) While
   (C) During
   (D) By the time of

4. _____ Social Security Act of 1935 was written to insure workers against unemployment.

   (A) The
   (B) What the
   (C) For the
   (D) After the

5. Chemists are not sure _____ .

   (A) how precisely can cold fusion occur
   (B) cold fusion can occur precisely how
   (C) precisely how cold fusion can occur
   (D) can cold fusion occur precisely how

6. Just off the Massachusetts coast _____ , a popular summer resort area.

   (A) Martha's Vineyard is
   (B) is where Martha's Vineyard
   (C) Martha's Vineyard
   (D) is Martha's Vineyard

7. Franchising offers many advantages to small business owners _____ problematic.

   (A) however it is
   (B) even though it is
   (C) despite its
   (D) it is

8. Although most cats hate to swim, _____ if necessary.

   (A) can they do so
   (B) so can they do
   (C) they do so can
   (D) they can do so

9. American author John Updike, _____ , spent his boyhood in Shillington, Pennsylvania.

   (A) was the only child of a high-school mathematics teacher
   (B) whom the only child of a high-school mathematics teacher
   (C) the only child of a high-school mathematics teacher
   (D) he was the only child of a high-school mathematics teacher

10. In practice, setting up a chain of command in a business can be a very complicated task, _____ it involves the interaction of real human beings.

    (A) because of
    (B) how
    (C) as
    (D) due to

11. When linguists encounter a new language, _____ work to identify all of the sounds it contains.

    (A) who
    (B) they
    (C) and
    (D) those

12. According to recent investigations, unselfish motives, such as true empathy, _____ , and commitment to a principle, sometimes surpass self-interest in influencing human behavior.

    (A) to have solidarity with others
    (B) others with solidarity
    (C) solidarity with others
    (D) one has solidarity with others

**GO ON TO THE NEXT PAGE**

13. _____ the lip of an open-pit copper mine, the huge tractors and cranes below look like toys, and people look like tiny ants scurrying about.

    (A) Where
    (B) While
    (C) That
    (D) From

14. Not only _____ atoms with their microscopes, but they now can also "feel" them with the aid of a versatile sensing device called the "magic wrist."

    (A) are today's scientists able to see
    (B) able to see today's scientists are
    (C) today's scientists are able to see
    (D) are able to see today's scientists

15. In the seventeenth century, North America was vast and unconquered, _____ only at great cost.

    (A) it promised riches but yielded its bounty
    (B) promising riches but yielding its bounty
    (C) by promising riches but by yielding its bounty
    (D) its riches were promised but its bounty yielded

**Directions:** In questions 16–40 each sentence has four underlined words or phrases. The four underlined parts of the sentence are marked (A), (B), (C), and (D). Identify the <u>one</u> underlined word or phrase that must be changed in order for the sentence to be correct. Then, on your answer sheet, find the number of the question and fill in the space that corresponds to the letter of the answer you have chosen.

Example I

The octopus <u>is</u> a unique animal <u>because</u> <u>they</u>
      A            B   C
has three <u>functioning</u> hearts.
         D

Sample Answer

(A) (B) ● (D)

The sentence should read, "The octopus is a unique animal because it has three functioning hearts." Therefore, you should choose answer (C).

Example II

The beagle, <u>one of the most</u> <u>ancient</u> breeds of
            A        B
dog <u>known</u>, <u>originating</u> in England.
   C     D

Sample Answer

(A) (B) (C) ●

The sentence should read, "The beagle, one of the most ancient breeds of dog known, originated in England." Therefore, you should choose answer (D).

Now begin work on the questions.

**GO ON TO THE NEXT PAGE**

16. <u>For make</u> <u>its</u> nest, the yellow-headed blackbird <u>weaves</u> a small cup and fastens <u>it</u> to reeds
       A    B                                   C                      D
    above water.

17. Native American <u>beaded</u> designs are often <u>characterized by</u> geometric <u>shaped</u> and <u>bright</u> colors.
                 A                      B                 C      D

18. The codfish <u>lays</u> <u>million</u> of eggs each year, <u>only</u> a small percentage <u>of which</u> actually hatch.
             A    B                   C                   D

19. When the body becomes <u>extremely</u> overheated, it <u>failure</u> to cool <u>itself</u> again, and sunstroke
                            A                   B          C
    <u>can occur</u>.
     D

20. The <u>preferring</u> of <u>many</u> Western cultures for <u>maintaining</u> a physical distance of <u>at least</u> three feet
        A       B                       C                       D
    during social interaction is well documented in anthropological studies.

21. <u>In chronicling</u> her months <u>as</u> a captive of the Wampanoag Indians, Mary Rowlandson
       A                           B
    <u>demonstrated</u> <u>his</u> narrative skill.
       C        D

22. The nests of <u>most</u> bird <u>species</u> are <u>strategic</u> placed to camouflage them <u>against predators</u>.
               A       B       C                         D

23. Few synthetic vitamins and minerals in pill supplements are  absorbed so efficiently <u>by the body</u>
                                                                        A
    <u>that are</u> those  <u>occurring</u> naturally <u>in foods</u>.
      B              C            D

24. On the one hand, most Americans <u>feel</u> that space exploration is a legitimate <u>and important</u>
                                 A                                   B
    national undertaking; <u>on the contrary</u>, they <u>worry about</u> the amount it costs.
                             C                D

25. Vitamin K <u>providing</u> the <u>necessary</u> impetus for the synthesis of <u>at least</u> two proteins <u>involved</u> in
              A         B                         C              D
    blood clotting.

26. If no fossil record <u>were</u> available, the next strongest evidence of the kinship among organisms
                     A
    would <u>to be</u>  similarities in the <u>embryonic</u> development of organisms <u>today</u>.
          B                     C                           D

27. The black cherry tree, <u>from which</u> fine cabinets and furniture <u>is</u> made, is found <u>all across</u> North
                       A                            B               C
    America, from Nova Scotia <u>to</u> Texas.
                          D

28. Research and <u>recommending</u> <u>concerning</u> the dangers of <u>smoking</u> are beginning to have an
                  A        B                  C
    impact on the tobacco <u>industry</u> in the United States.
                          D

29. Antarctic blue whales <u>can be</u> <u>100 foot long</u> and weigh <u>more than any</u> dinosaur that <u>ever</u> lived.
                     A       B                      C               D

30. Oil-base house paint is neither easy to work with <u>or</u> quick to clean up, <u>but</u> it is often <u>preferred to</u>
                                         A                  B              C
    latex paint <u>because of</u> its high sheen and durability.
             D

31. The colonists <u>who</u> first settled in New England <u>did so</u> <u>because</u> they felt there was <u>none</u> social
               A                           B     C                   D
    justice in their homeland of England.

32. Architect Louis Sullivan <u>commanded</u> the respect of <u>his</u> contemporaries for his work on the
                        A                   B
    <u>designed</u> of <u>the first</u> American skyscrapers.
      C       D

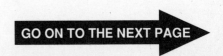
**GO ON TO THE NEXT PAGE**

33. <u>During</u> the 1850s, the Spanish colony of Cuba was <u>of interest</u> to Southerners, <u>who</u> felt they
       A                              B                   C
    needed it <u>for it</u> increasing political and economic power.
           D

34. Glucose is different from fructose <u>in its</u> structural formula, <u>but</u> the molecular formula for <u>these</u>
                                        A                   B                     C
    two sugars is the <u>similar</u>.
               D

35. A sealer <u>should be applied</u> <u>at</u> wood surfaces before they are varnished; <u>otherwise</u>, uneven
               A        B                                  C
    absorption of the varnish <u>may occur</u>.
                            D

36. The high temperatures <u>created</u> by fire are necessary <u>for to split</u> <u>open</u> the <u>seed-bearing</u> cones of
                           A                          B      C         D
    lodge pole pines.

37. Mormon leader Brigham Young was <u>too</u> brilliant and strong-willed <u>that</u> he was <u>able to organize</u>
                                     A                        B         C
    the most remarkable  religious migration in the annals <u>of</u> American history.
                                                             D

38. <u>Due to</u> her untimely death, the <u>talented</u> writer Sylvia Plath was never to know how well
     A                           B
    <u>would her work be</u> received <u>by</u> the American public.
        C                    D

39. From the Mexican War <u>toward</u> the Civil War, the major theme of American <u>political</u> history was
                        A                                            B
    a <u>growing sectionalism</u> <u>interacting</u> with a vigorous nationalism.
               C           D

40. In Western culture, <u>much</u> attention <u>been given</u> to the subject of social class conflict, <u>which</u>
                     A            B                                  C
    <u>may cause</u> revolution.
      D

**THIS IS THE END OF SECTION 2**

IF YOU FINISH BEFORE TIME IS CALLED, CHECK YOUR WORK
ON SECTION 2 ONLY.
DO NOT READ OR WORK ON ANY OTHER SECTION OF THE TEST.
THE SUPERVISOR WILL TELL YOU WHEN TO BEGIN
WORK ON SECTION 3.

SECTION 3
VOCABULARY AND READING COMPREHENSION
Time—45 minutes

This section is designed to measure your comprehension of standard written English. There are two types of questions in this section, with special directions for each type.

Directions:   In questions 1–30 each sentence has an underlined word or phrase. Below each sentence are four other words or phrases, marked (A), (B), (C), (D). You are to choose the one word or phrase that best keeps the meaning of the original sentence if it is substituted for the underlined word or phrase. Then, on your answer sheet, find the number of the question and fill in the space that corresponds to the letter you have chosen. Fill in the space so that the letter inside the oval cannot be seen.

Example

Ladybugs, small brightly colored beetles, feed on plant aphids and have considerable economic value in controlling pest populations.

Sample Answer

(A)  limiting
(B)  finding
(C)  increasing
(D)  ruling

The best answer is (A) because "Ladybugs, small brightly colored beetles, feed on plant aphids and have considerable economic value in limiting pest populations" is closest in meaning to the original sentence. Therefore, you should choose answer (A).

Now begin work on the questions.

1. Samuel Morse's most important contribution to the telegraph was a notched rod which would operate the lines of the sending device.

   (A)  receiver
   (B)  microphone
   (C)  matrix
   (D)  mechanism

2. In most cities crowded residential districts lie between the downtown factory area and the central business district.

   (A)  suburban
   (B)  rural
   (C)  shopping
   (D)  housing

3. A club is a group of people organized for some particular purpose, such as enjoyment and entertainment.

   (A)  perhaps
   (B)  for example
   (C)  specifically
   (D)  except for

4. One of the biggest problems in graphology is to discover which personality characteristics should be expected to show up in handwriting.

   (A)  reveal themselves
   (B)  clear themselves up
   (C)  resolve themselves
   (D)  deteriorate

GO ON TO THE NEXT PAGE

5. Cockles, a type of sea clam, are usually found burrowed in sand flats on the seashore.

   (A) lying on
   (B) swimming near
   (C) dug into
   (D) crawling on

6. The American Legion was formally founded at St. Louis on May 8, 1919, by a group of delegates representing the veterans of World War I.

   (A) officially
   (B) previously
   (C) specifically
   (D) ultimately

7. A clipper ship was a fast, slender vessel developed by American builders during the 1830s and 1840s.

   (A) wooden
   (B) seasoned
   (C) heavy
   (D) trim

8. The Great Wall of China, the world's greatest wall fortification, was completed in only 15 years.

   (A) separation
   (B) protection
   (C) extension
   (D) demarcation

9. Fungi helps man by causing decay so that rubbish doesn't accumulate endlessly.

   (A) immeasurably
   (B) indiscriminately
   (C) continually
   (D) tirelessly

10. Coaches served as the main means of public travel before the development of railroads.

    (A) replaced
    (B) supplemented
    (C) functioned as
    (D) looked like

11. The principle of the telephone depends on changing sound waves which have been carried in the air to vibrating electrical current.

    (A) undulating
    (B) vivacious
    (C) inexpensive
    (D) steady

12. The confusion over patents is often settled in courts of law.

    (A) lawsuits
    (B) misunderstanding
    (C) payment
    (D) liquidation

13. The Chesapeake Bay Bridge spans 21 miles across the Chesapeake Bay, linking the states of Maryland and Virginia.

    (A) entering
    (B) joining
    (C) crossing
    (D) extending

14. In countries where food is scarce, people have to spend most of their time getting enough to eat.

    (A) highly valued
    (B) well prepared
    (C) limited
    (D) expensive

15. When the Egyptians adopted the seven-day week, they named the days after five planets, the sun, and the moon.

    (A) sanctioned
    (B) considered
    (C) received
    (D) mentioned

**GO ON TO THE NEXT PAGE**

16. Vultures, often thought of as being sinister specters of death, are really shy, <u>inoffensive</u>, and downright helpful.

    (A) bothersome
    (B) harmless
    (C) repugnant
    (D) retiring

17. Warren G. Harding, whose presidential term was marred by scandal and corruption, is today <u>regarded</u> as a well-intentioned man who lacked leadership capabilities.

    (A) relayed
    (B) considered
    (C) denied
    (D) received

18. Some amphibians remain as tadpoles for a few weeks, or in some <u>cases</u>, for two years, before they look more like the mature animal.

    (A) instances
    (B) locations
    (C) environments
    (D) species

19. Television can influence our thoughts, our understanding, our likes and dislikes, our <u>manner</u> of speech, and even our dress.

    (A) politeness
    (B) style
    (C) speed
    (D) understanding

20. In modern times, of course, a press means something <u>altogether</u> different than it did in medieval times.

    (A) somewhat
    (B) completely
    (C) albeit
    (D) generally

21. Travel brochures offer potential tourists <u>concisely</u> written descriptions of places and attractions.

    (A) instructively
    (B) quickly
    (C) succinctly
    (D) marginally

22. <u>Traces</u> of ammonia from the decay of animal and plant matter are always found in the air.

    (A) Small amounts
    (B) Clouds
    (C) Scents
    (D) Marks

23. In the past, baths have served a primarily religious, social, or pleasurable function far more than <u>a hygienic</u> one.

    (A) a historical
    (B) an antiquated
    (C) a sanitary
    (D) a private

24. The thin metal diaphragm in the mouthpiece of the telephone <u>resembles</u> the human eardrum.

    (A) is similar to
    (B) amplifies
    (C) replaces
    (D) interacts with

25. Concern for the nature of human language is <u>characteristically</u> a function of twentieth-century thought.

    (A) virtually
    (B) sometimes
    (C) individually
    (D) typically

GO ON TO THE NEXT PAGE ▶

26. In television broadcasting many local stations are <u>affiliated with</u> the major networks.

    (A) associated with
    (B) in competition with
    (C) respected by
    (D) monitored by

27. A popular folklore character of the American Northwest is Paul Bunyan, <u>renowned</u> for his size and strength.

    (A) laughed at
    (B) mocked
    (C) famous
    (D) named

28. Of all the inventions of the late 1800s, the windmill was <u>deemed</u> most necessary for the survival of the prairie farmer.

    (A) judged
    (B) nominated
    (C) insinuated
    (D) suggested

29. The simplest type of telescope used by astronomers is called a refracting telescope, in which the <u>image</u> is inverted unless a special lens is utilized.

    (A) picture
    (B) distance
    (C) magnification
    (D) density

30. During many of the centuries that East African trade was <u>flourishing</u>, trade in western Europe was slowed almost to a standstill.

    (A) developing
    (B) thriving
    (C) decreasing
    (D) producing

**GO ON TO THE NEXT PAGE**

Directions: In the rest of this section you will read several passages. Each one is followed by several questions about it. For questions 31–60, you are to choose the <u>one</u> best answer, (A), (B), (C), or (D), to each question. Then, on your answer sheet, find the number of the question and fill in the space that corresponds to the letter of the answer you have chosen.

Answer all questions following a passage on the basis of what is <u>stated</u> or <u>implied</u> in that passage.

Read the following passage:

       The flamingo is a beautiful water bird with long legs, and a curving neck like a swan's. Most flamingos have deep red or flame-colored feathers with black quills. Some have pink or white feathers. The long legs and webbed feet are well suited
*Line*   for wading. The flamingo eats in a peculiar manner. It plunges its head
*(5)*   underwater and sifts the mud with a fine hairlike "comb" along the edge of its bent bill. In this way, it strains out small shellfish and other animals. The bird nests on a mound of mud with a hollow on top to hold its single egg. Flamingos are timid and often live together in large colonies. The birds once lived in the southern United States, but plume hunters killed them faster than they could breed, and the
*(10)*   flamingo no longer lives wild in the United States.

Example I

The flamingo can eat shellfish and other animals because of its

Sample Answer

(A) ● (C) (D)

(A) curved neck
(B) especially formed bill
(C) long legs
(D) brightly colored feathers

According to the passage, the flamingo sifts mud for food with "a fine hairlike 'comb' along the edge of its bent bill." Therefore, you should choose answer (B).

Example II

How many young would you expect the flamingo to raise at one time?

Sample Answer

(A) (B) ● (D)

(A) Several
(B) Two
(C) One
(D) Four

The passage states that the flamingo nests on a mound of mud with a "single" egg. Therefore, you should choose answer (C).

Now begin work on the questions.

**GO ON TO THE NEXT PAGE**

Questions 31–35

While most desert animals will drink water if confronted with it, for many of them the opportunity never comes. Yet all living things must have water, or they will expire. The herbivores find it in desert plants. The carnivores slake their thirst *Line* with the flesh and blood of living prey. One of the most remarkable adjustments, (5) however, has been made by the tiny kangaroo rat, who not only lives without drinking but also subsists on a diet of dry seeds containing about 5% free water. Like other animals, the kangaroo rat has the ability to manufacture water in its body by a metabolic conversion of carbohydrates. But it is notable for the parsimony with which it conserves its small supply by every possible means, expending (10) only minuscule amounts in its excreta and through evaporation from its respiratory tract.

31. What is the main idea of this passage?

   (A) The kangaroo rat is uniquely suited to desert life.
   (B) Animals need water to exist in the desert.
   (C) Herbivores and carnivores live together in the desert.
   (D) Animals' metabolic systems are complex.

32. Which of the following is NOT a source of water for the desert animals?

   (A) Desert plants
   (B) Metabolic conversion of carbohydrates in the body
   (C) The blood of other animals
   (D) Streams

33. The word *it* in line 3 refers to

   (A) a living thing
   (B) the desert
   (C) the opportunity
   (D) water

34. The author states that the kangaroo rat is known for all of the following EXCEPT

   (A) the economy with which it uses available water
   (B) living without drinking water
   (C) breathing slowly and infrequently
   (D) manufacturing water internally

35. The word *slake* in line 3 could best be replaced by which of the following?

   (A) ignore
   (B) satisfy
   (C) understand
   (D) enjoy

GO ON TO THE NEXT PAGE

Questions 36–42

Until recently, most American entrepreneurs were men. Discrimination against women in business, the demands of caring for families, and lack of business training had kept the number of women entrepreneurs small. Now, however,

*Line* businesses owned by women account for more than $40 billion in annual
(5) revenues, and this figure is likely to continue rising throughout the 1980s. As Carolyn Doppelt Gray, an official of the Small Business Administration, has noted, "The 1970s was the decade of women entering management, and the 1980s has turned out to be the decade of the woman entrepreneur."

What are some of the factors behind this trend? For one thing, as more women
(10) earn advanced degrees in business and enter the corporate world, they are finding obstacles. Women are still excluded from most executive suites. Charlotte Taylor, a management consultant, had noted, "In the 1970s women believed if they got an MBA and worked hard, they could become chairman of the board. Now they've found out that isn't going to happen, so they go out on their own."

(15) In the past, most women entrepreneurs worked in "women's" fields—cosmetics and clothing, for example. But this is changing. Consider ASK Computer Systems, a $22-million-a-year computer software business. It was founded in 1973 by Sandra Kurtzig, who was then a housewife with degrees in math and engineering. When Kurtzig founded the business, her first product was software that let weekly
(20) newspapers keep tabs on their newspaper carriers—and her office was a bedroom at home, with a shoebox under the bed to hold the company's cash. After she succeeded with the newspaper software system, she hired several bright computer-science graduates to develop additional programs. When these were marketed and sold, ASK began to grow. It now has 200 employees, and Sandra
(25) Kurtzig owns $66.9 million of stock.

Of course, many women who start their own businesses fail, just as men often do. They still face hurdles in the business world, especially problems in raising money; the banking and finance world is still dominated by men, and old attitudes die hard. Most businesses owned by women are still quite small.
(30) But the situation is changing; there are likely to be many more Sandra Kurtzigs in the years ahead.

GO ON TO THE NEXT PAGE

36. What is the main idea of this passage?

    (A) Women today are better educated than in the past, making them more attractive to the business world.
    (B) The computer is especially lucrative for women today.
    (C) Women are better at small businesses than men are.
    (D) Women today are opening more businesses of their own.

37. All of the following were mentioned in the passage as detriments to women in the business world EXCEPT

    (A) women were required to stay at home with their families
    (B) women lacked ability to work in business
    (C) women faced discrimination in business
    (D) women were not trained in business

38. According to the passage, Charlotte Taylor believes that women in the 1970s

    (A) were unrealistic about their opportunities in business management
    (B) were still more interested in education than business opportunities
    (C) had fewer obstacles in business than they do today
    (D) were unable to work hard enough to succeed in business

39. The author mentions the "shoebox under the bed" in the third paragraph in order to

    (A) show the frugality of women in business
    (B) show the resourcefulness of Sandra Kurtzig
    (C) point out that initially the financial resources of Sandra Kurtzig's business were limited
    (D) suggest that the company needed to expand

40. The word *hurdles* in line 27 can be best replaced by

    (A) fences
    (B) obstacles
    (C) questions
    (D) small groups

41. It can be inferred from the passage that the author believes that businesses operated by women are small because

    (A) women prefer a small, intimate setting
    (B) women can't deal with money
    (C) women are not able to borrow money easily
    (D) many women fail at large businesses

42. The author's attitude about the future of women in business is

    (A) skeptical
    (B) optimistic
    (C) frustrated
    (D) negative

**GO ON TO THE NEXT PAGE**

Questions 43–48

      This rapid transcontinental settlement and these new urban industrial circumstances of the last half of the 19th century were accompanied by the development of a national literature of great abundance and variety. New themes,
*Line* new forms, new subjects, new regions, new authors, new audiences all emerged in
(5) the literature of this half century. As a result, at the onset of World War I, the spirit and substance of American literature had evolved remarkably, just as its center of production had shifted from Boston to New York in the late 1880s and the sources of its energy to Chicago and the Midwest. No longer was it produced, at least in its popular forms, in the main by solemn, typically moralistic men from New
(10) England and the Old South; no longer were polite, well-dressed, grammatically correct, middle-class young people the only central characters in its narratives; no longer were these narratives to be set in exotic places and remote times; no longer, indeed, were fiction, poetry, drama, and formal history the chief acceptable forms of literary expression; no longer, finally, was literature read primarily by young,
(15) middle class women. In sum, American literature in these years fulfilled in considerable measure the condition Walt Whitman called for in 1867 in describing *Leaves of Grass:* it treats, he said of his own major work, each state and region as peers "and expands from them, and includes the world . . . connecting an American citizen with the citizens of all nations."

43. The main idea of this passage is

  (A) that the new American literature was less provincial than the old
  (B) that World War I caused a dramatic change in America
  (C) that centers of culture shifted from the East to the West
  (D) that most people were wary of the new literature

44. It can be inferred from lines 1–3 that the previous passage probably discussed

  (A) the importance of tradition to writers
  (B) new developments in industrialization and population shifts
  (C) the fashions and values of 19th-century America
  (D) the limitations of American literature to this time

45. The author uses the word *indeed* in line 13 for what purpose?

  (A) To emphasize the contrast he is making
  (B) For variety in a lengthy paragraph
  (C) To wind down his argument
  (D) To show a favorable attitude to these forms of literature

46. It can be inferred from the passage that the new literature

  (A) continued to be quite formal
  (B) enjoyed a great deal of prestige
  (C) broke with many literary traditions of the past
  (D) is seen as the high point of American literature

47. It can be inferred from the passage that Walt Whitman

  (A) disliked urban life
  (B) was disapproving of the new literature
  (C) wrote *Leaves of Grass*
  (D) was an international diplomat

48. This passage would probably be read in which of the following academic courses?

  (A) European history
  (B) American literature
  (C) Current events
  (D) International affairs

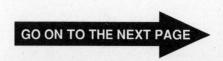
GO ON TO THE NEXT PAGE

Questions 49–56

When Daniel Boone died peacefully in bed in his son Nathan's elegant stone
Missouri farmhouse on September 26, 1820, the surge of emigrants along the
Oregon Trail was still a generation away. But Boone already exemplified the
*Line*    pioneer at his best. He was neither the physical giant (five feet nine) nor the
*(5)*     innocent child of nature that legend has made of him. He was an intelligent, soft-
spoken family man who cherished the same wife for 57 years. He befriended
Indians, preferred company to solitude, and when he told his wife it was time to
move because a newcomer had settled some 70 miles away, he was joking.

Pennsylvania-born, Boone was one of 11 children in a family of Quakers who
*(10)*    migrated to North Carolina. There Boone was recruited at age 40 to undertake a
scheme designed to open up Kentucky to settlers and establish it as a 14th colony.
He arranged a deal by which the Cherokees sold 20 million acres for 20,000 dollars,
worth of goods to Boone's employers, the Transylvania Company. It was all fair
and square—the Indians had an attorney, an interpreter, and the sound advice of
*(15)*    their squaws. The deal completed, Boone led a party from Tennessee through the
Cumberland Gap, hacked out the Wilderness Road, and set up a town—
Boonesboro—and a government. Elected a legislator, he introduced on the first
session's first day a bill to protect game against wanton slaughter, and a second
bill to "improve the breed of horses." He got 2,000 acres for his work, but after the
*(20)*    Revolution—in which Boone won considerable fame as a militia commander—the
scheme of the Transylvania Company was declared illegal and Boone lost his land.

Undaunted, he staked out more claims—and lost them because he impatiently
neglected to register his deeds. Ever hopeful, he accepted an invitation from
Spanish-held Missouri to come and settle there and bring others with him. The
*(25)*    Spanish gave him 8,500 acres and made him a judge. But the Louisiana Purchase,
which embraced Missouri, again left him—but not his children—landless. Old and
broke, Boone cheerfully continued hunting and trapping long after his hands
shook. Shortly before he died, he was talking knowledgeably with young men
about the joys to be experienced in settling California.

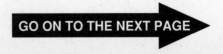

GO ON TO THE NEXT PAGE

3 • 3 • 3 • 3 • 3 • 3 • 3

49. What is the author's purpose in writing this passage?

    (A) To chronicle the life of a model pioneer
    (B) To romanticize the legend of Daniel Boone
    (C) To show Boone's many successes on the frontier
    (D) To trace Boone's explorations in Kentucky, Missouri, and Louisiana

50. It can be inferred that one area in which Boone was NOT successful was

    (A) politics
    (B) hunting and trapping
    (C) business
    (D) the military

51. It can be inferred from the passage that Boone died

    (A) a rich man
    (B) an eternal optimist
    (C) in California
    (D) a lonely trapper

52. According to the passage, where is Boone's namesake city located?

    (A) In North Carolina
    (B) In Translyvania
    (C) In Kentucky
    (D) In Missouri

53. The Transylvania Company wanted Boone to

    (A) settle Kentucky
    (B) be fair to the Indians
    (C) ensure animal rights
    (D) claim Missouri

54. According to the passage, the Louisiana Purchase

    (A) legitimized Boone's land claim in Missouri
    (B) revoked the earlier Spanish bequest to Boone
    (C) drove the Spanish from the East
    (D) excluded Missouri from its jurisdiction

55. What can be inferred from the passage about Boone's children?

    (A) They were better off financially than Boone.
    (B) They supported Boone's desire to settle new areas.
    (C) They lived in Kentucky.
    (D) They had no land due to Boone's bad investments.

56. The author's attitude toward Daniel Boone in the passage can be best described as

    (A) admiring
    (B) critical
    (C) admonishing
    (D) indifferent

GO ON TO THE NEXT PAGE

Questions 57–60

Reducing your intake of sweet food is one way to keep your teeth healthy. The least cavity-causing way to eat sweets is to have them with meals and not between. The number of times you eat sweets rather than the total amount
*Line* determines how much harmful acid the bacteria in your saliva produces. But the
*(5)* amount of sweets influences the quality of your saliva. Avoid, if you can, sticky sweets that stay in your mouth a long time. Also try to brush and floss your teeth after eating sugary foods. Even rinsing your mouth with water is effective. Whenever possible, eat foods with fiber, such as raw carrot sticks, apples, celery sticks, etc., that scrape off plaque, acting as a toothbrush. Cavities can be greatly
*(10)* reduced if these rules are followed when eating sweets.

57. Which of the following is the best title for this passage?

   (A) A Healthy Diet
   (B) Food with Fiber
   (C) Sweets and Cavities
   (D) Tooth Decay

58. What can be concluded from the passage about sweets?

   (A) All sweets should be avoided.
   (B) Sweets should be eaten with care.
   (C) It is better to eat sweets a little at a time throughout the day.
   (D) Sticky sweets are less harmful than other sweets.

59. According to the passage, the value of eating foods with fiber is that

   (A) they contain Vitamin A
   (B) they are less expensive than a toothbrush
   (C) they are able to remove the plaque from your teeth
   (D) they contain no sugar

60. The author of the passage states that the amount of acid produced by the bacteria in your saliva increases

   (A) with the amount of sweets you eat
   (B) with the number of times you eat sweets
   (C) if you eat sweets with your meals
   (D) if you eat sticky sweets

**THIS IS THE END OF SECTION 3**

IF YOU FINISH BEFORE TIME IS CALLED, CHECK YOUR WORK
ON SECTION 3 ONLY.
DO NOT READ OR WORK ON ANY OTHER SECTION OF THE TEST.

# TEST OF WRITTEN ENGLISH

## PRACTICE TEST TWO

### Time—30 minutes

The chart below shows the changing composition of the labor force in the United States over a 20-year period. What does the chart tell you about the changes? What does it tell you about the trend of the changes during this time period? Explain your conclusions, supporting them with details from the chart.

| OCCUPATION GROUP | PERCENT OF LABOR FORCE | |
|---|---|---|
| | 1958 | 1978 |
| Professional and Technical | 11.0 | 15.1 |
| Managers and Administrators | 10.8 | 10.7 |
| Clerical | 14.5 | 17.8 |
| Sales | 6.3 | 6.3 |
| Service | 11.9 | 13.7 |
| Blue-collar | 37.0 | 33.4 |
| Farm | 8.5 | 3.0 |
| Total | 100.0 | 100.0 |

### NOTES

Use this space to make your notes. Write the final version of your essay on lined paper. The Sample TWE Answer Sheet on page 192 is an example of the amount of writing space provided in the TOEFL Test.

# PRACTICE TEST THREE

## SECTION 1
## LISTENING COMPREHENSION

In this section of the test, you will have an opportunity to demonstrate your ability to understand spoken English. There are three parts to this section, with special directions for each part.

### Part A

Directions:   For each question in Part A, you will hear a short sentence. Each sentence will be spoken just one time. The sentences you hear will not be written out for you. Therefore, you must listen carefully to understand what the speaker says.

After you hear a sentence, read the four choices in your test book, marked (A), (B), (C), and (D), and decide which <u>one</u> is closest in meaning to the sentence you heard. Then, on your answer sheet, find the number of the question and fill in the space that corresponds to the letter of the answer you have chosen. Fill in the space so that the letter inside the oval cannot be seen.

Example I                                                                      Sample Answer

You will hear:                                                            Ⓐ Ⓑ ● Ⓓ

You will read:        (A)   Greg didn't bother to leave a tip.
                              (B)   Greg thought about typing a
                                       letter to his brother.
                              (C)   Greg didn't like to type.
                              (D)   My typing bothered Greg.

The speaker said, "Greg thought typing was a bother." Sentence (C), "Greg didn't like to type," is closest in meaning to the sentence you heard. Therefore, you should choose answer (C).

Example II                                                                   Sample Answer

You will hear:                                                            Ⓐ ● Ⓒ Ⓓ

You will read:        (A)   Everyone will be able to take this
                                       exam later.
                              (B)   Students should bring a calculator
                                       to this exam.
                              (C)   This test will be part of every
                                       student's final grade.
                              (D)   No one can calculate the grades
                                       for this test.

The speaker said, "Everyone needs a calculator for this test." Sentence (B), "Students should bring a calculator to this exam," is closest in meaning to the sentence you heard. Therefore, you should choose answer (B).

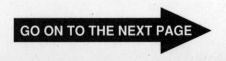

GO ON TO THE NEXT PAGE

1. (A) Was that tied right?
   (B) You should try this one on.
   (C) You are wearing a very colorful tie.
   (D) What time will you be home?

2. (A) Brian is too weak to work on this.
   (B) Brian must finish his work by next week.
   (C) Brian has two papers to write.
   (D) I was right about Brian's illness.

3. (A) She bought a new pair of glasses.
   (B) She took her glasses to someone to be fixed.
   (C) She had to change two classes.
   (D) She found it necessary to wear glasses.

4. (A) The shops have the students' books ready.
   (B) Half of the students bought their books.
   (C) The students are ready to shop for their books.
   (D) The students are done buying books.

5. (A) She visited me two days ago.
   (B) She and Lee make a nice couple.
   (C) She can't buy it for a while.
   (D) She passed by my house twice.

6. (A) George is feeling weak since he hurt himself running.
   (B) George is healing from the injury he got while running last week.
   (C) George injured his foot while trying to catch the bus.
   (D) George was driving a bus when he got hurt.

7. (A) I wasn't accepted into law school until the dean approved my application.
   (B) Only Dean received approval and was accepted into law school.
   (C) Dean tried to prove that the law should be accepted.
   (D) I helped the dean decide upon some new school regulations.

8. (A) You'll see us tonight at the office.
   (B) Take your letter right to the post office.
   (C) The post office is around the corner.
   (D) You'll be posted at the corner tonight.

9. (A) Nothing has been set up for today.
   (B) She does not get upset very easily.
   (C) She needs to set things up today.
   (D) Recently she has been getting upset very easily.

10. (A) How much have you grown?
    (B) You certainly have grown.
    (C) How will you get the call?
    (D) How tall are you?

11. (A) Ted's aunt wrote him a very touching letter.
    (B) Ted took note of his aunt's kindness.
    (C) Ted wrote his aunt a letter she appreciated.
    (D) Ted sang a touching song for his aunt.

12. (A) Jane has worked at the gym for some time.
    (B) Jane and Jim work together quite often.
    (C) Jane exercises with Jim several times a week.
    (D) Jane exercises at the gym quite often.

13. (A) He passed by the new port and stopped at the old one.
    (B) He was asked for his passport because no one knew him.
    (C) He was lost without his passport.
    (D) He sent for a new passport because he lost the original one.

14. (A) He's going to graduate from night school soon.
    (B) He's trying very hard to be successful in graduate school.
    (C) He may not go to graduate school because it's too hard.
    (D) He's trying to study today so he can go with us tonight.

GO ON TO THE NEXT PAGE

15. (A) It took me 15 minutes to find these books.
    (B) These mystery books cost me 25 cents each.
    (C) After history class, I spent 3 hours down at the track.
    (D) Why does he spend so much time down at the track?

16. (A) Don't you think that's a noisy class?
    (B) It sounds like a glass is breaking, doesn't it?
    (C) This class will probably be a very good one.
    (D) You don't think the glass will break, do you?

17. (A) Carol clearly accepts and understands our problem.
    (B) Carol wants us to solve this problem without her help.
    (C) Our instructions were not clear enough for Carol to understand.
    (D) Our own understanding of Carol's expectations is clearly wrong.

18. (A) What are you going to do after you turn in your work?
    (B) You're going to assign a project today, aren't you?
    (C) Won't you turn in your work today?
    (D) Didn't you hand in your project?

19. (A) Sandy's been using up all the fuel in the lab working on her experiment.
    (B) Sandy's been working very hard to finish her work.
    (C) Sandy's been staying out late so her project isn't finished.
    (D) Sandy is finished in the lab every night at midnight.

20. (A) Parts of his story are true.
    (B) He didn't correct the story.
    (C) He must rewrite the entire story.
    (D) None of his story is true.

GO ON TO THE NEXT PAGE

## Part B

<u>Directions:</u> In Part B you will hear short conversations between two speakers. At the end of each conversation, a third person will ask a question about what was said. You will hear each conversation and question about it just one time. Therefore, you must listen carefully to understand what each speaker says. After you hear a conversation and the question about it, read the four possible answers in your test book and decide which <u>one</u> is the best answer to the question you heard. Then, on your answer sheet, find the number of the question and fill in the space that corresponds to the letter of the answer you have chosen.

Look at the following example.

You will hear:

You will read:

(A) At last winter is almost over.
(B) She doesn't like winter weather very much.
(C) This winter's weather is similar to last winter's weather.
(D) Winter won't last as long this year as it did last year.

<u>Sample Answer</u>

From the conversation you learn that the woman thinks the weather this winter is almost the same as the weather last winter. The best answer to the question "What does the woman mean?" is (C), "This winter's weather is similar to last winter's weather." Therefore, you should choose answer (C).

21. (A) Happy.
    (B) Frustrated.
    (C) Sleepy.
    (D) Full.

22. (A) In a dentist's office.
    (B) At the employment office.
    (C) In a pharmacy.
    (D) In a coffee shop.

23. (A) John likes old movies more than Bill does.
    (B) John likes old movies, but Bill doesn't.
    (C) Both John and Bill like old movies.
    (D) Old movies are really enjoyable.

24. (A) He wants to talk about the project.
    (B) He thinks the project is fine.
    (C) He agrees with the woman.
    (D) The woman shouldn't be worried.

25. (A) Continue with work.
    (B) Hold his breath.
    (C) Breathe deeply.
    (D) Rest for a short time.

26. (A) He didn't get the grant he wanted.
    (B) He's going to choose another university.
    (C) He wants the woman to help him.
    (D) He isn't pleased with the university he has chosen.

27. (A) She has to look for the library.
    (B) The library is only a little farther.
    (C) The man has found the library.
    (D) She doesn't know where the library is.

28. (A) Ask the man to fix the lawn mower.
    (B) Try to fix the lawn mower herself.
    (C) Take the lawn mower out of the garage.
    (D) Stop working in the garage.

29. (A) To a beauty salon.
    (B) To a furniture store.
    (C) To a library.
    (D) To a clothing store.

**GO ON TO THE NEXT PAGE** ➤

1 · 1 · 1 · 1 · 1 · 1 · 1

30. (A) It only has two chapters.
    (B) The last part won't contain any new material.
    (C) He doesn't think Charles will ever finish it.
    (D) He might be able to help Charles write a summary of it.

31. (A) Take his typewriter to the library.
    (B) Buy a typewriter.
    (C) Borrow a typewriter from the woman.
    (D) Go to the library to use a typewriter.

32. (A) Find a friend to take her to the party.
    (B) Wait until she's feeling better to go to the party.
    (C) Go to the party for a short time.
    (D) Find the papers for the man to sign.

33. (A) His car lost the race.
    (B) He wasn't able to buy the car.
    (C) He can't help the woman choose a car.
    (D) Someone hit his car from behind.

34. (A) He isn't very interested in the concert.
    (B) The concert is too much for him to do.
    (C) He is quite interested in the tickets.
    (D) He couldn't see much of the concert.

35. (A) Annoyed.
    (B) Hungry.
    (C) Tired.
    (D) Happy.

**GO ON TO THE NEXT PAGE**

Part C

Directions:   In this part of the test, you will hear short talks and conversations. After each of them, you will be asked some questions. You will hear the talks and conversations and the questions about them just one time. They will not be written out for you. Therefore, you must listen carefully to understand what each speaker says.

After you hear a question, read the four possible answers in your test book and decide which <u>one</u> is the best answer to the question you heard. Then, on your answer sheet, find the number of the question and fill in the space that corresponds to the letter of the answer you have chosen.

Answer all questions on the basis of what is <u>stated</u> or <u>implied</u> in the talk or conversation.

    Listen to this sample talk.

      You will hear:

Now look at the following example.

      You will hear:

<u>Sample Answer</u>

● Ⓑ Ⓒ Ⓓ

      You will read:
    (A)  Only bumblebees can fertilize red clover plants.
    (B)  Bumblebees protect red clover from plant eating insects.
    (C)  Bumblebees bring water to red clover plants on their tongues.
    (D)  Bumblebees keep mice and other animals away from red clover plants.

The best answer to the question "Why is it impossible to raise red clover where there are no bumblebees?" is (A), "Only bumblebees can fertilize red clover plants." Therefore, you should choose answer (A).

    Now look at the next example.

      You will hear:

<u>Sample Answer</u>

Ⓐ Ⓑ Ⓒ ●

      You will read:
    (A)  They both make honey.
    (B)  They both build combs.
    (C)  Both of them are found in underground nests.
    (D)  They both live through the winter.

The best answer to the question "According to the speaker, in what way are the queen wasp and the queen bee similar?" is (D), "They both live through the winter." Therefore, you should choose answer (D).

36. (A)  A businessman.
    (B)  A professor.
    (C)  A distributor.
    (D)  A student.

37. (A)  Distribution of goods and services.
    (B)  Factories.
    (C)  Today's homework.
    (D)  Advertising.

38. (A)  The movement of goods from their sources to their destinations.
    (B)  The arrangement of products on the shelves.
    (C)  The circulation of advertisements.
    (D)  The manufacturing of goods.

**GO ON TO THE NEXT PAGE** ➡

39. (A) A guest speaker might arrive.
    (B) Class might be cancelled.
    (C) There might be a short quiz.
    (D) Homework might be collected.

40. (A) Advertising as an important aspect
        of marketing.
    (B) A comparison between wholesalers
        and retailers.
    (C) The manufacture of goods.
    (D) The roles of consumers.

41. (A) Pigments used in paint production.
    (B) Steps in chlorophyll production.
    (C) The loss of trees due to disease.
    (D) Reasons for autumn leaf color.

42. (A) A change in the weather.
    (B) A radio program.
    (C) A botany lecture.
    (D) The woman's hopes to save a
        dying tree.

43. (A) Bright autumn leaf color is due to
        frost and cold.
    (B) Pigments from leaves are used in the
        production of paint.
    (C) Sunlight is necessary in the
        production of bright leaf color.
    (D) The true color of leaves is brown.

44. (A) Red.
    (B) Brown.
    (C) Green.
    (D) Orange.

45. (A) Chlorophyll.
    (B) Bright sunlight.
    (C) Different chemical pigments.
    (D) Nutrient production.

46. (A) A teacher.
    (B) A museum guide.
    (C) A curator.
    (D) A receptionist.

47. (A) Changing exhibits.
    (B) Permanent displays.
    (C) The tipi village.
    (D) The library service.

48. (A) It is too busy today.
    (B) It is too far away.
    (C) It is too dangerous.
    (D) It is still being built.

49. (A) The portrait gallery.
    (B) The research library.
    (C) The sculpture gardens.
    (D) The Indian museum.

50. (A) Because of the large number
        of visitors.
    (B) Because of construction in part of
        the museum.
    (C) So that visitors could shop for gifts.
    (D) To give everyone a needed rest.

## THIS IS THE END OF THE LISTENING COMPREHENSION SECTION OF THE TEST

THE NEXT PART OF THE TEST IS SECTION 2. TURN TO THE
DIRECTIONS FOR SECTION 2 IN YOUR TEST BOOK.
READ THEM, AND BEGIN WORK.
DO NOT READ OR WORK ON ANY OTHER SECTION OF THE TEST.

  STOP STOP STOP STOP STOP STOP STOP

## SECTION 2
## STRUCTURE AND WRITTEN EXPRESSION

Time—25 minutes

This section is designed to measure your ability to recognize language that is appropriate for standard written English. There are two types of questions in this section, with special directions for each type.

<u>Directions:</u>   Questions 1–15 are incomplete sentences. Beneath each sentence you will see four words or phrases, marked (A), (B), (C), and (D). Choose the <u>one</u> word or phrase that best completes the sentence. Then, on your answer sheet, find the number of the question and fill in the space that corresponds to the letter of the answer you have chosen. Fill in the space so that the letter inside the oval cannot be seen.

Example I

Most American families _____ at least one automobile.

Sample Answer
● Ⓑ Ⓒ Ⓓ

   (A)  have
   (B)  in
   (C)  that
   (D)  has

The sentence should read, "Most American families have at least one automobile." Therefore, you should choose answer (A).

Example II

_____ recent times, the discipline of biology has expanded rapidly into a variety of subdisciplines.

Sample Answer
Ⓐ Ⓑ Ⓒ ●

      (A)  It is since
      (B)  When
      (C)  Since it is
      (D)  In

The sentence should read, "In recent times, the discipline of biology has expanded into a variety of subdisciplines." Therefore, you should choose answer (D).

Now begin work on the questions.

1. _____ fall naturally into two classes, which can be further subdivided into several subclasses.

   (A)  There are vitamins
   (B)  Vitamins that
   (C)  Vitamins
   (D)  After vitamins

2. The incidence of anorexia nervosa, _____ , is growing in industrially advanced societies.

   (A)  is an eating disorder
   (B)  an eating disorder which
   (C)  an eating disorder
   (D)  for which an eating disorder

3. In the 1960s, *pop art* _____ to discover artistic significance in the commercial artifacts of the consumer culture.

   (A)  seeking
   (B)  to seek
   (C)  has sought
   (D)  sought

**GO ON TO THE NEXT PAGE**

4. Air _____ the carbon dioxide necessary for photosynthesis enters leaves through tiny surface openings.
   (A) contains
   (B) contained
   (C) containing
   (D) it contains

5. Overexposure to the sun can produce _____ can some toxic chemicals.
   (A) more than damage to the skin
   (B) more damage than to the skin
   (C) damage more than to the skin
   (D) more damage to the skin than

6. The Federal Reserve System, _____ under President Wilson, plays a key role in regulating the U.S. economy.
   (A) the establishment in 1913
   (B) was established in 1913
   (C) established in 1913
   (D) in 1913 they established it

7. In the 1960s, due in part to the invention of air conditioning, the population of the United States _____ a dramatic geographical shift southward.
   (A) experiencing
   (B) was experienced
   (C) to experience
   (D) experienced

8. Antarctica is larger _____ , but it has no native human population.
   (A) than Europe or Australia does
   (B) Europe or Australia
   (C) of Europe or Australia
   (D) than Europe or Australia

9. Whole-grain food products _____ in most large supermarkets across the United States and Canada.
   (A) now can purchase
   (B) can now be purchased
   (C) now to purchase
   (D) the purchase of which

10. A dividend is _____ the only benefit a corporation can offer its shareholders.
    (A) no
    (B) nor
    (C) none
    (D) not

11. _____ all citrus fruit originated with the Chinese orange.
    (A) That the belief
    (B) The belief that
    (C) To believe that
    (D) It is believed that

12. The year 1732 saw the first appearance of *Poor Richard's Almanac*, _____ Benjamin Franklin created the character of Poor Richard.
    (A) there
    (B) in which
    (C) in it
    (D) which in

13. _____ more susceptible to bacterial contamination than other types of meat because it has more surface area exposed to bacteria laden air.
    (A) Ground meat
    (B) Ground meat is
    (C) Ground meat that is
    (D) Ground meat being

14. Over the past several decades, radio telescopes _____ of the universe from the one disclosed by ordinary telescopes.
    (A) have given scientists quite a different view
    (B) have quite a different view given scientists
    (C) quite a different view have given scientists
    (D) have they given scientists quite a different view

15. Nestled along the shoreline of Hudson Bay _____ .
    (A) are several recently settled Inuit communities
    (B) several recently settled Inuit communities are there
    (C) near several recently settled Inuit communities
    (D) is where several recently settled Inuit communities

**GO ON TO THE NEXT PAGE**

Directions:   In questions 16–40 each sentence has four underlined words or phrases. The four underlined parts of the sentence are marked (A), (B), (C), and (D). Identify the <u>one</u> underlined word or phrase that must be changed in order for the sentence to be correct. Then, on your answer sheet, find the number of the question and fill in the space that corresponds to the letter of the answer you have chosen.

Example I

The octopus <u>is</u> a unique animal <u>because</u> <u>they</u>
      A             B     C

has three <u>functioning</u> hearts.
        D

Sample Answer

The sentence should read, "The octopus is a unique animal because it has three functioning hearts." Therefore, you should choose answer (C).

Example II

The beagle, <u>one of the most</u> <u>ancient</u> breeds of
           A        B

dog <u>known</u>, <u>originating</u> in England.
    C      D

Sample Answer

The sentence should read, "The beagle, one of the most ancient breeds of dog known, originated in England." Therefore, you should choose answer (D).

Now begin work on the questions.

16. The field cricket is <u>quite</u> <u>injury</u> to crops and <u>vegetation</u> and does most of its <u>harmful</u> work at night.
                     A    B                C                      D

17. Perhaps <u>the most</u> unique thing <u>about</u> carbon atoms <u>are</u> their ability <u>to combine</u> with themselves.
            A                  B              C              D

18. Works <u>wrote</u> by Vladimir Nabokov <u>often</u> contain heroes and heroines <u>who</u> <u>have lived</u> in many places.
        A                      B                            C    D

19. Organisms and their cells live <u>by maintaining</u> a <u>constant</u> exchange <u>of elemental</u>, ions, minerals
                               A        B              C

and <u>gases</u>.
    D

20. For the past <u>few years</u>, researchers <u>have perfecting</u> <u>their</u> control over the movements of cells and
              A                        B        C

microbes by <u>using</u> low-power laser beams.
          D

21. The mountain sheep <u>is known for</u> its <u>incredible</u> agility, <u>timid</u>, and ability <u>to withstand</u> severe cold.
                      A         B         C                  D

22. The chimpanzee possesses <u>hand tool</u>, the sticky termite stick, <u>with which</u> <u>it</u> digs termites <u>out of</u>
                           A                            B      C            D

logs and stumps.

23. The different layers of the Grand Canyon <u>contain</u> a variety of fossils, <u>including</u> algae and
                                      A                      B

seaweed <u>from</u> early <u>historically</u> periods.
         C           D

24. The United States government <u>use</u> price supports and <u>cost</u> <u>subsidies</u> to <u>raise</u> farm prices and profits.
                          A                    B    C       D

25. The basic factors <u>that</u> enhance health and <u>longevity</u> include vigorous exercise, <u>hereditary</u>, and <u>diet</u>.
                 A                      B                      C      D

26. Fission tracking <u>is</u> a new artifact <u>dating</u> method <u>who</u> promises <u>to have</u> important archeological
               A                B            C        D

applications in the future.

**GO ON TO THE NEXT PAGE**

27. <u>Biologically</u> produced ceramics, <u>alike</u> those made by mollusks <u>such as</u> the sea urchin, remain
       A            B                      C
    superior <u>to those</u> produced synthetically.
            D

28. <u>Contemporary</u> poet James Merrill <u>writes</u> autobiographical verse that <u>building on</u> remembrances
         A                      B                         C
    of <u>his</u> childhood.
      D

29. Many New England farmers <u>supplement</u> their incomes with the <u>sold</u> of maple syrup <u>tapped</u>
                            A                      B                 C
    from <u>sugar maples</u> growing on their farmland.
         D

30. When <u>attempt</u> <u>to explain</u> <u>children's</u> food preferences, researchers are faced <u>with</u> contradictions.
         A       B     C                                        D

31. Glaciologists <u>now suspect</u> that the Antarctic ice sheet <u>unstable is</u>, but they are <u>not yet</u> certain to
               A                              B              C
    what extent this instability <u>might cause</u> problems.
                         D

32. Human infants are <u>not</u> usually <u>able to</u> walk by <u>selves</u> until they reach eleven or twelve <u>months</u> of age.
                  A        B        C                                D

33. Scholars of historical change <u>feels</u> <u>that</u> the velocity of history <u>has been</u> greatly accelerated by the
                             A    B                      C
    onward rush of science and technology <u>during</u> the twentieth century.
                                  D

34. Psychologists and psychiatrists <u>are trained</u> to encourage <u>their</u> patients <u>to talk for</u> the things that
                               A                    B          C
    are causing them <u>difficulty</u>.
                D

35. Food contamination <u>is monitored</u> by the Food and Drug Administration, <u>which</u> periodically
                      A                                        B
    <u>conducts</u> <u>controlled strictly</u> inspections of foodstuffs.
      C          D

36. <u>From the time</u> he was a child, author Herman Melville <u>had</u> <u>a interest</u> in <u>the sea</u>.
        A                                     B   C     D

37. Booker T. Washington, head of <u>the first</u> industrial school for African Americans, <u>was</u> as
                                A                                          B
    <u>popular with</u> Southerners <u>than he</u> was with Northerners.
     C                      D

38. Peacocks are <u>among</u> the <u>most exotic</u> birds in nature; <u>its</u> long tail feathers <u>fan out</u> to reveal a
                  A       B                    C                 D
    profusion of vivid colors.

39. In the <u>latter half</u> of the nineteenth century, physical techniques <u>making it</u> possible <u>to determine</u>
           A                                        B          C
    the chemical constitution <u>of stars</u>.
                         D

40. In seeking out <u>its</u> representative writers, twentieth-century America seems <u>to be</u> searching for
               A                                                B
    someone who <u>chronicle</u> the chaos and lack of direction <u>reflected</u> in some contemporary values.
              C                                  D

---

**THIS IS THE END OF THE LISTENING COMPREHENSION SECTION OF THE TEST**

THE NEXT PART OF THE TEST IS SECTION 2. TURN TO THE
DIRECTIONS FOR SECTION 2 IN YOUR TEST BOOK.
READ THEM, AND BEGIN WORK.
DO NOT READ OR WORK ON ANY OTHER SECTION OF THE TEST.

SECTION 3
VOCABULARY AND READING COMPREHENSION
Time—45 minutes

This section is designed to measure your comprehension of standard written English. There are two types of questions in this section, with special directions for each type.

Directions:   In questions 1–30 each sentence has an underlined word or phrase. Below each sentence are four other words or phrases, marked (A), (B), (C), (D). You are to choose the <u>one</u> word or phrase that <u>best keeps the meaning</u> of the original sentence if it is substituted for the underlined word or phrase. Then, on your answer sheet, find the number of the question and fill in the space that corresponds to the letter you have chosen. Fill in the space so that the letter inside the oval cannot be seen.

Example

Ladybugs, small brightly colored beetles, feed on plant aphids and have considerable economic value in <u>controlling</u> pest populations.

(A)  limiting
(B)  finding
(C)  increasing
(D)  ruling

Sample Answer

● Ⓑ Ⓒ Ⓓ

The best answer is (A) because "Ladybugs, small brightly colored beetles, feed on plant aphids and have considerable economic value in limiting pest populations" is closest in meaning to the original sentence. Therefore, you should choose answer (A).

Now begin work on the questions.

1. Today we know that heat is the <u>motion</u> of atoms and molecules in objects.

   (A)  relation
   (B)  mixture
   (C)  movement
   (D)  number

2. Fog forms as the moisture in warm air condenses, or turns to small water drops, when it <u>strikes</u> cooler air.

   (A)  batters
   (B)  meets
   (C)  controls
   (D)  drives

3. Coatis live in the <u>dense</u> jungles of Mexico and Central and South America.

   (A)  hot
   (B)  thick
   (C)  green
   (D)  rainy

4. Our bodies <u>continuously</u> break down and build up structures, with tissues and organs replacing their cells in an ongoing process.

   (A)  often
   (B)  constantly
   (C)  quickly
   (D)  impartially

5. As you probably know from the <u>appeals</u> being made for funds to fight cancer, cancer is a great menace to the health and life of mankind.

   (A)  requests
   (B)  remarks
   (C)  posters
   (D)  supplies

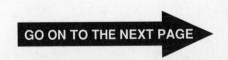
GO ON TO THE NEXT PAGE

**Practice Test Three**    83

6. Carnivorous plants, which <u>trap</u> insects and other small animals, live in many parts of the world.
   (A) ensnare
   (B) find
   (C) join
   (D) engage

7. The development of the American system of telegraphy is <u>largely</u> the result of the efforts of two men: Joseph Henry and Samuel Morse.
   (A) partially
   (B) equally
   (C) undoubtedly
   (D) mainly

8. Practically all languages spoken on earth today can be traced by scholars back to some common source, an ancestor language which has many <u>descendants</u>.
   (A) documents
   (B) offshoots
   (C) memories
   (D) causes

9. The coast guard is the nation's oldest continuous seagoing <u>force</u>.
   (A) military unit
   (B) fleet
   (C) station
   (D) attraction

10. Between the twilight zone on the forest floor and the quilt of green spread under the sun, there is a hidden but <u>lively</u> world.
    (A) beautiful
    (B) muted
    (C) active
    (D) human

11. Fossils are not, as some people think, the <u>remains</u> of bodies buried ages ago.
    (A) reminders
    (B) pictures
    (C) residue
    (D) mysteries

12. Hummingbirds have a "sweet tooth," so any flower high in nectar is sure to get their <u>attention</u>.
    (A) benefit
    (B) reward
    (C) interest
    (D) care

13. The single region of the earth that has earthquakes most <u>frequently</u> is Japan.
    (A) often
    (B) predictably
    (C) pervasively
    (D) severely

14. <u>Unlike</u> so many other great developments, the automobile cannot be considered the invention of any one person.
    (A) Similar to
    (B) Compared to
    (C) Related to
    (D) In contrast to

15. The roots of plants which grow on the prairies can <u>withstand</u> fires, which sometimes sweep across the plains, and remain alive to send up new shoots.
    (A) avoid
    (B) anticipate
    (C) tolerate
    (D) withhold

16. One of the <u>principal</u> properties of fluorescent materials is that they can receive invisible radiations, such as x rays and ultraviolet rays, and give off light.
    (A) unique
    (B) known
    (C) complex
    (D) most important

17. In technical language, an ego state may be described <u>operationally</u> as a set of coherent behavior patterns.
    (A) simply
    (B) medically
    (C) functionally
    (D) correctly

18. Soldiers in tropical countries must <u>contend with</u> disease-spreading insects and troublesome flies as well as a debilitating climate.
    (A) protect
    (B) suffer from
    (C) fight against
    (D) respect

GO ON TO THE NEXT PAGE

19. The northern coast of the United States is sunk in <u>vast</u> bays and straits, from the Shelikof Strait to Puget Sound.
    (A) magnificent
    (B) large
    (C) varied
    (D) long

20. Some fungi <u>consist of</u> a single cell.
    (A) turn into
    (B) combine with
    (C) result from
    (D) are made of

21. Grain is the seed of such plants as wheat, rice, rye, and oats and is the largest <u>single</u> food item used throughout the world.
    (A) individual
    (B) useful
    (C) unique
    (D) simple

22. Travel brochures offer potential tourists <u>concisely</u> written descriptions of places and attractions.
    (A) cleverly
    (B) interestingly
    (C) succinctly
    (D) marginally

23. Patriotic songs may be either legendary or composed, and they often <u>stem from</u> some historical crisis.
    (A) refer to
    (B) simulate
    (C) portray
    (D) arise from

24. Stephen Collins Foster, one of America's best-loved songwriters, wrote "Oh, Susanna" in 1846 and saw it become the <u>favorite</u> song of the forty-niners in the California gold rush.
    (A) most useful
    (B) related
    (C) preferred
    (D) original

25. The art of writing is one of the <u>highlights</u> in the contributions to the development of civilization.
    (A) major points
    (B) mysteries
    (C) beginnings
    (D) justifications

26. Unless control measures are carried out by everyone in a community, it is impossible to <u>get rid of</u> the housefly.
    (A) destroy
    (B) avoid
    (C) cope with
    (D) study

27. Once diagnosed, diabetes needs treatment to <u>stabilize</u> the blood-sugar level and keep it within strict limits.
    (A) balance
    (B) infuse
    (C) analyze
    (D) augment

28. The function of the flywheel, a heavy wheel attached to the shaft of an engine, is to keep a steady speed when forces <u>driving</u> the engine shaft are not constant.
    (A) steering
    (B) motioning
    (C) urging
    (D) propelling

29. There were several reasons for making the sod house as <u>impervious</u> as possible: tight construction helped keep out the snow in winter, the rain in spring, and the wind-blown dust in summer.
    (A) safe
    (B) cost effective
    (C) warm
    (D) impermeable

30. William Howard Taft, twenty-seventh president of the United States was a <u>modest</u> man with none of the sense of drama and color that wins the hearts of many persons.
    (A) happy
    (B) sour
    (C) humble
    (D) honorable

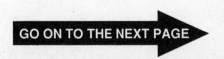
GO ON TO THE NEXT PAGE

<u>Directions:</u>  In the rest of this section you will read several passages. Each one is followed by several questions about it. For questions 31–60, you are to choose the <u>one</u> best answer, (A), (B), (C), or (D), to each question. Then, on your answer sheet, find the number of the question and fill in the space that corresponds to the letter of the answer you have chosen.

Answer all questions following a passage on the basis of what is <u>stated</u> or <u>implied</u> in that passage.

Read the following passage:

> The flamingo is a beautiful water bird with long legs, and a curving neck like a
> swan's. Most flamingos have deep red or flame-colored feathers with black quills.
> Some have pink or white feathers. The long legs and webbed feet are well suited
> *Line* for wading. The flamingo eats in a peculiar manner. It plunges its head
> *(5)* underwater and sifts the mud with a fine hairlike "comb" along the edge of its
> bent bill. In this way, it strains out small shellfish and other animals. The bird nests
> on a mound of mud with a hollow on top to hold its single egg. Flamingos are
> timid and often live together in large colonies. The birds once lived in the southern
> United States, but plume hunters killed them faster than they could breed, and the
> *(10)* flamingo no longer lives wild in the United States.

Example I                                                                          <u>Sample Answer</u>

The flamingo can eat shellfish and other                                           Ⓐ ● Ⓒ Ⓓ
animals because of its

(A) curved neck
(B) especially formed bill
(C) long legs
(D) brightly colored feathers

According to the passage, the flamingo sifts mud for food with "a fine hairlike 'comb' along the edge of its bent bill." Therefore, you should choose answer (B).

Example II                                                                         <u>Sample Answer</u>

How many young would you expect the                                                Ⓐ Ⓑ ● Ⓓ
flamingo to raise at one time?

(A) Several
(B) Two
(C) One
(D) Four

The passage states that the flamingo nests on a mound of mud with a "single" egg. Therefore, you should choose answer (C).

Now begin work on the questions.

**GO ON TO THE NEXT PAGE**

Questions 31–35

     In the spring of 1886, a 30-year-old sodbuster who had worked briefly as a photographer back East hit upon the idea of producing an album of his fellow settlers. For the next 15 years, as the pioneer era drew to a close, Solomon D.

*Line* Butcher crisscrossed Custer County, Nebraska, in a wagon that served as his
*(5)* studio. He announced his forays with notices in the local newspaper: "Farmers, have your farm photos taken for Butcher's Pioneer History."

     The fact that Butcher was himself a farmer provided rapport with his subjects. But his genius as a photographer lay in allowing them to pose as they wished, against scenes of their own choosing. The portraits that resulted convey the
*(10)* dignity of pioneers in challenging circumstances, and they remain a classic record of a resolute breed.

31. The topic of this passage is

(A) early farmers in Nebraska
(B) photography in 1886
(C) pioneer history
(D) Butcher's photography of pioneers

32. The author mentions all of the following as jobs held by Solomon D. Butcher EXCEPT

(A) farmer
(B) settler
(C) photographer
(D) newspaperman

33. According to the article, what was Butcher most noted for?

(A) His advertising techniques
(B) His compatibility with his clients
(C) The poses and settings of his portraits
(D) The technical ability he demonstrated in photography

34. The author implies in the passage that Butcher's photography was

(A) realistic
(B) expensive
(C) colorful
(D) pretentious

35. The word *they* in line 10 refers to

(A) the scenes
(B) the circumstances
(C) the portraits
(D) the pioneers

GO ON TO THE NEXT PAGE

Questions 36–41

During the period of urban expansion following the Civil War, speculative builders discovered a bonanza in the form of the row house. Designed for single-family occupancy, these dwellings cost relatively little to construct because they
*Line* shared common walls with their neighbors and because many could be erected
(5) side by side on a narrow street frontage. Along New York's gridiron of streets and avenues rose block after block of row houses, which, by the 1880s, were almost invariably faced with brownstone. In contrast, wooden row houses on the West Coast appeared light and airy with their coats of bright paint. San Francisco developed a particularly successful row vernacular, suitable for rich and poor
(10) alike, as typified by clusters of homes like the Rountree group, which featured Queen Anne elements in their pitched roofs and heavily decorated exteriors. Although critics likened the facades of such structures to the "puffing, paint and powder of our female friends," the houses were efficiently planned, sanitary, and well-lighted. Virtually every dwelling boasted one or more bay windows, which
(15) were as important to sun-loving San Franciscans as brownstone fronts were to New Yorkers. As an English traveler observed, California architecture, "with all the windows gracefully leaping out at themselves," should rightly be called the "bay-window order."

36. The main purpose of the author in this passage is

(A) to contrast two versions of a similar architectural form
(B) to persuade people to live in row houses
(C) to argue for the excellence of California row houses
(D) to describe early housing in urban areas

37. According to the passage, why did speculative builders profit from row houses?

(A) Because they cost very little to build
(B) Because they were for single families
(C) Because they were well-constructed
(D) Because they were attractive

38. All of the following can be inferred about row houses from the passage EXCEPT

(A) they provided for high-density housing
(B) they housed people of different ethnic groups
(C) they provided a new and popular form of architectural design
(D) they had no front yards

39. What can be inferred from the passage about New York row houses?

(A) They were less colorful than row houses on the West Coast
(B) They were windowless
(C) They were smaller than California row houses
(D) They were less similar in appearance than row houses in California

40. In lines 12–14 critics of California row houses commented on their

(A) excessive use of bay windows
(B) ostentatious decoration
(C) repetitive nature
(D) lack of light

41. The author of the passage implies that the most important feature for Californians living in row houses was

(A) the color
(B) the price
(C) the windows
(D) the heavily decorated exteriors

GO ON TO THE NEXT PAGE

Questions 42–47

Since water is the basis of life, composing the greater part of the tissues of all living things, the crucial problem of desert animals is to survive in a world where sources of flowing water are rare. And since man's inexorable necessity is to
*Line* absorb large quantities of water at frequent intervals, he can scarcely comprehend
(5) that many creatures of the desert pass their entire lives without a single drop.

Uncompromising as it is, the desert has not eliminated life but only those forms unable to withstand its desiccating effects. No moist-skinned, water-loving animals can exist there. Few large animals are found: the giants of the North American desert are the deer, the coyote, and the bobcat. Since desert country is
(10) open, it holds more swift-footed, running, and leaping creatures than the tangled forest. Its population are largely nocturnal, silent, filled with reticence, and ruled by stealth. Yet they are not emaciated. Having adapted to their austere environment, they are as healthy as animals anywhere in the world.

The secret of their adjustment lies in a combination of behavior and physiology.
(15) None could survive if, like mad dogs and Englishmen, they went out in the midday sun; many would die in a matter of minutes. So most of them pass the burning hours asleep in cool, humid burrows underneath the ground, emerging to hunt only by night. The surface of the sun-baked desert averages around 150 degrees, but 18 inches down the temperature is only 60 degrees.

42. What is the topic of this passage?

(A) Desert plants
(B) Life underground
(C) Animal life in a desert environment
(D) Man's life in the desert

43. *Desiccating* in line 7 means

(A) drying
(B) humidifying
(C) killing
(D) life threatening

44. The author mentions all of the following as examples of the behavior of desert animals EXCEPT

(A) animals sleep during the day
(B) animals dig homes underground
(C) animals are noisy and aggressive
(D) animals are watchful and quiet

45. The author states that one characteristic of animals who live in the desert is that they

(A) are smaller and fleeter than forest animals
(B) are less healthy than animals who live in different places
(C) can hunt in temperatures of 150 degrees
(D) live in an accommodating environment

46. The word *they* in line 12 refers to

(A) the forest animals
(B) the desert population
(C) large animals
(D) water-loving animals

47. Which of the following generalizations is supported by the passage?

(A) Water is the basis of life.
(B) All living things adjust to their environments.
(C) Desert life is colorful.
(D) Healthy animals live longer lives.

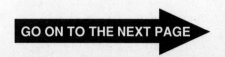
GO ON TO THE NEXT PAGE

Questions 48–54

The influx of Americans into Oregon in the 1840s ignited a dispute between Britain and the United States that, in its more intemperate phases, was accompanied by shrill demands in both countries for war. The argument
*Line*   originated in the fact that the boundaries of Oregon had never been clearly fixed.
(5)    The name vaguely embraced the territory west of the Rockies between the northern boundary of Mexican-held California and the southern edge of Russian-held Alaska, which at the time extended south to parallel 54° 40'. In 1818 when America proposed a boundary at the 49th parallel—an extension of the border with Canada that already existed east of the Rockies—and the British suggested a
(10)   line farther south, statesmen of both nations avoided the resulting impasse by agreeing to accept temporary "joint occupancy."
         But by the early 1840s, the issue could no longer be avoided: Oregon fever and Manifest Destiny had become potent political forces. Though many eastern Americans considered Oregon country too remote to become excited about,
(15)   demands for its occupation were shouted with almost religious fervor. Senator Thomas Hart Benton, for one, urged Congress to muster "thirty or forty thousand American rifles beyond the Rocky Mountains that will be our effective negotiators." The Democratic Party made "54° 40' or fight" an issue of the 1844 presidential election and just managed to install James K. Polk, an ardent expansionist, in the
(20)   White House. But despite their seeming intransigence, neither Polk nor the British government wanted to fight. And just about the time that Polk learned that the land lying north of the 49th parallel was useless for agriculture, the British decided the American market for goods was worth far more than Oregon's fast-dying fur trade. So they quietly settled for the 49th parallel, the boundary that the United
(25)   States had proposed in the first place.

48. What is the main idea of this passage?

(A) The disagreement over the boundaries of Oregon was peacefully solved.
(B) The United States wanted more land than it needed.
(C) Politicians in 1840 favored war with Britain.
(D) The United States ended up sharing Oregon with Canada.

49. As used in line 4, the word *fixed* could best be replaced by

(A) repaired
(B) adjusted
(C) built
(D) established

50. In line 12 the phrase *the issue* refers to

(A) what to do with the Americans living in Oregon
(B) claiming Alaska as part of the United States
(C) setting the Oregon boundary
(D) going to war with Britain

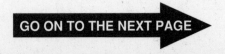
GO ON TO THE NEXT PAGE

51. The confrontation with Britain over Oregon boundaries came to a head in the early 1840s for all the following reasons EXCEPT

   (A) more people were living in Oregon at that time
   (B) the expansionists made the situation a political issue
   (C) all people were united in favoring the expansion and settlement of Oregon
   (D) Manifest Destiny was a major political force at this time

52. It can be inferred from the passage that Senator Thomas Hart Benton

   (A) was a temperate man
   (B) supported the occupation of Oregon by force
   (C) felt negotiation was the best policy
   (D) proposed and approved the final boundary decision

53. The 49th parallel was accepted by both parties in the border dispute for all of the following reasons EXCEPT

   (A) the dying fur trade in Oregon
   (B) the attraction of the American market for goods
   (C) the condition of the land north of 49°
   (D) the desire for a good fight

54. It can be inferred from the passage that in the final boundary settlement the United States

   (A) got the land that it had originally demanded
   (B) got less land than it had originally demanded
   (C) got more land than it had originally demanded
   (D) had no interest in the land involved in the dispute

**GO ON TO THE NEXT PAGE**

Questions 55–60

For all their great diversity of shapes and sizes, glaciers can be divided into two essential types: valley glaciers, which flow downhill from mountains and are shaped by the constraints of topography, and ice sheets, which flow outward in all
*Line* directions from domelike centers of accumulated ice to cover vast expanses of
(5) terrain. Whatever their type, most glaciers are remnants of great shrouds of ice that covered the earth eons ago. In a few of these glaciers the oldest ice is very ancient indeed: the age of parts of the Antarctic sheet may exceed 500,000 years.

Glaciers are born in rocky wombs above the snow line, where there is sufficient winter snowfall and summer cold for snow to survive the annual melting. The
(10) long gestation period of a glacier begins with the accumulation and gradual transformation of snowflakes. Soon after they reach the ground, complex snowflakes are reduced to compact, roughly spherical ice crystals, the basic components of a glacier. As new layers of snow and firn, snow that survives the melting of the previous summer, accumulate, they squeeze out most of the air
(15) bubbles trapped within and between the crystals below. This process of recrystallization continues throughout the life of the glacier.

The length of time required for the creation of glacier ice depends mainly upon the temperature and the rate of snowfall. In Iceland, where snowfall is heavy and summer temperatures are high enough to produce plenty of meltwater, glacier ice
(20) may come into being in a relatively short time—say, ten years. In parts of Antarctica, where snowfall is scant and the ice remains well below its melting temperature year-round, the process may require hundreds of years.

The ice does not become a glacier until it moves under its own weight, and it cannot move significantly until it reaches a critical thickness —the point at which
(25) the weight of the piled-up layers overcomes the internal strength of the ice and the friction between the ice and the ground. This critical thickness is about 60 feet. The fastest moving glaciers have been gauged at not much more than two and a half miles per year, and some cover less than 1/100 inch in that same amount of time. But no matter how infinitesimal the flow, movement is what distinguishes a
(30) glacier from a mere mass of ice.

GO ON TO THE NEXT PAGE

55. This passage mainly discusses

    (A) the size and shape of glaciers
    (B) the formation of glaciers
    (C) why glaciers move
    (D) two types of glaciers

56. Why does the author mention the Antarctic ice sheet in the first paragraph?

    (A) It is a slow-moving glacier.
    (B) One would expect glaciers in this part of the world.
    (C) It contains some of the oldest ice in existence.
    (D) It is an example of a well-formed ice sheet.

57. In order to describe the development of glaciers, the author uses the analogy of

    (A) birth
    (B) snowflakes
    (C) crystals
    (D) Iceland

58. According to the passage, what is one of the differences between valley glaciers and ice sheets?

    (A) Ice sheets move faster than valley glaciers.
    (B) While valley glaciers flow downhill, ice sheets flow in all directions.
    (C) Valley glaciers are thicker than ice sheets because of the restricting land formations.
    (D) Valley glaciers are not as old as ice sheets.

59. In line 23, what does *it* refer to?

    (A) glacier
    (B) ice
    (C) weight
    (D) critical thickness

60. According to the passage, the characteristic that identifies a glacier is

    (A) the critical thickness of the ice
    (B) the amount of firn accumulated
    (C) the movement of the ice
    (D) the weight of the ice

**THIS IS THE END OF SECTION 3**

IF YOU FINISH BEFORE TIME IS CALLED, CHECK YOUR WORK
ON SECTION 3 ONLY
DO NOT READ OR WORK ON ANY OTHER SECTION OF THE TEST.

STOP STOP STOP STOP STOP STOP STOP

# TEST OF WRITTEN ENGLISH

## PRACTICE TEST THREE

Time—30 minutes

Some people believe that students should receive specific letter grades (A, B, C, D, F) to evaluate their performance in courses. Others believe that students should receive a written evaluation of their strengths and weaknesses. Discuss these two points of view. In which way would you prefer to be evaluated? Explain your reasons.

### NOTES

Use this space to make your notes. Write the final version of your essay on lined paper. The Sample TWE Answer Sheet on page 192 is an example of the amount of writing space provided in the TOEFL Test.

# PRACTICE TEST FOUR

## SECTION 1
## LISTENING COMPREHENSION

In this section of the test, you will have an opportunity to demonstrate your ability to understand spoken English. There are three parts to this section, with special directions for each part.

### Part A

Directions:   For each question in Part A, you will hear a short sentence. Each sentence will be spoken just one time. The sentences you hear will not be written out for you. Therefore, you must listen carefully to understand what the speaker says.

After you hear a sentence, read the four choices in your test book, marked (A), (B), (C), and (D), and decide which <u>one</u> is closest in meaning to the sentence you heard. Then, on your answer sheet, find the number of the question and fill in the space that corresponds to the letter of the answer you have chosen. Fill in the space so that the letter inside the oval cannot be seen.

Example I                                          Sample Answer

You will hear:                                      Ⓐ Ⓑ ● Ⓓ

You will read:      (A)  Greg didn't bother to leave a tip.
                    (B)  Greg thought about typing a
                         letter to his brother.
                    (C)  Greg didn't like to type.
                    (D)  My typing bothered Greg.

The speaker said, "Greg thought typing was a bother." Sentence (C), "Greg didn't like to type," is closest in meaning to the sentence you heard. Therefore, you should choose answer (C).

Example II                                         Sample Answer

You will hear:                                      Ⓐ ● Ⓒ Ⓓ

You will read:      (A)  Everyone will be able to take this
                         exam later.
                    (B)  Students should bring a calculator
                         to this exam.
                    (C)  This test will be part of every
                         student's final grade.
                    (D)  No one can calculate the grades
                         for this test.

The speaker said, "Everyone needs a calculator for this test." Sentence (B), "Students should bring a calculator to this exam," is closest in meaning to the sentence you heard. Therefore, you should choose answer (B).

**GO ON TO THE NEXT PAGE** ➡

1. (A) You'll see later.
   (B) It's getting late.
   (C) Good bye for now.
   (D) Did you see your letter?

2. (A) Business isn't too good right now, is it?
   (B) Why don't we start our own business?
   (C) I think we should get started.
   (D) Let's go down to the office.

3. (A) The teacher wants to meet with Chris.
   (B) Chris bought some meat from the butcher.
   (C) Chris and his teacher went to get something to eat.
   (D) Some meat can be bought at the butcher's.

4. (A) Please hand me that.
   (B) I'd like to give you that.
   (C) I applaud you for that.
   (D) I'd like to help you with that.

5. (A) I had to go congratulate my brother.
   (B) My brother will graduate soon.
   (C) I will go to my brother's graduation next semester.
   (D) My brother wants to go to a different school.

6. (A) Larry didn't take today's quiz.
   (B) Today's quiz was worth one point.
   (C) Larry didn't understand today's quiz.
   (D) Larry's missing quiz was found today.

7. (A) Claire is all ready to complete her paper.
   (B) Claire has already found some writing paper.
   (C) Claire's paper is not ready yet.
   (D) Claire's paper has been completed.

8. (A) Paul doesn't paint anymore.
   (B) I admire the painting Paul has finished.
   (C) Paul refuses to look at the painting.
   (D) Paul is looking at the painting.

9. (A) The course wasn't supposed to be so hard.
   (B) The class was as difficult as had been predicted.
   (C) It was difficult to be accepted into the course.
   (D) The class was different than it was supposed to be.

10. (A) Pam will pick us up for the party after she finishes running a few errands.
    (B) Pam is going shopping for party supplies.
    (C) Pam's score was the highest of all the people she knew at the party.
    (D) Pam will come to the party after she finishes jogging.

11. (A) I watched an art student buy this portfolio.
    (B) I gave this portfolio to an art student.
    (C) An art student helped me present this portfolio.
    (D) An art student gave me this portfolio.

12. (A) The robbers returned to look for more books.
    (B) They were asked to return to Robert's by tomorrow.
    (C) They were supposed to take the books back to Robert.
    (D) Robert suggested that they take turns reading the books.

13. (A) Did you start the game?
    (B) You couldn't have been the star of the play.
    (C) I'm fairly certain that you were the star of the play.
    (D) You weren't playing when the game started, were you?

14. (A) I don't receive letters from Pat anymore.
    (B) That just isn't right for me.
    (C) I had one letter from Pat this week.
    (D) The pack on the right is used.

GO ON TO THE NEXT PAGE

15. (A) Jessica now works in Cleveland.
    (B) Before Jessica graduated, she got a job.
    (C) Jessica will soon leave to go back to school.
    (D) Jessica will finish school in Cleveland.

16. (A) Hasn't he had plenty of time to adjust to his schedule?
    (B) He shouldn't have the same schedule now that he used to have.
    (C) Does he need to schedule use of it now?
    (D) He's getting accustomed to his schedule.

17. (A) You certainly are an excellent musician.
    (B) Being a professional magician is hard work!
    (C) You aren't a professional magician, are you?
    (D) I don't believe that you are a professional musician.

18. (A) He claims that he cannot move forward.
    (B) No one knows what has happened to his foot.
    (C) Undeniably, he tried very hard.
    (D) He didn't tell anyone that he was famous.

19. (A) Let's see if we can go in my car.
    (B) I ran to get my car washed.
    (C) My car seems to be running low on gas.
    (D) I can't get my car started.

20. (A) You've read a lot of the required books.
    (B) You shouldn't have required two books.
    (C) You haven't read very many of the required books.
    (D) Are there only two books required for the course?

GO ON TO THE NEXT PAGE

## Part B

<u>Directions:</u>   In Part B you will hear short conversations between two speakers. At the end of each conversation, a third person will ask a question about what was said. You will hear each conversation and question about it just one time. Therefore, you must listen carefully to understand what each speaker says. After you hear a conversation and the question about it, read the four possible answers in your test book and decide which <u>one</u> is the best answer to the question you heard. Then, on your answer sheet, find the number of the question and fill in the space that corresponds to the letter of the answer you have chosen.

Look at the following example.

You will hear:

You will read:
  (A)  At last winter is almost over.
  (B)  She doesn't like winter weather very much.
  (C)  This winter's weather is similar to last winter's weather.
  (D)  Winter won't last as long this year as it did last year.

Sample Answer

From the conversation you learn that the woman thinks the weather this winter is almost the same as the weather last winter. The best answer to the question "What does the woman mean?" is (C), "This winter's weather is similar to last winter's weather." Therefore, you should choose answer (C).

21. (A)  Someone is already using his vacuum.
    (B)  He's having trouble with his vacuum.
    (C)  He will not need the vacuum to clean out his car.
    (D)  He is willing to lend the woman his vacuum.

22. (A)  In a hotel.
    (B)  In a furniture store.
    (C)  In a campground.
    (D)  In a private home.

23. (A)  There is one apartment that is worse than this one.
    (B)  She doesn't like the size of this apartment at all.
    (C)  She would like to see the next apartment.
    (D)  She has never seen a worse apartment.

24. (A)  She can't understand why the man is thirsty.
    (B)  The man ought to go to the laundromat.
    (C)  The laundromat is too far away.
    (D)  She will not wash the man's clothes for him.

25. (A)  She'll take no more than six courses.
    (B)  She's not interested in hearing about the man's life.
    (C)  She will not enroll in so many classes.
    (D)  She'll get her new glasses before fall.

26. (A)  Get a better doctor.
    (B)  Go see a doctor.
    (C)  Try not to hurt her shoulder.
    (D)  Look carefully at her shoulder.

27. (A) She can't figure out what is wrong with the car.
    (B) She is shocked by what the man has said.
    (C) She did not hear what the man said.
    (D) She can't see what is behind the car.

28. (A) It's Carol's turn to bake one.
    (B) He doesn't know when Carol baked it.
    (C) He would like to taste it.
    (D) He will take it to Carol.

29. (A) He has to be home by eight.
    (B) He doesn't have time to eat right now.
    (C) He's going to see the woman later.
    (D) He doesn't want to gain any weight.

30. (A) She doesn't understand the man's question.
    (B) She'll have the test ready in a few days.
    (C) She has a few questions about the man's schedule.
    (D) The man may not take the test early.

31. (A) She didn't think the professor's joke was very funny.
    (B) She paid a hundred dollars for her new glasses.
    (C) She couldn't hear what was being said in class very well.
    (D) She had heard the professor speak many times.

32. (A) It will carry him far.
    (B) It is certain to improve with time.
    (C) It is somewhat limited.
    (D) It has developed since he began singing opera.

33. (A) Can he stop and count the sandwiches?
    (B) Did she pay for his sandwiches?
    (C) Are his sandwiches included in the ones that were counted?
    (D) Did she put his sandwiches in the picnic basket for him?

34. (A) She thinks it would be a good idea to go swimming.
    (B) She wants to talk to the man.
    (C) She'll loan the heater to the man.
    (D) The heat doesn't bother her that much.

35. (A) Both Professor Andrews and Professor Larson refuse late work.
    (B) Professor Andrews will accept late work, but Professor Larson won't.
    (C) Professor Larson will take everything except her papers to the lake.
    (D) Professor Larson and Professor Andrews both live near the lake.

GO ON TO THE NEXT PAGE

## Part C

<u>Directions:</u>   In this part of the test, you will hear short talks and conversations. After each of them, you will be asked some questions. You will hear the talks and conversations and the questions about them just one time. They will not be written out for you. Therefore, you must listen carefully to understand what each speaker says.

After you hear a question, read the four possible answers in your test book and decide which <u>one</u> is the best answer to the question you heard. Then, on your answer sheet, find the number of the question and fill in the space that corresponds to the letter of the answer you have chosen.

Answer all questions on the basis of what is <u>stated</u> or <u>implied</u> in the talk or conversation.

Listen to this sample talk.

You will hear:

Now look at the following example.

You will hear:                                                                         Sample Answer

You will read:   (A)  Only bumblebees can fertilize red            ● Ⓑ Ⓒ Ⓓ
                         clover plants.
                   (B)  Bumblebees protect red clover from
                         plant eating insects.
                   (C)  Bumblebees bring water to red clover
                         plants on their tongues.
                   (D)  Bumblebees keep mice and other animals
                         away from red clover plants.

The best answer to the question "Why is it impossible to raise red clover where there are no bumblebees?" is (A), "Only bumblebees can fertilize red clover plants." Therefore, you should choose answer (A).

Now look at the next example.

You will hear:                                                                         Sample Answer

You will read:   (A)  They both make honey.                          Ⓐ Ⓑ Ⓒ ●
                   (B)  They both build combs.
                   (C)  Both of them are found in
                         underground nests.
                   (D)  They both live through the winter.

The best answer to the question "According to the speaker, in what way are the queen wasp and the queen bee similar?" is (D), "They both live through the winter." Therefore, you should choose answer (D).

36. (A)  In a furniture store.
    (B)  In the woman's apartment.
    (C)  In the man's car.
    (D)  At a party.

37. (A)  Have a party.
    (B)  Go on a long vacation.
    (C)  Buy a new bed.
    (D)  Move away.

38. (A)  Help the woman clean her apartment.
    (B)  Exercise with the woman.
    (C)  Help the woman buy a bed.
    (D)  Explain what he meant.

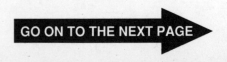

GO ON TO THE NEXT PAGE

39. (A) She is not a good housekeeper.
    (B) She has found a larger apartment.
    (C) She has a lot more cleaning to do.
    (D) She wants to have a clean apartment.

40. (A) He would like to shake the woman's hand.
    (B) He is stronger than the woman.
    (C) He would like to offer the woman his help.
    (D) He will give the woman whatever she needs.

41. (A) The man will take her.
    (B) She'll drive her car.
    (C) She'll take a taxi.
    (D) She'll walk.

42. (A) A librarian.
    (B) A tour guide.
    (C) A professor.
    (D) Alexander Boyd's secretary.

43. (A) In the library.
    (B) In an auditorium.
    (C) On the campus grounds.
    (D) In the greenhouse of the biology building.

44. (A) Library science students.
    (B) Students interested in attending this college.
    (C) Librarians who want to know about the library collection.
    (D) Students who will be graduating from the college soon.

45. (A) The person who designed the library building.
    (B) The author of several books in the library.
    (C) The first director of the library.
    (D) The biology professor after whom the library is named.

46. (A) To the biology building.
    (B) To the reference section of the library.
    (C) To the cafeteria.
    (D) To the admissions office.

47. (A) That the woman was going to empty her trash.
    (B) That the woman would save her glass containers for him.
    (C) That the woman would go for a bicycle ride with him.
    (D) That the woman was saving her used bottles and cans for recycling.

48. (A) Saving money.
    (B) Reusing materials that have already been used.
    (C) Taking the same bicycle route more than once.
    (D) Disposing of trash.

49. (A) It is too expensive.
    (B) It takes too much time.
    (C) She doesn't have very many recyclable items.
    (D) She can't remember to do it.

50. (A) Go for a walk with the man.
    (B) Start saving money.
    (C) Start recycling again.
    (D) Help the man recycle his cans and bottles.

---

**THIS IS THE END OF THE LISTENING COMPREHENSION SECTION OF THE TEST**

THE NEXT PART OF THE TEST IS SECTION 2. TURN TO THE
DIRECTIONS FOR SECTION 2 IN YOUR TEST BOOK.
READ THEM, AND BEGIN WORK.
DO NOT READ OR WORK ON ANY OTHER SECTION OF THE TEST.

SECTION 2
STRUCTURE AND WRITTEN EXPRESSION

Time—25 minutes

This section is designed to measure your ability to recognize language that is appropriate for standard written English. There are two types of questions in this section, with special directions for each type.

Directions:   Questions 1–15 are incomplete sentences. Beneath each sentence you will see four words or phrases, marked (A), (B), (C), and (D). Choose the one word or phrase that best completes the sentence. Then, on your answer sheet, find the number of the question and fill in the space that corresponds to the letter of the answer you have chosen. Fill in the space so that the letter inside the oval cannot be seen.

Example I

Most American families _____ at least one automobile.

(A)  have
(B)  in
(C)  that
(D)  has

Sample Answer

● Ⓑ Ⓒ Ⓓ

The sentence should read, "Most American families have at least one automobile." Therefore, you should choose answer (A).

Example II

_____ recent times, the discipline of biology has expanded rapidly into a variety of subdisciplines.

(A)  It is since
(B)  When
(C)  Since it is
(D)  In

Sample Answer

Ⓐ Ⓑ Ⓒ ●

The sentence should read, "In recent times, the discipline of biology has expanded into a variety of subdisciplines." Therefore, you should choose answer (D).

Now begin work on the questions.

1. Copper tubing is the preferred choice of plumbers _____ noncorrosive.

(A)  since it is
(B)  because of
(C)  it is
(D)  insofar as

2. _____ cultural diffusion refers to the spread of customs or practices from one culture to another.

(A)  To phrase
(B)  Phrased
(C)  To the phrase
(D)  The phrase

3. _____ born, a baby kangaroo measures less than three inches in length.

(A)  One is
(B)  When is one
(C)  Is one
(D)  When it is

4. _____ daily promotes physical as well as emotional well-being in people of all ages.

(A)  Having exercised
(B)  Those who exercise
(C)  Exercising
(D)  For exercising

GO ON TO THE NEXT PAGE

5. The financial manager's job _____ among the many sources of finance for the best interest rates available.

   (A) to shop around is
   (B) to shop around it is
   (C) is it to shop around
   (D) is to shop around

6. Spectrographs _____ possible for phoneticians to analyze the human voice and its speech qualities.

   (A) make
   (B) make it
   (C) makes it
   (D) are made

7. Trace minerals are _____ are elements needed in greater quantities.

   (A) as important to healthy human tissue as
   (B) most important to healthy human tissue
   (C) to healthy human tissue as important
   (D) important to healthy human tissue

8. Balinese cats, which are a cross between Siamese and long-haired cats, _____ medium length silky coats of fur.

   (A) they have
   (B) have
   (C) which have
   (D) having

9. _____ when a person doesn't eat enough fruit and vegetables.

   (A) Depleting gradually, potassium can occur
   (B) Gradual potassium depletion can occur
   (C) Since potassium can gradually be depleted
   (D) Since gradually depleting potassium can occur

10. Anthropologist Guy Swenson _____ that witchcraft beliefs are prevalent in societies in which social groups interact without formal mechanisms for social control.

    (A) he found
    (B) found
    (C) finding
    (D) was found

11. Declared an endangered species in the United States, _____ .

    (A) people have gathered the ginseng root almost to the point of extinction
    (B) the ginseng root has been gathered almost to the point of extinction
    (C) the near extinction of the ginseng root is due to excessive gathering
    (D) gathering the ginseng root almost to the point of extinction

12. The sudden expansion of heated air associated with lightning produces _____ often heard during a storm.

    (A) thunder is the rumbling sound
    (B) the rumbling sound, thunder is
    (C) the rumbling sound, thunder, that
    (D) thunder, the rumbling sound

13. Henry Ford revolutionized production management by _____ into small steps on a moving line.

    (A) breaking down auto assembly
    (B) broken down auto assembly
    (C) he broke down auto assembly
    (D) auto assembly breaking down

14. In carpentry, _____ *ceiling joists* refers to boards hung down from unfinished ceilings as the backbone from which finishing materials can be hung.

    (A) to the term
    (B) is termed
    (C) the term
    (D) to term

15. _____ the 35 years between the end of the Civil War and the turn of the century, the population of the United States doubled and manufacturing production increased sevenfold.

    (A) Into
    (B) In
    (C) At
    (D) To

**GO ON TO THE NEXT PAGE**

<u>Directions:</u>  In questions 16–40 each sentence has four underlined words or phrases. The four underlined parts of the sentence are marked (A), (B), (C), and (D). Identify the <u>one</u> underlined word or phrase that must be changed in order for the sentence to be correct. Then, on your answer sheet, find the number of the question and fill in the space that corresponds to the letter of the answer you have chosen.

Example I

The octopus <u>is</u> a unique animal <u>because</u> <u>they</u>
          A                        B          C
has three <u>functioning</u> hearts.
              D

Sample Answer

(A) (B) ● (D)

The sentence should read, "The octopus is a unique animal because it has three functioning hearts." Therefore, you should choose answer (C).

Example II

The beagle, <u>one of the most</u> <u>ancient</u> breeds of
              A                    B
dog <u>known</u>, <u>originating</u> in England.
        C          D

Sample Answer

(A) (B) (C) ●

The sentence should read, "The beagle, one of the most ancient breeds of dog known, originated in England." Therefore, you should choose answer (D).

Now begin work on the questions.

16. One important agent of <u>erosion</u> is the glacier, which is an <u>accumulated</u> of snow <u>slowly pressed</u> <u>into</u> ice.
                            A                                      B                    C            D

17. Ethnolinguists <u>study</u> language as <u>it</u> relates to society, <u>culture</u>, and human <u>behaving</u>.
                    A              B                      C                      D

18. It has <u>long</u> been known <u>as</u> an entire cluster of galaxies may sometimes <u>lie</u> buried <u>within</u> a vast,
            A                    B                                              C            D
dense ball of gas.

19. Paleoanthropologists <u>believe</u> that prehistoric man was <u>innate</u> a gentle, <u>cooperative</u>,
                          A                                    B                  C
food-sharing <u>creature</u>.
              D

20. Many corporate advisors feel <u>that</u> companies <u>that</u> provide their employees with <u>recreational</u> time
                                  A                    B                                      C
and facilities <u>safe</u> money on health insurance in the long run.
                D

21. Metal and glass containers can <u>be recycled</u>, <u>and</u> several states are <u>currently contemplating</u>
                                    A                B                            C
mandatory recycling laws <u>for either</u>.
                          D

22. The desire <u>to</u> species preservation is a primary <u>motivator</u> for <u>many</u> kinds of animal behavior,
                A                                        B            C
<u>including</u> reproduction.
  D

23. <u>In</u> 1987, molecular biologist L. Mark Lagrimini of Ohio State University cloned the gene <u>in that</u>
    A                                                                                            B
codes for <u>a type of</u> peroxidase <u>found</u> in tobacco plants.
            C                          D

24. <u>To fit</u> <u>on</u> an ecosystem, an organism <u>must be able</u> to adapt or <u>become</u> a part of it.
    A      B                                        C                        D

25. Arteries with <u>poorly</u> blood flow can leave <u>the</u> heart muscle <u>starved for</u> oxygen, a condition <u>that</u>
                  A                                B                        C                                D
often leads to heart attack.

26. Christopher Columbus first <u>seen</u> Native Americans <u>when</u> he <u>discovered</u> the Caribbean Islands
                                A                          B            C
<u>on</u> October 12, 1492.
  D

GO ON TO THE NEXT PAGE

27. Alpine Saint Bernards are <u>too</u> good at <u>following</u> the scent of man, even in snow, that they
       A          B
<u>are used</u> by ski patrols <u>as</u> rescue dogs.
  C           D

28. The writing of Elizabeth Stoddard was praised <u>by her</u> contemporaries because <u>they</u> was
                          A                      B
dramatic and direct, <u>possessing</u> a frankness <u>unlike that</u> of most other writing of the time.
                C              D

29. <u>Newspapers metropolitan</u> that <u>pride themselves</u> on the quality of <u>their</u> opinion articles often
       A               B                   C
have large staffs to write and edit the <u>editorial page</u>.
                        D

30. <u>Theoretical</u> biologist Aristid Lindenmayer <u>is</u> known <u>for him</u> description of the developmental
  A                         B     C
processes <u>in multicellular</u> structures.
        D

31. <u>When</u> the Panic of 1857, some U.S. citizens who <u>had been</u> rich or comfortable became poor <u>while</u>
  A                           B                        C
a few others, <u>capitalizing</u> on economic shifts, became richer.
          D

32. Many artists receive <u>promote</u> backing <u>from</u> government agencies <u>as well as</u> from private
               A          B                 C
<u>individuals</u> and firms.
  D

33. Dr. Frank Conrad's <u>musical</u> radio broadcasts in 1919 led Westinghouse <u>open</u> the first fully
               A                               B
<u>licensed</u> commercial broadcasting system in the United States <u>on</u> November 2, 1920.
  C                                     D

34. The rocks of the Cambrian period <u>of prehistory</u> <u>were formed</u> 500 to 600 million <u>year</u> <u>ago</u>.
                          A        B                  C   D

35. Organisms that are related <u>are</u> usually identifiable by <u>at less</u> some similarities in <u>anatomical</u>
                    A                    B                C
structure and embryonic <u>development</u>.
                   D

36. <u>With</u> the development of underwater breathing equipment, helmeted divers <u>can now</u> descend
  A                                               B
six hundred <u>foot</u> if they breathe a <u>special</u> mixture of gases.
           C               D

37. <u>According to</u> Cherokee legend, a woman <u>named</u> Grandmother Spider <u>brought</u> to her people the
    A                             B                     C
light of intelligence and <u>to experience</u>.
                   D

38. Many of the mammals <u>that</u> dwell in the desert are active only at <u>a night</u> <u>as</u> the intense heat of a
                A                            B    C
desert day can be fatal to <u>warm-blooded</u> animals.
                    D

39. The building blocks of the proteins necessary <u>for</u> life are amino acids, <u>much</u> of which cannot be
                                  A                 B
synthesized by the body <u>and</u> must be included <u>in</u> the diet.
                C               D

40. The cytoskeleton of a cell provides <u>structural</u> support <u>also</u> coordinates <u>cell</u> division, <u>growth</u>,
                          A           B           C        D
and morphology.

**THIS IS THE END OF SECTION 2**

IF YOU FINISH BEFORE TIME IS CALLED, CHECK YOUR WORK
ON SECTION 2 ONLY.
DO NOT READ OR WORK ON ANY OTHER SECTION OF THE TEST.
THE SUPERVISOR WILL TELL YOU WHEN TO BEGIN
WORK ON SECTION 3.

## SECTION 3
## VOCABULARY AND READING COMPREHENSION
### Time—45 minutes

This section is designed to measure your comprehension of standard written English. There are two types of questions in this section, with special directions for each type.

<u>Directions:</u>   In questions 1–30 each sentence has an underlined word or phrase. Below each sentence are four other words or phrases, marked (A), (B), (C), (D). You are to choose the <u>one</u> word or phrase that <u>best keeps the meaning</u> of the original sentence if it is substituted for the underlined word or phrase. Then, on your answer sheet, find the number of the question and fill in the space that corresponds to the letter you have chosen. Fill in the space so that the letter inside the oval cannot be seen.

Example

<u>Sample Answer</u>

Ladybugs, small brightly colored beetles, feed on plant aphids and have considerable economic value in <u>controlling</u> pest populations.

(A) limiting
(B) finding
(C) increasing
(D) ruling

The best answer is (A) because "Ladybugs, small brightly colored beetles, feed on plant aphids and have considerable economic value in limiting pest populations" is closest in meaning to the original sentence. Therefore, you should choose answer (A).

Now begin work on the questions.

1. A true folk dance should be popular only with a <u>limited</u> group of people.

(A) restricted
(B) large
(C) skillful
(D) musical

2. Although fluoridation of water is known to have <u>beneficial</u> effects on tooth development and resistance to tooth decay, some persons argue against it on religious grounds.

(A) unusual
(B) helpful
(C) documented
(D) marginal

3. The lack of gravity on the moon's surface makes extensive exploration by people wearing space suits <u>unwieldy</u> and impractical.

(A) unwholesome
(B) hot
(C) awkward
(D) time-consuming

4. Though the dog has been loved and <u>respected</u> by most peoples of the world, there are some exceptions.

(A) admired
(B) domesticated
(C) tolerated
(D) neglected

GO ON TO THE NEXT PAGE

5. Writers who know Africa well often paint pictures of its landscapes and climates that leave far more <u>lasting</u> impressions than maps.

(A) enduring
(B) accurate
(C) vivid
(D) general

6. The first cities probably had only a few thousand persons, because all food had to be grown on nearby farms and <u>transported</u> on foot or in small boats.

(A) conveyed
(B) sold
(C) eaten
(D) packaged

7. Free and open debate is necessary in a democracy in order to <u>reach</u> sound decisions and to protect minority groups.

(A) vote on
(B) record
(C) achieve
(D) grasp

8. Scientists believe that prehistoric man <u>did not mind</u> severe heat or cold.

(A) was not aware of
(B) was not affected by
(C) did not tolerate
(D) did not think about

9. In warm climates people often wear white because it <u>reflects</u> the hot rays of the sun and makes them feel cooler.

(A) retains
(B) compliments
(C) relays
(D) throws off

10. In the heat of the midday sun, the desert seems <u>devoid of</u> life to an unknowing visitor.

(A) part of
(B) bustling with
(C) empty of
(D) unconcerned with

11. Pioneer families, grown <u>weary of</u> their covered wagons, nevertheless had to live in them for weeks while building their log cabins.

(A) sentimental about
(B) tired of
(C) accustomed to
(D) impressed with

12. People who smoke get a great deal of <u>satisfaction</u> from it.

(A) hassle
(B) money
(C) pleasure
(D) irritation

13. Coal is one of the most important <u>sources</u> of energy for our modern civilization.

(A) beginnings
(B) uses
(C) developments
(D) bases

14. Seismological observations, or the recording of earthquakes, obtain information on the <u>nature</u> and distribution of earthquakes.

(A) time
(B) origin
(C) duration
(D) characteristics

15. The <u>proliferation</u> of motel chains in the 1950s was a response to more Americans traveling farther distances by car.

(A) decoration
(B) increase
(C) advertisement
(D) use

**GO ON TO THE NEXT PAGE**

16. Although the stars in the flag of the United States are sometimes counted according to dates the states were admitted to the nation, there is no legal basis for this <u>practice</u>.

    (A) use
    (B) manner
    (C) accounting
    (D) procedure

17. The origins and evolution of language will probably always remain in the realm of <u>speculation</u>.

    (A) science
    (B) conjecture
    (C) specialization
    (D) linguistics

18. A nesting meadowlark sometimes chooses <u>a spot</u> in a clump of grass near a stream where she goes to bathe.

    (A) a branch
    (B) a place
    (C) an entrance
    (D) a mate

19. Holistic approaches to health suggest that we are healthy when our body, mind, and spirit exist in a <u>harmoniously</u> balanced state of well-being.

    (A) energetically
    (B) compatibly
    (C) musically
    (D) artificially

20. Certain insects <u>mimic</u> the actions of their predators, thereby developing protective devices.

    (A) imitate
    (B) observe
    (C) avoid
    (D) figure out

21. American football, which developed from rugby, was first played in the United States in 1875, <u>pitting</u> Harvard against Yale in the new running game.

    (A) observing
    (B) matching
    (C) opening
    (D) defeating

22. Soon after the financial success of the Model T, Henry Ford announced that from then on his company would <u>share</u> its profits with its employees.

    (A) divide
    (B) save
    (C) invest
    (D) spend

23. The Finger Lakes, a series of long, narrow lakes in western New York State, received their name because they <u>stretch out</u> like fingers of a hand.

    (A) extend
    (B) intertwine
    (C) interact
    (D) flow

24. Labor unions are important because they can <u>exert</u> substantial pressure on wages and working conditions not only for themselves but also for all workers.

    (A) try
    (B) mention
    (C) find
    (D) apply

25. Nature herself probably provided man with his first bridge when a tree fell <u>across</u> some stream.

    (A) above
    (B) within
    (C) on top of
    (D) over

**GO ON TO THE NEXT PAGE**

26. Tomatoes, peppers, and eggplant are all members of the same family and require <u>essentially</u> the same climatic conditions to grow.

    (A) most importantly
    (B) basically
    (C) precisely
    (D) in part

27. Stephen Crane is interesting as a writer because he <u>deftly</u> used words and images as if he were a painter or composer.

    (A) usually
    (B) skillfully
    (C) sarcastically
    (D) discreetly

28. The desert roadrunner, a small, picturesque bird of the southwest, spends most of its time on the ground, darting <u>warily</u> among the cactus and mesquite in search of food.

    (A) quickly
    (B) guardedly
    (C) awkwardly
    (D) carelessly

29. Dwarf evergreens tend to be densely foliated and compact in form, keeping them relatively free of leaves and other windblown <u>debris</u>.

    (A) trash
    (B) birds
    (C) flowers
    (D) seeds

30. Lack of money in the federal budget often makes it difficult to have <u>efficiently</u> enforced regulations.

    (A) comprehensively
    (B) intrusively
    (C) effectively
    (D) selectively

GO ON TO THE NEXT PAGE

Directions:   In the rest of this section you will read several passages. Each one is followed by several questions about it. For questions 31–60, you are to choose the <u>one</u> best answer, (A), (B), (C), or (D), to each question. Then, on your answer sheet, find the number of the question and fill in the space that corresponds to the letter of the answer you have chosen.

Answer all questions following a passage on the basis of what is <u>stated</u> or <u>implied</u> in that passage.

Read the following passage:

The flamingo is a beautiful water bird with long legs, and a curving neck like a swan's. Most flamingos have deep red or flame-colored feathers with black quills. Some have pink or white feathers. The long legs and webbed feet are well suited for wading. The flamingo eats in a peculiar manner. It plunges its head underwater and sifts the mud with a fine hairlike "comb" along the edge of its bent bill. In this way, it strains out small shellfish and other animals. The bird nests on a mound of mud with a hollow on top to hold its single egg. Flamingos are timid and often live together in large colonies. The birds once lived in the southern United States, but plume hunters killed them faster than they could breed, and the flamingo no longer lives wild in the United States.

*Line* (5) ... (10)

Example I

Sample Answer

The flamingo can eat shellfish and other animals because of its

(A) ● (C) (D)

(A)  curved neck
(B)  especially formed bill
(C)  long legs
(D)  brightly colored feathers

According to the passage, the flamingo sifts mud for food with "a fine hairlike 'comb' along the edge of its bent bill." Therefore, you should choose answer (B).

Example II

Sample Answer

How many young would you expect the flamingo to raise at one time?

(A) (B) ● (D)

(A)  Several
(B)  Two
(C)  One
(D)  Four

The passage states that the flamingo nests on a mound of mud with a "single" egg. Therefore, you should choose answer (C).

Now begin work on the questions.

**GO ON TO THE NEXT PAGE**

Questions 31–37

Swans are among the most beautiful of North American waterfowl and have always enjoyed the admiration and even the protection of bird lovers. Of the six species in the swan genus, only two are native to North America. The trumpeter swan, the largest of the group, breeds in the northern United States and Alaska and was nearly wiped out during the nineteenth-century craze for elaborately feathered hats. The whistling swan, which winters in large flocks on the Chesapeake Bay, has recently been renamed the tundra swan because it breeds and summers on the northernmost tundra regions of the continent.

Recently, populations of mute swans—an exotic species introduced to North America from Europe in the early 1900s—have begun increasing by an alarming 30 to 40 percent annually in some states. Most wildlife biologists today believe the majestic white creatures, with their tendency to destroy a pond's plant life and drive away native waterfowl, might create havoc on the scale of the gypsy moth, starling, or English sparrow.

Both native species of swans are wild and require large areas of uninhabited summer ground for nesting and feeding. Mutes, however, semi-domesticated and accustomed to people, can nest in pairs of as many as three or four on one small coastal pond, which can burden delicate and environmentally essential brackish ponds.

31. The author's main purpose in this passage is to
    (A) interest people in wildlife biology
    (B) describe swans of North America
    (C) prevent extinction of a swan species
    (D) forewarn an environmental problem

32. According to the passage, the main issue concerning mute swans is that they are
    (A) not native to North America
    (B) semi-domesticated
    (C) increasing very rapidly
    (D) possessive of their habitat

33. The author states that the native species of swans can live best
    (A) in close contact with people
    (B) in the southern part of the United States
    (C) in unpopulated areas
    (D) in a similar habitat to mute swans

34. The passage comments on all features of swans EXCEPT their
    (A) life span
    (B) breeding and nesting habits
    (C) habitats
    (D) origins

35. Which swan was close to extinction?
    (A) The mute swan
    (B) The whistling swan
    (C) The trumpeter swan
    (D) The tundra swan

36. From the passage it can be concluded that mute swans are
    (A) more numerous than other types of swans
    (B) a problem for coastal ponds
    (C) welcome in most parts of North America
    (D) unattractive in appearance

37. It can be inferred from the passage that the author
    (A) approves of all swans
    (B) is concerned about mute swans
    (C) is a wildlife biologist
    (D) prefers trumpeter swans

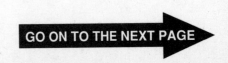

GO ON TO THE NEXT PAGE

Questions 38–41

The earliest system of writing is usually attributed to the Sumerians of
Mesopotamia during the end of the fourth millennium B.C. There, officials of such
Sumerian city-states as Uruk had developed a system of recording numerals,
*Line* pictographs, and ideographs on specially prepared clay surfaces.
*(5)*     Although the clay blanks used by the Uruk scribes are universally referred to as
tablets, a word with the connotation of flatness, they are actually convex.
Individual characters were inscribed in the clay by means of a stylus made of
wood, bone, or ivory, with one end blunt and the other pointed. The characters
were basically of two kinds. Numerical signs were impressed into the clay; all
*(10)* other signs, pictographs, and ideographs alike, were incised with the pointed end
of the stylus. The repertory of characters used by the Uruk scribes was large; it is
estimated at no fewer than 1,500 separate signs.

38. This passage mainly discusses

(A)  the Uruk writing system
(B)  the Sumerians of Mesopotamia
(C)  writing instruments of the
      Uruk scribes
(D)  the materials used in early
      writing systems

39. The word *there* in line 2 refers to

(A)  the Sumerian city states
(B)  Mesopotamia
(C)  Uruk
(D)  the fourth millennium B.C.

40. Which of the following terms does NOT
refer to something on which early writing
was inscribed?

(A)  Clay surfaces
(B)  Characters
(C)  Clay blanks
(D)  Tablets

41. According to the passage, how were
pictographs recorded?

(A)  They were cut into the clay.
(B)  They were painted onto the surface.
(C)  They were pressed into the clay.
(D)  They were brushed onto the surface.

**GO ON TO THE NEXT PAGE**

Questions 42–47

In addition to providing energy, fats have several other functions in the body. The fat-soluble vitamins—A, D, E, and K—are dissolved in fats, as their name implies. Good sources of these vitamins have high oil or fat content, and the
Line vitamins are stored in the body's fatty tissues. In the diet, fats cause food to remain
(5) longer in the stomach, thus increasing the feeling of fullness for some time after a meal is eaten. Fats add variety, taste, and texture to foods, which accounts for the popularity of fried foods. Fatty deposits in the body have an insulating and protective value. The curves of the human female body are due mostly to strategically located fat deposits.
(10) Whether a certain amount of fat in the diet is essential to human health is not definitely known. When rats are fed a fat-free diet, their growth eventually ceases, their skin becomes inflamed and scaly, and their reproductive systems are damaged. Two fatty acids, linoleic and arachidonic acids, prevent these abnormalities and hence are called essential fatty acids. They also are required by
(15) a number of other animals, but their roles in human beings are debatable. Most nutritionists consider linoleic fatty acid an essential nutrient for humans.

42. This passage probably appeared in which of the following?

(A) A diet book
(B) A book on basic nutrition
(C) A cookbook
(D) A popular women's magazine

43. According to the passage, all the following vitamins are stored in the body's fatty tissue EXCEPT

(A) A
(B) D
(C) B
(D) E

44. The author states that fats serve all of the following body functions EXCEPT to

(A) promote a feeling of fullness
(B) insulate and protect the body
(C) provide energy
(D) control weight gain

45. According to the author of the passage, which of the following is true for rats when they are fed a fat-free diet?

(A) They stop growing
(B) They have more babies
(C) They lose body hair
(D) They require less care

46. Linoleic fatty acid is mentioned in the passage as

(A) an essential nutrient for humans
(B) more useful than arachidonic acid
(C) preventing weight gain in rats
(D) a nutrient found in most foods

47. That humans should all have some fat in their diets is, according to the author,

(A) a commonly held view
(B) not yet a proven fact
(C) only true for women
(D) proven to be true by experiments on rats

GO ON TO THE NEXT PAGE

Questions 48–52

In our discussion of dance, it might be valuable to contrast style with another word often employed by dancers: technique. To have technique is to possess the physical expertise to perform whatever steps a given work may contain, be they
*Line* simple or complex. Some dances may contain only the most elementary steps.
(5) Choreographers influenced by minimalist art or by the stripped-down productions associated with the experimental Judson Dance Theater of the 1900s have put together dances that consist of nothing but such basic actions as walking or running. Anyone who can walk or run for the duration of those pieces therefore possesses the necessary technique to perform them.
(10) If technique is the ability to perform steps, style refers to the way steps are organized and shaped, both by the choreographer who has invented them and by the dancers who perform them. Many things can affect the style of a work: for instance, the historical period and geographical locale in which it is set and the social status of its characters. The style of an abstract dance may also be
(15) determined by a choreographer's predilections: Some choreographers are fond of lyrical movements, whereas others prefer sharp, glittering steps. Individual performing styles may be influenced by such considerations as a dancer's temperament and the way that the dancer habitually accents or times certain movements on stage.

48. The main purpose of this passage is to

(A) explain the necessity of technique in dance
(B) contrast technique and style in dance
(C) describe the differences between choreographers and dancers
(D) contrast modern and classical dance

49. It can be assumed that the paragraph preceding this passage most probably discusses

(A) art
(B) theater
(C) dance
(D) opera

50. It can be inferred from the passage that the author believes dancers in the Judson Dance Theater exhibited

(A) dance technique containing mostly elementary steps
(B) complex dance technique
(C) technique similar to classical ballet
(D) technique different from that influenced by minimalist art

51. Which of the following was NOT mentioned as something that might affect style in dance?

(A) The amount of practice time
(B) Temperament
(C) Preference for certain movements
(D) The historical setting of the work

52. The word *work* in line 12 can best be replaced by

(A) job
(B) musical composition
(C) dance group
(D) choreographed dance

GO ON TO THE NEXT PAGE

Questions 53–60

For its sudden destruction of crops, farmers call hail the "white plague." "It wipes you out in the passing of a cloud," complained a Colorado farm boy bitterly. "Half an hour ago you had a half-section of wheat—320 acres—ready to harvest
*Line*    and haul to town. Now you haven't got a penny."
(5)      Thousands of hailstorms occur each year, especially in the moist, temperate climates of the middle latitudes. In the United States alone, crop damage from hail totals about one billion dollars a year, with a further $75 million in losses attributable to livestock deaths and property damage.

The groundwork for such devastation is laid innocently enough, deep within a
(10)    thunderstorm's cumulus cloud. There, at frigid altitudes above 15,000 feet, the air is at first so pure that water droplets can exist at temperatures well below the freezing point without turning to ice.

As the storm's convection currents become more powerful, however, they sweep tiny particles of dust and ice upward into the cloud. Each of these foreign
(15)    bodies—a potential hailstone nucleus—begins to collide with supercooled water droplets, which freeze to it on impact. Buffeted about by a series of updrafts and downdrafts, the hailstone gathers layer upon layer of ice. When it has grown so heavy that even the strongest updraft cannot sustain it, the mature hailstone plummets to earth.

(20)    While weak storms produce small stones that melt before reaching the ground, severe thunderstorms are capable of generating hail the size of eggs, baseballs, or even grapefruit. When a particularly violent storm ravaged Coffeyville, Kansas, on September 3, 1970, residents collected scores of unusually large hailstones, including one that measured nearly six inches in diameter and weighed 1 2/3
(25)    pounds. When the amazing specimen was sent to Colorado's National Center for Atmospheric Research, meteorologists confirmed that it set a new record for size— and calculated that, in its final stages of growth, the stone had required an updraft of 100 miles per hour to keep it in the air.

GO ON TO THE NEXT PAGE

53. A good title for this passage would be

    (A) The White Plague
    (B) Heavy Stones
    (C) Severe Storms
    (D) An Amazing Specimen

54. In line 2, the phrase "It wipes you out" means

    (A) hail has a cleansing effect
    (B) you feel tired after a hailstorm
    (C) hailstorms can cause financial ruin
    (D) a hailstorm will make you
       feel depressed

55. It can be inferred from the passage that hailstorms would most likely occur in which of the following climates?

    (A) A dry climate
    (B) A tropical climate
    (C) An arctic climate
    (D) A moderate climate

56. According to the passage, water droplets are able to exist as water when temperatures are below freezing because of

    (A) the high altitude
    (B) the pure air
    (C) the cumulus cloud
    (D) the convection currents

57. The formation of a hailstone can be best described as

    (A) sudden
    (B) cumulative
    (C) severe
    (D) sustaining

58. According to the passage, the hailstone falls to earth

    (A) immediately
    (B) when the downdraft is very strong
    (C) when it is heavier than the updraft
    (D) after the winds die down

59. It can be inferred from the passage that some hailstones melt before reaching the ground because of their

    (A) weight
    (B) size
    (C) nucleus
    (D) immaturity

60. The word *it* in line 26 refers to

    (A) the National Center for
       Atmospheric Research
    (B) the size
    (C) the specimen
    (D) the storm

**THIS IS THE END OF SECTION 3**

IF YOU FINISH BEFORE TIME IS CALLED, CHECK YOUR WORK
ON SECTION 3 ONLY.
DO NOT READ OR WORK ON ANY OTHER SECTION OF THE TEST.

# TEST OF WRITTEN ENGLISH

## PRACTICE TEST FOUR

Time—30 minutes

The graph below shows the share of car sales in the United States of a major U.S. car manufacturer and a major imported-car manufacturer over a period of years. Discuss the information you get from this graph. Support your conclusions with details from the graph.

Shares of Car Sales in the U.S.

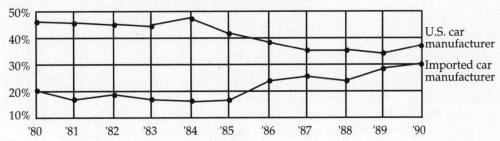

### NOTES

Use this space to make your notes. Write the final version of your essay on lined paper. The Sample TWE Answer Sheet on page 192 is an example of the amount of writing space provided in the TOEFL Test.

GO ON TO THE NEXT PAGE

# PRACTICE TEST FIVE

## SECTION 1
## LISTENING COMPREHENSION

In this section of the test, you will have an opportunity to demonstrate your ability to understand spoken English. There are three parts to this section, with special directions for each part.

### Part A

Directions:   For each question in Part A, you will hear a short sentence. Each sentence will be spoken just one time. The sentences you hear will not be written out for you. Therefore, you must listen carefully to understand what the speaker says.

After you hear a sentence, read the four choices in your test book, marked (A), (B), (C), and (D), and decide which <u>one</u> is closest in meaning to the sentence you heard. Then, on your answer sheet, find the number of the question and fill in the space that corresponds to the letter of the answer you have chosen. Fill in the space so that the letter inside the oval cannot be seen.

Example I

You will hear:

        Sample Answer

        Ⓐ Ⓑ ● Ⓓ

You will read:    (A)  Greg didn't bother to leave a tip.
                (B)  Greg thought about typing a
                        letter to his brother.
                (C)  Greg didn't like to type.
                (D)  My typing bothered Greg.

The speaker said, "Greg thought typing was a bother." Sentence (C), "Greg didn't like to type," is closest in meaning to the sentence you heard. Therefore, you should choose answer (C).

Example II

You will hear:

        Sample Answer

        Ⓐ ● Ⓒ Ⓓ

You will read:    (A)  Everyone will be able to take this
                        exam later.
                (B)  Students should bring a calculator
                        to this exam.
                (C)  This test will be part of every
                        student's final grade.
                (D)  No one can calculate the grades
                        for this test.

The speaker said, "Everyone needs a calculator for this test." Sentence (B), "Students should bring a calculator to this exam," is closest in meaning to the sentence you heard. Therefore, you should choose answer (B).

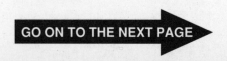

GO ON TO THE NEXT PAGE

1. (A) I believe I've been working
       long enough.
   (B) I'll probably take a walk in a while.
   (C) It's too late to think about going for
       a walk.
   (D) I should probably continue working a
       while longer.

2. (A) My parents are 40 years old.
   (B) I haven't seen my parents for
       four years.
   (C) My parents have been married 40 years.
   (D) Fourteen people came to my
       parents' party.

3. (A) It certainly is a nice day.
   (B) What are you doing today?
   (C) You look beautiful today.
   (D) What day is it today?

4. (A) I couldn't understand their directions.
   (B) I don't think they saw my truck.
   (C) They didn't follow my instructions.
   (D) I think they understood what I
       wanted them to do.

5. (A) A group of friends entered the
       room together.
   (B) The music started when they were
       walking in.
   (C) The music had been playing for a
       long time when they arrived.
   (D) They played together in the band.

6. (A) We need to brush it right now.
   (B) Let's not rush through this.
   (C) We aren't rushed now because we
       began this early enough.
   (D) We should have started this earlier.

7. (A) Frank doesn't know very much about
       this town.
   (B) Very few people know Frank.
   (C) Almost everyone knows Frank.
   (D) Nobody wants to get to know Frank.

8. (A) He had another massage while he
       was here.
   (B) He couldn't hear the message well
       enough to understand what it said.
   (C) He couldn't remember whether or not
       he had listened to the message before.
   (D) He was surprised by what the
       message said.

9. (A) Someone had already borrowed one
       of the books I was looking for.
   (B) I thought I could write a check for
       both books.
   (C) I can't wait to look at the books I got.
   (D) I'm out of checks, so I can't buy the
       books I wanted.

10. (A) There are 5 or 6 students in the
        history class.
    (B) History 506 will meet on Tuesday
        afternoons.
    (C) We will meet on Tuesday at 1:30 to
        hear his story.
    (D) Only one student out of 30 wants to
        meet on Thursday.

11. (A) Dave went to the library twice to try
        to find the article.
    (B) Dave tried two different times to find
        Art in the library.
    (C) Dave looked at the article twice in
        the library.
    (D) Dave and Ben are going to look for
        an article.

12. (A) I think you can get accustomed to
        dormitory food.
    (B) Don't you think dormitory food is bad?
    (C) I heard this food was grown in the
        garden next door.
    (D) Don't you think Judy has grown since
        she's been living in a dorm?

GO ON TO THE NEXT PAGE

13. (A) The well was tested as he thought it should be.
    (B) He was wrong about the difficulty of the test.
    (C) He thought he was well, but he has a pain in his chest.
    (D) He did as well on the test as he had expected.

14. (A) The doctor will try to treat the cut on your back.
    (B) The cut was expensive to treat.
    (C) Doctors are trying to save money.
    (D) Doctors are becoming more and more costly.

15. (A) She'll be touched when you give her your new dress.
    (B) You don't have a new address yet, so she can't reach you.
    (C) If you tell her where you live, she'll contact you.
    (D) She can fix your new dress as soon as you give it to her.

16. (A) I am actually not responsible for the athletic facilities.
    (B) I don't like sports very much.
    (C) I honestly wasn't a very careful athlete.
    (D) Honesty is important in any sports activity.

17. (A) You must talk to the professor about your project before you begin.
    (B) Get the professor to help you start your project.
    (C) You should improve your project before you begin.
    (D) You don't need the professor's approval for your project.

18. (A) Rick is feeling bitter because he couldn't play in the concert.
    (B) Rick felt it would be better to meet us at the concert.
    (C) Rick isn't sure how he feels about going to the concert.
    (D) Because Rick isn't feeling well, he won't go with us tonight.

19. (A) No matter what the weather is like, we'll play soccer tomorrow.
    (B) Let's wait until tomorrow to play soccer, in case it rains today.
    (C) If it rains tomorrow, we won't play soccer.
    (D) There aren't any soccer players for the game tomorrow.

20. (A) They both lost a lot of weight because they were so disappointed.
    (B) Pat received a scholarship, but Chris did not.
    (C) Pat was disappointed that Chris received the scholarship.
    (D) They both tried not to show how unhappy they were.

GO ON TO THE NEXT PAGE

Part B

Directions: In Part B you will hear short conversations between two speakers. At the end of each conversation, a third person will ask a question about what was said. You will hear each conversation and question about it just one time. Therefore, you must listen carefully to understand what each speaker says. After you hear a conversation and the question about it, read the four possible answers in your test book and decide which <u>one</u> is the best answer to the question you heard. Then, on your answer sheet, find the number of the question and fill in the space that corresponds to the letter of the answer you have chosen.

Look at the following example.

You will hear:

You will read:

(A) At last winter is almost over.
(B) She doesn't like winter weather very much.
(C) This winter's weather is similar to last winter's weather.
(D) Winter won't last as long this year as it did last year.

Sample Answer

From the conversation you learn that the woman thinks the weather this winter is almost the same as the weather last winter. The best answer to the question "What does the woman mean?" is (C), "This winter's weather is similar to last winter's weather." Therefore, you should choose answer (C).

21. (A) She isn't sure what she wants.
    (B) She will certainly have a party.
    (C) She is sure about her part for tonight.
    (D) She would like to go to the party.

22. (A) On a subway.
    (B) In an airport.
    (C) In an airplane.
    (D) In a bus station.

23. (A) Hungry.
    (B) Angry.
    (C) Tired.
    (D) Happy.

24. (A) He doesn't know how much the dinner cost.
    (B) He is not worried about what the woman owns.
    (C) He doesn't own the diner.
    (D) The woman doesn't need to pay for her meal.

25. (A) She fell and hurt herself.
    (B) She hasn't been able to complete her work.
    (C) She finished her term papers on time.
    (D) She actually left her papers behind.

26. (A) She never minds repeating herself.
    (B) She doesn't want to repeat what she said.
    (C) She accepts the man's apology.
    (D) She didn't hear the man.

27. (A) He mailed it for George.
    (B) He sent it to the woman.
    (C) He received it in the mail.
    (D) George mailed it.

28. (A) She figured the problem out in her head.
    (B) She was ahead of the other students until today.
    (C) She didn't think carefully about the problem.
    (D) She used her calculator to do the problem.

**GO ON TO THE NEXT PAGE**

29. (A) The man had finished the laundry.
    (B) The laundry still needed to be washed.
    (C) There were no dirty shirts in the laundry.
    (D) All the man's clothes were clean.

30. (A) He will lend the woman his book.
    (B) He threw the book away.
    (C) He doesn't like his sociology book.
    (D) The woman should buy her own book.

31. (A) He isn't sure when the school year will end.
    (B) He doesn't want to start writing right away.
    (C) He needs to read his book before the end of the year.
    (D) He's all booked up until the end of the year.

32. (A) He doesn't like museums.
    (B) He's tired of touring this museum.
    (C) He thinks a hundred miles is too far to go for a tour.
    (D) He is excited about going to the museum.

33. (A) He didn't understand what she was singing about.
    (B) He has a few questions about her performance.
    (C) He isn't sure what to ask her.
    (D) She was definitely the best performer in the show.

34. (A) He might break the handle on his glass.
    (B) He has an advanced physical illness.
    (C) The class might be too difficult for him.
    (D) His hands have been bothering him.

35. (A) Her award wasn't as impressive as it seems.
    (B) She encouraged other people from her school to apply for the scholarship.
    (C) Her school has won a number of scholarships.
    (D) She hopes to win the scholarship she applied for.

GO ON TO THE NEXT PAGE

Part C

Directions: In this part of the test, you will hear short talks and conversations. After each of them, you will be asked some questions. You will hear the talks and conversations and the questions about them just one time. They will not be written out for you. Therefore, you must listen carefully to understand what each speaker says.

After you hear a question, read the four possible answers in your test book and decide which <u>one</u> is the best answer to the question you heard. Then, on your answer sheet, find the number of the question and fill in the space that corresponds to the letter of the answer you have chosen.

Answer all questions on the basis of what is <u>stated</u> or <u>implied</u> in the talk or conversation.

Listen to this sample talk.

You will hear:

Now look at the following example.

You will hear:                                                    Sample Answer

You will read:  (A)  Only bumblebees can fertilize red             ● Ⓑ Ⓒ Ⓓ
                         clover plants.
                (B)  Bumblebees protect red clover from
                         plant eating insects.
                (C)  Bumblebees bring water to red clover
                         plants on their tongues.
                (D)  Bumblebees keep mice and other animals
                         away from red clover plants.

The best answer to the question "Why is it impossible to raise red clover where there are no bumblebees?" is (A), "Only bumblebees can fertilize red clover plants." Therefore, you should choose answer (A).

Now look at the next example.

You will hear:                                                    Sample Answer

You will read:  (A)  They both make honey.                         Ⓐ Ⓑ Ⓒ ●
                (B)  They both build combs.
                (C)  Both of them are found in
                         underground nests.
                (D)  They both live through the winter.

The best answer to the question "According to the speaker, in what way are the queen wasp and the queen bee similar?" is (D), "They both live through the winter." Therefore, you should choose answer (D).

36. (A)  A television announcer.
    (B)  A member of a research team.
    (C)  A teacher.
    (D)  A network executive.

37. (A)  To present information about several
             Hawaiian volcanoes.
    (B)  To explain a research project about an
             underwater volcano.
    (C)  To demonstrate the latest use of
             underwater cables.
    (D)  To discuss a study of ocean life near
             underwater volcanoes.

38. (A)  Geologists will bring it back.
    (B)  It will be sent back by cable.
    (C)  It will be sent by mail.
    (D)  It will be sent back through
             seismometers.

**GO ON TO THE NEXT PAGE** ▶

**Practice Test Five**    123

39. (A) Because it is related to work being
        done in class.
    (B) Because she helped produce it.
    (C) Because she is excited about it.
    (D) Because it is a public television
        broadcast.

40. (A) Differences between anthropology
        and biology.
    (B) Biological approaches to the study of
        human beings.
    (C) Differences in two approaches to
        anthropological study.
    (D) Family structure in cultures all over
        the world.

41. (A) She didn't see the man there.
    (B) The first lecture was more difficult
        than she had expected.
    (C) The course had a different name than
        she had expected.
    (D) She thought she would be studying
        physical anthropology.

42. (A) Ancient human tools.
    (B) The relationship between parents and
        children in different societies.
    (C) Food crops in various cultures.
    (D) Height differences in people from
        different cultures.

43. (A) Because he heard it was easier.
    (B) Because he is interested in
        human cultures.
    (C) Because he's a biology major.
    (D) Because it is a required course for him.

44. (A) She is happy about the writing
        assignments it involves.
    (B) She would rather be in class with
        the man.
    (C) She is not sure yet how she feels
        about it.
    (D) She likes it.

45. (A) Manmade fibers for clothing.
    (B) Rayon.
    (C) How nylon is made.
    (D) Clothing care.

46. (A) Since 1939.
    (B) For a little over a century.
    (C) For approximately 20 years.
    (D) Since nylon was first invented.

47. (A) It is inexpensive to produce.
    (B) It is more durable than other
        manmade fibers.
    (C) It remains a very popular clothing fiber.
    (D) It is easy to produce in great quantities.

48. (A) It shrinks.
    (B) It fades.
    (C) It wrinkles.
    (D) It turns pink.

49. (A) It does not wash well.
    (B) It is manmade.
    (C) It loses its color in sunlight.
    (D) It is not very comfortable to wear.

50. (A) Talk about the production of nylon.
    (B) Leave the factory.
    (C) Take a break.
    (D) Go into the rayon production room.

**THIS IS THE END OF THE LISTENING COMPREHENSION SECTION OF THE TEST**

THE NEXT PART OF THE TEST IS SECTION 2. TURN TO THE
DIRECTIONS FOR SECTION 2 IN YOUR TEST BOOK.
READ THEM, AND BEGIN WORK.
DO NOT READ OR WORK ON ANY OTHER SECTION OF THE TEST.

## SECTION 2
## STRUCTURE AND WRITTEN EXPRESSION

Time—25 minutes

This section is designed to measure your ability to recognize language that is appropriate for standard written English. There are two types of questions in this section, with special directions for each type.

Directions: Questions 1–15 are incomplete sentences. Beneath each sentence you will see four words or phrases, marked (A), (B), (C), and (D). Choose the one word or phrase that best completes the sentence. Then, on your answer sheet, find the number of the question and fill in the space that corresponds to the letter of the answer you have chosen. Fill in the space so that the letter inside the oval cannot be seen.

Example I

Most American families _____ at least one automobile.

(A) have
(B) in
(C) that
(D) has

Sample Answer

● Ⓑ Ⓒ Ⓓ

The sentence should read, "Most American families have at least one automobile." Therefore, you should choose answer (A).

Example II

_____ recent times, the discipline of biology has expanded rapidly into a variety of subdisciplines.

(A) It is since
(B) When
(C) Since it is
(D) In

Sample Answer

Ⓐ Ⓑ Ⓒ ●

The sentence should read, "In recent times, the discipline of biology has expanded into a variety of subdisciplines." Therefore, you should choose answer (D).

Now begin work on the questions.

1. _____ growing awareness of social ills, Edna Saint Vincent Millay wrote increasingly more somber poetry during her later years.
   (A) A
   (B) Because her
   (C) When a
   (D) Due to her

2. _____ categorized as lipids.
   (A) Fats and also oils
   (B) While fats and oils
   (C) Fats and oils are
   (D) Fats and oils

3. The role of the mass media in influencing public policy decisions, maintaining or changing the status quo of our society, and _____ outlets for all types of views is enormous.
   (A) as it provides
   (B) to provide
   (C) provide
   (D) providing

GO ON TO THE NEXT PAGE

4. _____ earth might be experiencing a global warming trend which could have devastating climatic effects.
   (A) In the
   (B) The
   (C) Where the
   (D) Whole

5. Depressant drugs _____ historically have been known to be addictive are called narcotics.
   (A) and
   (B) which
   (C) they
   (D) about which

6. _____ young, Eugene O'Neill traveled with his father's theatrical company, and the stage was an important part of his life.
   (A) When was he
   (B) He was
   (C) Was he
   (D) When he was

7. Vitamins are organic compounds _____ and must be ingested to maintain proper bodily functions.
   (A) that they can't be produced by the body
   (B) the body can't produce them
   (C) that can't be produced by the body
   (D) not produced them by the body

8. _____ , business managers plan the tasks that their employees are to carry out.
   (A) It is the organizing process
   (B) They process the organizing
   (C) While the organizing process
   (D) Through the organizing process

9. Copper is the favored metal for electricians' wire because of _____ .
   (A) it is an excellent conductor
   (B) its excellent conductivity
   (C) excellent conductivity of it
   (D) so conductive is it

10. Chemicals in paint that pose a fire hazard _____ as combustible, flammable, or extremely flammable.
   (A) are listed
   (B) listed
   (C) being listed
   (D) they are listed

11. Scientists believe that the beaver's instinct to build dams is more complex than _____ other animal instinct.
   (A) most
   (B) all
   (C) any
   (D) these

12. Considered unique and exotic, _____ .
   (A) over 4,000 American households keep the llama as a pet
   (B) there are over 4,000 American households that keep the llama as a pet
   (C) the llama is kept as a pet in over 4,000 American households
   (D) the llama kept as a pet in over 4,000 American households

13. Anxiety about uncontrollable situations is thought to cause _____ .
   (A) to fitfully sleep
   (B) fitful sleep
   (C) fitful in sleep
   (D) sleep fitfully

14. One of the most influential Virginians of colonial times, _____ in England.
   (A) the education received by William Bird
   (B) was the education that William Bird received
   (C) William Bird was educated
   (D) the education that William Bird received

15. By careful seeding, weathermakers can encourage two small clouds to merge into one big cloud _____ produce a powerful thunderstorm.
   (A) so
   (B) these
   (C) which
   (D) and

GO ON TO THE NEXT PAGE

<u>Directions:</u>   In questions 16–40 each sentence has four underlined words or phrases. The four underlined parts of the sentence are marked (A), (B), (C), and (D). Identify the <u>one</u> underlined word or phrase that must be changed in order for the sentence to be correct. Then, on your answer sheet, find the number of the question and fill in the space that corresponds to the letter of the answer you have chosen.

Example I

The octopus <u>is</u> a unique animal <u>because</u> <u>they</u>
           A         B    C
has three <u>functioning</u> hearts.
          D

<u>Sample Answer</u>

Ⓐ Ⓑ ● Ⓓ

The sentence should read, "The octopus is a unique animal because it has three functioning hearts." Therefore, you should choose answer (C).

Example II

The beagle, <u>one of the most</u> <u>ancient</u> breeds of
           A           B
dog <u>known</u>, <u>originating</u> in England.
     C       D

<u>Sample Answer</u>

Ⓐ Ⓑ Ⓒ ●

The sentence should read, "The beagle, one of the most ancient breeds of dog known, originated in England." Therefore, you should choose answer (D).

Now begin work on the questions.

16. The <u>tiny nucleus</u> of <u>an atom</u> is held together by <u>forces powerful</u> capable <u>of unleashing</u> great energy.
          A          B                    C               D

17. <u>Because of</u> their <u>beautiful</u> coloration, palomino horses <u>does</u> often chosen <u>as</u> show horses for parades.
     A           B                         C            D

18. The <u>discovering</u> of quarks, <u>minute</u> particles of matter, has <u>led to</u> a new age in particle <u>physics</u>.
       A                 B                   C                  D

19. Thanksgiving Day, a <u>uniquely</u> North American holiday, <u>is celebrated</u> in the United States on the
                     A                           B
<u>four</u> Thursday <u>in</u> November.
 C         D

20. A square is <u>a</u> <u>geometric</u> shape which is as long <u>as is</u> tall and which <u>has</u> four right angles.
            A  B                    C             D

21. The incidence <u>of which</u> is now <u>referred to</u> as cryovolcanism, or ice volcanoes, <u>is</u> quite high on the
               A         B                                    C
surface of Triton, <u>one of the</u> moons of Neptune.
               D

22. Contemporary poet Allen Ginsberg prides <u>him</u> for his ability to create poetry <u>which</u> invites
                                 A                             B
<u>complete</u> emotional and physical <u>participation</u> by its audience.
 C                          D

23. The <u>amount of</u> red meat needed <u>to provision</u> sufficient protein <u>for maintaining</u> good health is
      A                  B                          C
estimated at <u>less than</u> four ounces per day.
             D

24. Neither oil drilling <u>or</u> gas <u>exploration</u> can <u>be prevented</u> from <u>steadily changing</u> the face of the Arctic.
                 A         B            C             D

25. <u>However</u> unavoidable the Civil War may have been, it was more devastating <u>also</u> exhausting
    A                                                        B
<u>than</u> any European war <u>between</u> 1815 and 1914.
 C              D

26. Water and petroleum are the <u>only</u> two liquids <u>what</u> occur in <u>large</u> quantities <u>in</u> nature.
                          A           B         C     D

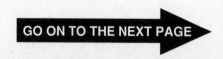

**GO ON TO THE NEXT PAGE**

27. <u>Allowing</u> children to help plan and prepare family meals provides enjoyable <u>learning</u>
     A                                                                                        B
experiences that later <u>encouraging</u> them to eat the foods they <u>have prepared</u>.
                             C                                              D

28. <u>According to</u> many economists, international specialization in the production of some goods,
     A
<u>such as</u> cars and computers, <u>increase</u> world efficiency and output, <u>making</u> all nations richer.
     B                                C                                         D

29. <u>Solar astronomers</u> have <u>recently</u> observed bursts of coherent radio waves coming <u>from</u> a specific
     A                            B                                                               C
<u>locations</u> on the sun's surface.
     D

30. <u>In accordance the</u> wishes of <u>most of his electorate</u>, President Franklin D. Roosevelt
     A                                 B
<u>postponed entering</u> the Second World War <u>until</u> December 11, 1941.
     C                                              D

31. Substances <u>such as</u> DDT become <u>more concentrated</u> in each <u>successively</u> level in <u>an</u>
                    A                          B                          C                       D
ecological pyramid.

32. The rate of stomach cancer is <u>lowest</u> in countries <u>where</u> people <u>don't eat</u> processed meat
                                      A                          B              C
products than in nations where such foods <u>are consumed</u>.
                                                D

33. <u>Unlike most</u> liquids, which contract when they <u>solidify</u>, water expands <u>by</u> nine <u>percentage</u>
     A                                                   B                              C              D
when it freezes.

34. Raindrops <u>falling</u> on the ocean <u>reduce</u> the number of breaking waves, thereby <u>calming</u> <u>roughness</u> water.
                 A                          B                                                   C          D

35. The languages <u>spoken by</u> the Alaskan Eskimos <u>and</u> the Inuit of northern Canada are <u>such</u> similar
                      A                                    B                                          C
as to be mutually <u>intelligible</u>.
                       D

36. <u>According to</u> a Keynesian economist, <u>expects</u> economic conditions to worsen can bring about
     A                                          B
behavior <u>which</u> in fact causes these conditions <u>to worsen</u>.
              C                                            D

37. <u>Desiring</u> to leave their own marks of identity inside the White House, most presidents' wives
     A
<u>redecorate</u> at least some portion of <u>its</u> rooms <u>as soon as</u> arrival there.
     B                                        C              D

38. <u>Generally</u> speaking, proteins that come from <u>animal</u> sources are complete whereas <u>those that</u>
     A                                                    B                                          C
come from <u>another</u> sources are incomplete proteins.
              D

39. Even <u>although</u> he is best <u>remembered</u> as a writer, Walt Whitman was <u>also</u> a <u>newspaper</u>
             A                        B                                            C          D
publisher, teacher, and farmer.

40. The <u>first</u> <u>domesticated</u> bird <u>in</u> earth was probably <u>the</u> goose.
            A          B                    C                            D

**THIS IS THE END OF SECTION 2**

IF YOU FINISH BEFORE TIME IS CALLED, CHECK YOUR WORK
ON SECTION 2 ONLY.
DO NOT READ OR WORK ON ANY OTHER SECTION OF THE TEST.
THE SUPERVISOR WILL TELL YOU WHEN TO BEGIN
WORK ON SECTION 3.

SECTION 3
VOCABULARY AND READING COMPREHENSION
Time—45 minutes

This section is designed to measure your comprehension of standard written English. There are two types of questions in this section, with special directions for each type.

<u>Directions:</u>  In questions 1–30 each sentence has an underlined word or phrase. Below each sentence are four other words or phrases, marked (A), (B), (C), (D). You are to choose the <u>one</u> word or phrase that <u>best keeps the meaning</u> of the original sentence if it is substituted for the underlined word or phrase. Then, on your answer sheet, find the number of the question and fill in the space that corresponds to the letter you have chosen. Fill in the space so that the letter inside the oval cannot be seen.

Example                                                    Sample Answer

Ladybugs, small brightly colored beetles, feed on          ● Ⓑ Ⓒ Ⓓ
plant aphids and have considerable economic value
in <u>controlling</u> pest populations.

    (A)  limiting
    (B)  finding
    (C)  increasing
    (D)  ruling

The best answer is (A) because "Ladybugs, small brightly colored beetles, feed on plant aphids and have considerable economic value in limiting pest populations" is closest in meaning to the original sentence. Therefore, you should choose answer (A).

Now begin work on the questions.

1. Steamship lines <u>connect</u> Chicago with all important Great Lakes ports.
    (A)  mention
    (B)  note
    (C)  join
    (D)  span

2. There seems to be rather widespread agreement on the <u>overall</u> objectives of foreign assistance.
    (A)  limited
    (B)  numerous
    (C)  mentioned
    (D)  general

3. There is a complex <u>chain</u> of events which trigger the production of the hormone glucagon to function in controlling the amount of blood sugar.
    (A)  concentration
    (B)  sequence
    (C)  initiation
    (D)  interaction

4. In man, the circulatory system consists of the heart, which <u>pumps</u> the blood through the body, and the arteries, veins, and tinier blood vessels called capillaries, through which the blood travels.
    (A)  carries
    (B)  forces
    (C)  inserts
    (D)  meanders

5. An insecticide called DDT has been used with <u>some</u> success in killing flies.
    (A)  acclaimed
    (B)  minimal
    (C)  limited
    (D)  hopeful

6. Until a few years ago, <u>virtually</u> all telephones used in the United States belonged to the AT&T system.
    (A)  practically
    (B)  relatively
    (C)  apparently
    (D)  usually

**GO ON TO THE NEXT PAGE** ▶

7. The sky is especially clear on cold, sparkling winter nights, and it is at those times the <u>fainter</u> stars are seen in great profusion.

    (A) smaller
    (B) dimmer
    (C) less important
    (D) newer

8. Chihuahuas may be almost any color, and they <u>appear</u> in two varieties, long-haired and short-haired.

    (A) seem
    (B) show
    (C) visualize
    (D) come

9. One reason that oxen were among the first animals to be domesticated was that the males were very <u>docile</u> and could therefore be used for doing heavy work.

    (A) strong
    (B) manageable
    (C) large
    (D) intelligent

10. In the early 1920s, even people of <u>modest</u> means were able to build homes in the country.

    (A) moderate
    (B) shy
    (C) aspiring
    (D) tasteful

11. Because icebergs extend so far below the surface of the ocean, they don't <u>drift</u> with the winds but instead follow the ocean currents.

    (A) topple
    (B) move
    (C) join
    (D) conflict

12. A great many legends exist about <u>various</u> fish that have lived to a ripe old age.

    (A) healthy
    (B) many
    (C) different
    (D) famous

13. Corporations use advertising to get a larger market <u>share</u>.

    (A) advantage
    (B) portion
    (C) resource
    (D) appeal

14. The most common form of compass is a magnetic needle <u>supported on</u> a pivot so that it is free to swing in all directions.

    (A) favored by
    (B) impressed upon
    (C) attached to
    (D) embossed on

15. A citadel is a high, walled fortress built to <u>defend</u> a city.

    (A) identify
    (B) beautify
    (C) protect
    (D) surround

16. The <u>first</u> lighthouses were low towers on which were placed metal baskets full of flaming wood or charcoal.

    (A) basic
    (B) leading
    (C) earliest
    (D) most effective

17. Root growth is affected by soil conditions and <u>availability</u> of water.

    (A) composition
    (B) accessibility
    (C) liability
    (D) use

18. The permanently frozen ground greatly affects the character of the Alaskan wilderness, seriously <u>impeding</u> drainage and determining to a large extent the pattern of vegetation.

    (A) upholding
    (B) threatening
    (C) obstructing
    (D) speeding up

GO ON TO THE NEXT PAGE

19. <u>Given</u> the inconveniences, that the early pioneers grew to love their simple homes is a credit to their spirit and courage.
    (A) Discounting
    (B) Taking account of
    (C) Above and beyond
    (D) Justifying

20. With the <u>advent</u> of the motor car, travel became more accessible to the population in general.
    (A) success
    (B) arrival
    (C) necessity
    (D) revision

21. People who live close to others must be careful not to <u>interfere with</u> their neighbors' lives.
    (A) inquire about
    (B) intrude upon
    (C) talk about
    (D) complain about

22. Originally invented by the Chinese before the Christian era, gunpowder was first used by European nations in the 14th century, <u>hence</u> enabling them to spread their influence into the rest of the world.
    (A) at the moment
    (B) quickly
    (C) therefore
    (D) previously

23. The treacherous <u>shoals</u> off the coast of Cape Hatteras are sometimes referred to as the "Graveyard of the Atlantic."
    (A) ships
    (B) waters
    (C) sand dunes
    (D) lighthouses

24. It is important to distinguish between the market demand curve and the demand curve confronting <u>a firm</u>.
    (A) a company
    (B) a pitcher
    (C) an economy
    (D) a production

25. Regulatory boards set up to protect consumers from contaminated and adulterated food are not <u>quite</u> as effective as we would like them to be.
    (A) usually
    (B) closely
    (C) practically
    (D) entirely

26. One <u>disproved</u> theory of how infants learn language was that they learned to speak by mimicking their parents.
    (A) unpopular
    (B) early
    (C) distinguished
    (D) invalidated

27. Using foster parents, scientists continue to hatch whooping cranes in the wild, but the success of the project is viewed with <u>skepticism</u>.
    (A) hope
    (B) doubt
    (C) certainty
    (D) surprise

28. When the Barnum & Bailey Circus returned to the United States from Europe, it found a strong rival had <u>sprung up</u> in the Ringling Brothers circus.
    (A) appeared
    (B) conspired
    (C) joined
    (D) starred

29. Within a wintering hive, a <u>cluster</u> of bees moves slowly about on the comb, eating the stored honey, which is their energy source.
    (A) line
    (B) mass
    (C) migration
    (D) mission

30. Consumers are reluctant to borrow money when current and future income <u>prospects</u> are uncertain or distinctly unfavorable.
    (A) investments
    (B) bargains
    (C) possibilities
    (D) clients

**GO ON TO THE NEXT PAGE**

**Directions:**   In the rest of this section you will read several passages. Each one is followed by several questions about it. For questions 31–60, you are to choose the <u>one</u> best answer, (A), (B), (C), or (D), to each question. Then, on your answer sheet, find the number of the question and fill in the space that corresponds to the letter of the answer you have chosen.

Answer all questions following a passage on the basis of what is <u>stated</u> or <u>implied</u> in that passage.

Read the following passage:

      The flamingo is a beautiful water bird with long legs, and a curving neck like a swan's. Most flamingos have deep red or flame-colored feathers with black quills. Some have pink or white feathers. The long legs and webbed feet are well suited
*Line*
(5) for wading. The flamingo eats in a peculiar manner. It plunges its head underwater and sifts the mud with a fine hairlike "comb" along the edge of its bent bill. In this way, it strains out small shellfish and other animals. The bird nests on a mound of mud with a hollow on top to hold its single egg. Flamingos are timid and often live together in large colonies. The birds once lived in the southern United States, but plume hunters killed them faster than they could breed, and the
(10) flamingo no longer lives wild in the United States.

Example I

The flamingo can eat shellfish and other animals because of its

Sample Answer

(A)  curved neck
(B)  especially formed bill
(C)  long legs
(D)  brightly colored feathers

According to the passage, the flamingo sifts mud for food with "a fine hairlike 'comb' along the edge of its bent bill." Therefore, you should choose answer (B).

Example II

How many young would you expect the flamingo to raise at one time?

Sample Answer

(A)  Several
(B)  Two
(C)  One
(D)  Four

The passage states that the flamingo nests on a mound of mud with a "single" egg. Therefore, you should choose answer (C).

Now begin work on the questions.

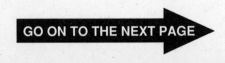

GO ON TO THE NEXT PAGE

Questions 31–35

Long ago prehistoric man began to domesticate a number of wild plants and animals for his own use. This not only provided more abundant food but also allowed more people to live on a smaller plot of ground. We tend to forget that all
*Line* of our present-day pets, livestock, and food plants were taken from the wild and
(5)     developed into the forms we know today.

As centuries passed and human cultures evolved and blossomed, humans began to organize their knowledge of nature into the broad field of natural history. One aspect of early natural history concerned the use of plants for drugs and medicine. The early herbalists sometimes overworked their imaginations in this
(10)     respect. For instance, it was widely believed that a plant or part of a plant that resembled an internal organ would cure ailments of that organ. Thus, an extract made from a heart-shaped leaf might be prescribed for a person suffering from heart problems.

Nevertheless, the overall contributions of these early observers provided the
(15)     rudiments of our present knowledge of drugs and their uses.

31. The best title for this passage would be

(A) Cures from Plants
(B) The Beginnings of Natural History
(C) Prehistoric Man
(D) Early Plants and Animals

32. According to the passage, domestication of plants and animals probably occurred because of

(A) need for more readily available food
(B) lack of wild animals and plants
(C) early man's power as a hunter
(D) the desire of prehistoric man to be nomadic

33. It can be inferred from the passage that an herbalist is which of the following?

(A) A dreamer
(B) An early historian
(C) Someone who uses plants in medicine
(D) A farmer

34. Which of the following statements can be inferred from the passage?

(A) The shape of a plant is indicative of its ability to cure ailments of a similarly shaped organ.
(B) Early herbalists were unimaginative.
(C) The work of early herbalists has nothing to do with present-day medicine.
(D) There is little relation between a cure for illness and the physical shape of a plant.

35. This passage would most likely lead to a more specific discussion in the field of

(A) zoology
(B) biology
(C) anatomy
(D) astrology

GO ON TO THE NEXT PAGE

Questions 36–42

Simply being bilingual does not qualify someone to interpret. Interpreting is not merely a mechanical process of converting one sentence in language A into the same sentence in language B. Rather, it's a complex art in which thoughts and

*Line*
(5)
idioms that have no obvious analogues from tongue to tongue—or words that have multiple meanings—must quickly be transformed in such a way that the message is clearly and accurately expressed to the listener.

At one international conference, an American speaker said, "You can't make a silk purse out of a sow's ear," which meant nothing to the Spanish audience. The interpretation was, "A monkey in a silk dress is still a monkey"—an idiom that the

(10)
Spanish understood and that conveyed the same idea.

There are two kinds of interpreters, simultaneous and consecutive, each requiring separate talents. The former, sitting in an isolated booth, usually at a large multilingual conference, speaks to listeners who wear headphones, interpreting what a foreign-language speaker says as he says it—actually a

(15)
sentence behind. Consecutive interpreters are the ones most international negotiators use. They are mainly employed for smaller meetings without sound booths, headphones, and other high-tech gear. Equally taxing in its own way, consecutive interpretation also requires two-person teams. A foreign speaker says his piece while the interpreter, using a special shorthand, takes notes and during a

(20)
pause, tells the client what was said.

36. What is the purpose of this passage?

(A) To explain the scope of interpreting
(B) To differentiate between simultaneous and consecutive interpreters
(C) To state the qualifications of an interpreter
(D) To point out the importance of an interpreter

37. The author implies that most people are of the opinion that the skill of interpreting is

(A) simpler than it really is
(B) very complex and demanding
(C) highly valued and admired
(D) based on principles of business

38. The example of the expression "You can't make a silk purse out of a sow's ear" in line 8 is used to

(A) show the differences in language A and language B
(B) stress the importance of word-for-word translation
(C) emphasize the need for translation of the meaning of the utterance
(D) point out the difference in attributes of animals in English and Spanish

39. It can be inferred from the passage that a necessary prerequisite of being a translator is

(A) being a linguist
(B) being bilingual
(C) being able to use high-tech equipment
(D) working well with people

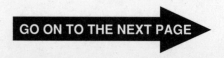
GO ON TO THE NEXT PAGE

40. According to the passage, which of the following would a consecutive interpreter be used for?

    (A) A business transaction between two foreign speakers
    (B) A large meeting of many nations
    (C) A translation of a foreign book
    (D) An interpretation of a major literary work

41. Based on the description given in the passage, what would a simultaneous interpreter be most in need of?

    (A) A dictionary or phrase book
    (B) Advanced technical style in writing
    (C) Headphones and a booth
    (D) Shorthand skills and a notepad

42. What is one difference mentioned in the passage between a consecutive interpreter and a simultaneous interpreter?

    (A) The money they are paid
    (B) The size of group with whom they work
    (C) Their proficiency in the language
    (D) The type of dictionary they use

**GO ON TO THE NEXT PAGE** ▶

Questions 43–48

Watching for wildlife in the forest, we rarely see past the surface of things. Standing on the ground floor, we scan the leafy rafters, entirely overlooking the living world in the soil beneath our feet.

*Line*
(5)
The forest's basement is a secret world. As different from our own world as water is from air, the soil seems quiet, even dead. But life bustles down below: a cubic inch of topsoil may contain billions of creatures.

Predators and prey roam beneath as well as above the forest floor. Furthermore, those upstairs and downstairs forest denizens live closely linked lives. Soil-dwelling bacteria and fungi break down dead organic matter into molecules that
(10)
aboveground plants use for food. Those plants, as well as animals, mature and die, leaving more organic matter to fuel the folks downstairs.

Like a well-insulated house, the soil protects its tenants from extreme temperatures and from rain and snow. It also provides a bulwark against predators that roam the surface world. But the dense, protecting soil also limits
(15)
mobility. Soil creatures must be specially equipped in order to travel easily through their dark, constricting realm.

Earthworms and ants are the champion earth-movers, creating channels that allow air and water to enter the soil. While ants travel relatively far from their nests, earthworms work small areas, reprocessing vast amounts of soil into fertile
(20)
"waste." In a single year, as much as 36 tons of soil may pass through the alimentary tracts of all the earthworms living in an acre of soil.

43. The main topic of this passage is

(A) life in the forest soil
(B) the life cycle of ants and worms
(C) a description of a forest scene
(D) the habits of the forest animals

44. It can be inferred from the passage that the forest soil is

(A) densely inhabited
(B) sparsely inhabited
(C) devoid of life
(D) unknown to man

45. According to the passage, what is the main function of bacteria and fungi?

(A) To help aerate the soil
(B) To provide food for plant life
(C) To kill mature plants
(D) To build walls in the soil

46. According to the passage, the soil offers creatures who live underground protection from all of the following EXCEPT

(A) enemies
(B) bad weather
(C) bacteria and fungi
(D) extreme heat and cold

47. According to the passage, it could be expected that ants

(A) move more earth than earthworms
(B) are more mobile than earthworms
(C) live only above ground
(D) perform similar functions to fungi

48. The author uses which analogy to discuss the soil of the forest?

(A) A laboratory
(B) A tunnel
(C) A vehicle
(D) A building

**GO ON TO THE NEXT PAGE**

Questions 49–54

Over the years from the seventeenth century through the nineteenth and beyond, as one style and fashion in building succeeded another, two very modest but highly distinctive types of dwellings flourished continuously—the log cabin and the Cape Cod cottage. Completely unpretentious in design, both varieties enjoyed widespread popularity, and their derivatives are still with us today.

While visiting Cape Cod in 1800, the president of Yale, Timothy Dwight, observed that nearly all the homes of this whaling and shipbuilding center were one and one-half stories, with central chimneys, small windows, and gabled roofs. He referred to these dwellings as "Cape Cod houses," a type which originated with the Pilgrims, and which today can be found everywhere from Palo Alto to Provincetown. The shingled exteriors of these cottages usually weathered to a silvery gray. In Cape communities, where pretension was abhorred, and where the homes of captain and crewman were undifferentiated, even painted clapboards were considered "showy." As one Bostonian put it, "Cape Cod residences have a peculiarity. . . . The houses and their surroundings seem of an unsuitable inferiority of style to those who live in them . . . [men] whose sons and daughters visit and marry in the best circles. . . . There is . . . a remarkable republican simplicity in the style of buildings; little distinction that betokens wealth; and equality that extends to everything."

*Line* (5)

(10)

(15)

49. This passage mainly discusses
(A) two types of houses
(B) the effect of the weather on house types
(C) the Cape Cod house
(D) peculiarities of the Cape Cod communities

50. From the passage, which of the following can be inferred about log cabins and Cape Cod cottages?
(A) They were the only available housing in the 17th and 18th centuries.
(B) They can still be seen today as a popular housing form.
(C) They often appeared in high-fashion magazines.
(D) They appealed to people who desired a distinctive style.

51. The passage characterizes the Cape Cod house as
(A) poorly built and inferior
(B) free from affectation
(C) strange and unsuitable
(D) large and airy

52. In line 14, the word *showy* could best be replaced by which of the following?
(A) Not functional
(B) Unusual
(C) Pretentious
(D) Inferior

53. In lines 14–19, what was the Bostonian commenting on?
(A) The craftsmanship of the era that produced the Cape Cod
(B) The lack of social class distinction represented by the Cape Cod cottage
(C) His particular distaste for the Cape Cod style
(D) The high cost of the house for such a simple style

54. What will the following section of this text probably discuss?
(A) The Pilgrims' homes in England
(B) The opinion of the Bostonian about other styles of houses
(C) A modern architectural style house
(D) The log cabin

GO ON TO THE NEXT PAGE

Questions 55–60

Generally recognized as one of the significant musical artists of this century, Aaron Copland succeeded so well in assimilating the materials of American folk song into his own highly personal style that, in the eyes of the world, he came to be regarded as "the" American composer of his time.

*Line*
*(5)*    The son of a Russian-Jewish immigrant to America, Copland was born on November 14, 1900, in Brooklyn. By the time he was 15, he had decided to become a composer. In 1921 he went to France, where he became the student of Nadia Boulanger, a brilliant teacher who shaped the outlook of an entire generation of American musicians.

*(10)*    In his growth as a composer, Copland mirrored the important trends of his time. After his return from Paris, he worked with jazz rhythms. There followed a period during which he was strongly influenced by Stravinski's neoclassicism, turning toward an abstract style. In 1935, however, Copland took a change of direction that began the most productive phase of his career. He realized that a new public for
*(15)*    modern music was being created by the new media of radio, phonograph, and film scores. Copland was therefore led to what became a most significant development after the 1930s: the attempt to simplify the new music in order that it would have meaning for a large public.

The decades that followed saw the production of the scores that spread
*(20)*    Copland's fame throughout the United States and the rest of world. Notable among these were three ballets based on American folk material, an orchestral piece based on Mexican melodies and rhythms, and a series of film scores. Typical too of the Copland style are two major works that were written in time of war—both drawing on the life and speeches of Abraham Lincoln for their inspiration.

*(25)*    In his later years, Copland refined his treatment of Americana. "I no longer feel the need of seeking out conscious Americanism. Because we live here and work here, we can be certain that when our music is mature it will also be American in quality." As composer, teacher, and conductor, Copland succeeded in expressing "the deepest reactions of the American consciousness to the American scene."

GO ON TO THE NEXT PAGE

55. According to the passage, Copland is mostly famous for

    (A) the range of types of compositions he produced
    (B) the treatment of American topics in his music
    (C) his study with the famous French teacher, Nadia Boulanger
    (D) his ability as a conductor

56. All of the following are mentioned in the passage as types of compositions Copland produced EXCEPT

    (A) orchestral music
    (B) film scores
    (C) ballets
    (D) operas

57. Which of the following did the author cite as having a major influence on the most productive phase of Copland's career?

    (A) His work with the French teacher, Nadia Boulanger
    (B) The realization of a new public created by new media
    (C) Stravinski's neoclassicism
    (D) The war

58. According to the passage, in the decade after the 1930s Copland's compositions became

    (A) more abstract
    (B) more complex
    (C) more refined
    (D) more simplified

59. In line 21, the word *these* refers to

    (A) ballets
    (B) scores
    (C) decades
    (D) United States

60. With which of the following generalizations can it be inferred that Copland would agree?

    (A) American composers must consciously work with American topics.
    (B) Only mature composers can produce American music.
    (C) American composers' mature music will surely produce music reflective of America.
    (D) American folk material has little place in American music.

**THIS IS THE END OF SECTION 3**

IF YOU FINISH BEFORE TIME IS CALLED, CHECK YOUR WORK
ON SECTION 3 ONLY.
DO NOT READ OR WORK ON ANY OTHER SECTION OF THE TEST.

## PRACTICE TEST FIVE

Time—30 minutes

Exercise is an important part of a healthy lifestyle. Some people prefer to join an exercise program or to do exercises at home. Others prefer to get their exercise through sports and athletic activities. In which of these ways do you prefer to get exercise? Give reasons for your preference.

## NOTES

Use this space to make your notes. Write the final version of your essay on lined paper. The Sample TWE Answer Sheet on page 192 is an example of the amount of writing space provided in the TOEFL Test.

# TAPESCRIPTS
# AND
# ANSWER KEYS

These Tapescripts and Answer Keys are designed to provide teachers and students with help in understanding the TOEFL test questions in this book.

To understand better the questions in Section One of each of the practice tests, extensive use should be made of the tapescripts. They will provide you with a written version of exactly what was said on the practice test tapes, so you can compare what was actually said to what you thought you heard. It is often helpful to read along with the tapescript while listening to the taped version of questions missed.

To understand better the questions in Section Two of each of the practice tests, annotations have been provided for each answer. Similarly, annotations are provided for each of the answers to the reading comprehension questions in Section Three.

Next to each correct annotated answer, you will find a checkpoint number (e.g., R✔7 or G✔22). These numbers refer you to *The Heinemann TOEFL Preparation Course*, where you will find further explanations and exercises for each point tested in the practice tests. By studying the course book checkpoint study and exercises for the questions you miss, you will gain a better understanding of why you missed them. You will also learn valuable language skills and test-taking strategies for the next TOEFL test you take.

# PRACTICE TEST ONE TAPESCRIPT

## SECTION 1
## LISTENING COMPREHENSION

In this section of the test, you will have an opportunity to demonstrate your ability to understand spoken English. There are three parts to this section, with special directions for each part.

### Part A

Directions: For each question in Part A, you will hear a short sentence. Each sentence will be spoken just one time. The sentences you hear will not be written out for you. Therefore, you must listen carefully to understand what the speaker says.

After you hear a sentence, read the four choices in your test book, marked (A), (B), (C), and (D), and decide which one is closest in meaning to the sentence you heard. Then, on your answer sheet, find the number of the question and fill in the space that corresponds to the letter of the answer you have chosen. Fill in the space so that the letter inside the oval cannot be seen.

### Example I

You will hear:  Greg thought typing was a bother.

You will read:  (A)  Greg didn't bother to leave a tip.
(B)  Greg thought about typing a letter to his brother.
(C)  Greg didn't like to type.
(D)  My typing bothered Greg.

The speaker said, "Greg thought typing was a bother." Sentence (C), "Greg didn't like to type," is closest in meaning to the sentence you heard. Therefore, you should choose answer (C).

### Example II

You will hear:  Everyone needs a calculator for this test.

You will read:  (A)  Everyone will be able to take this exam later.
(B)  Students should bring a calculator to this exam.
(C)  This test will be part of every student's final grade.
(D)  No one can calculate the grades for this test.

The speaker said, "Everyone needs a calculator for this test." Sentence (B), "Students should bring a calculator to this exam," is closest in meaning to the sentence you heard. Therefore, you should choose answer (B).

1.  What can I do for you?
2.  Sarah bought a bicycle and toured the state.
3.  He's not here right now.
4.  Their apartment has a nice view, doesn't it.
5.  If Frank comes, ask him to wait for me here.
6.  Mary told herself not to worry about the exam.
7.  On the whole, Jack hasn't let success go to his head.
8.  It was Craig who finally won the bet.
9.  She thinks she'll finish her paper by Tuesday.
10.  You like this music? But it's jazz!
11.  I don't believe they saw the stop sign.
12.  Professor Clyburn turned a deaf ear to our request.
13.  If they had read the book, they would have understood the movie better.
14.  The doctor made her stop taking her medication.
15.  No sooner had she begun her presentation than the microphone broke.
16.  They call each other every evening to keep up on the latest news.
17.  I didn't retain much of the material covered in my geology course.
18.  Judy can't ever seem to get used to the snow.
19.  Kathy used to drive a car to school, but now she lives close enough to ride her bike.
20.  Paula has an eye for detail.

## Part B

<u>Directions:</u> In Part B you will hear short conversations between two speakers. At the end of each conversation, a third person will ask a question about what was said. You will hear each conversation and question about it just one time. Therefore, you must listen carefully to understand what each speaker says. After you hear a conversation and the question about it, read the four possible answers in your test book and decide which <u>one</u> is the best answer to the question you heard. Then, on your answer sheet, find the number of the question and fill in the space that corresponds to the letter of the answer you have chosen.

Look at the following example.

You will hear: **Man:** What's the weather been like there this winter?

**Woman:** About the same as last.

**Question:** What does the woman mean?

You will read: (A) At last winter is almost over.
(B) She doesn't like winter weather very much.
(C) This winter's weather is similar to last winter's weather.
(D) Winter won't last as long this year as it did last year.

From the conversation you learn that the woman thinks the weather this winter is almost the same as the weather last winter. The best answer to the question "What does the woman mean?" is (C), "This winter's weather is similar to last winter's weather." Therefore, you should choose answer (C).

21. M: What would you say to a few days off?
    W: Super!
    Q: What does the woman mean?

22. M: This food sure is spicy!
    W: No kidding!
    Q: What does the woman mean?

23. W: Wasn't that a great lecture?
    M: I've seen better.
    Q: What does the man mean?

24. W: That's a fantastic stereo system! It must have been expensive!
    M: I bought it on sale.
    Q: What does the man imply about his stereo?

25. M: You look different. Did you change your hair?
    W: Yes. I had it cut last week.
    Q: What does the woman mean?

26. W: Could you please bring me a bowl of soup and a salad?
    M: Right away!
    Q: What does the man mean?

27. M: Have you come up with a guest speaker for the banquet?
    W: Not so far, but I'm working on it.
    Q: What does the woman mean?

28. M: Someone's here to see you.
    W: What?
    Q: What does the woman want to know?

29. M: Can you tell me how to use this pay telephone?
    W: The instructions are written on the poster right next to it.
    Q: What will the man probably do next?

30. W: How did you do at getting contributions for the scholarship?
    M: Well, we're still short two hundred dollars.
    Q: What does the man mean?

31. W: Are you going to be able to come with us to the game?
    M: I'm afraid not. I have to work late.
    Q: What does the man mean?

32. W: Sam, are you the one who picked up the picnic table for us?
    M: No, I got Tony to do it.
    Q: What does Sam say about the table?

33. W: When are you going to move into the dorm, Randy?
    M: I'm not sure. I'd like to be able to wait until after summer vacation.
    Q: What does Randy mean?

34. W: Thanks for fixing that broken chair.
    M: The glue isn't dry yet. The legs are still unstable.
    Q: What does the man say about the chair?

35. M: This assignment is too much! I'll never get it done!
    W: No need to panic. Just take it one step at a time.
    Q: What does the woman think the man should do?

## Part C

Directions:  In this part of the test, you will hear short talks and conversations. After each of them, you will be asked some questions. You will hear the talks and conversations and the questions about them just one time. They will not be written out for you. Therefore, you must listen carefully to understand what each speaker says.

After you hear a question, read the four possible answers in your test book and decide which <u>one</u> is the best answer to the question you heard. Then, on your answer sheet, find the number of the question and fill in the space that corresponds to the letter of the answer you have chosen.

Answer all questions on the basis of what is <u>stated</u> or <u>implied</u> in the talk or conversation.

Listen to this sample talk.

You will hear:

The familiar black and yellow bumblebee is often found in fields of red clover. It is the only bee with a tongue long enough to fertilize this plant, so it is impossible to raise red clover where there are no bumblebees.

Like the queen wasp, the queen bee is the only member of her colony that lives through the winter. She starts a new colony in her underground nest every spring by laying from 400 to 1,000 eggs in wax cells, or "combs." Bumblebees also produce honey. Their nests are often dug up and the contents eaten by bears, mice, and other animals.

Now look at the following example.

You will hear:

Why is it impossible to raise red clover where there are no bumblebees?

You will read:  (A) Only bumblebees can fertilize red clover plants.
(B) Bumblebees protect red clover from plant eating insects.
(C) Bumblebees bring water to red clover plants on their tongues.
(D) Bumblebees keep mice and other animals away from red clover plants.

The best answer to the question "Why is it impossible to raise red clover where there are no bumblebees?" is (A), "Only bumblebees can fertilize red clover plants." Therefore, you should choose answer (A).

Now look at the next example.

You will hear:

According to the speaker, in what way are the queen wasp and the queen bee similar?

You will read:  (A) They both make honey.
(B) They both build combs.
(C) Both of them are found in underground nests.
(D) They both live through the winter.

The best answer to the question "According to the speaker, in what way are the queen wasp and the queen bee similar?" is (D), "They both live through the winter." Therefore, you should choose answer (D).

Questions 36 through 40 refer to the following conversation.

W: Hi, Fred. I didn't see you in Professor Densmore's class this morning.
M: Well, I spent half the night in the computer lab trying to write a psychology paper that's due today. I finally did get to sleep around 3:00 this morning, but I didn't hear my alarm when it went off at 6:30.
W: Still always putting things off until the last minute, huh. Wasn't that paper assigned a couple of months ago?
M: Well, yes, but, you know how fast time can get away from you.
W: Right. Well, anyway, you missed a good lecture this morning. I think you would have found it especially interesting.
M: Oh, yeah? Why?
W: As I remember, you're interested in volcanoes. Well, today Professor Densmore's lecture was all about Mount Saint Helen's in Washington state.
M: It really is a shame that I missed that! Oh, well, at least I got my psychology paper finished.
W: Yeah. By the way, what did you write about?
M: The personality traits of people who are prone to procrastination—you know, that fine art of postponing things you have to do.
W: Oh! So, I guess you understand <u>yourself</u> a bit better now that you've finished this paper, right?
M: Well, I hadn't thought of it that way, but, you know, I guess you might be right!

36. Who is the woman in this conversation?
37. Why didn't Fred go to his morning class?
38. What was Fred doing last night?
39. What does Professor Densmore most likely teach?
40. What does the woman probably think about Fred?

Questions 41 through 45 are based on the following talk.

Come on in and have a seat on the bleachers. I know that many of you came here today because you are athletes and you're interested in developing strong bodies. Coach Ward asked me to join you this morning to talk about food and strength. You might ask just what you should eat to increase your strength. Well, the most important factor in increasing your strength is not what you eat as much as how you train. Strength can be gained only through progressive-resistance weight training. How much strength you gain depends on the intensity and type of weight training you do.

It is commonly thought that large amounts of protein or amino acids are necessary to build muscles. However, although an adequate protein intake is certainly important in gaining strength and muscle, so is your intake of other nutrients, including carbohydrates and vitamins. Additionally, if your calorie intake is not adequate, the protein you eat will be used for energy instead of for building muscle mass.

The athlete who cuts back on food to lose weight and then takes vitamin and mineral supplements may be getting more than the needed amount of vitamins and minerals but would not be able to increase or even maintain muscle mass. An adequate diet is essential to maintaining energy, developing muscle mass, and increasing endurance and strength.

41. Where does this talk take place?
42. What is the purpose of this talk?
43. What does the speaker think is most important for gaining strength?
44. What does the speaker say about weight loss?
45. According to the speaker, what is commonly thought about protein?

Questions 46 through 50 refer to the following conversation.

W: Sam, where are you going with all that climbing gear? To the mountains?
M: That's what most people think, but actually I'm involved in an up-and-coming new sport—tree climbing.
W: Really? I know that kids climb trees, and people climb trees as part of their jobs, but a new sport? . . . Tell me more about it.

M: Well, there is now an organization, Tree Climbers International, which was founded in 1984 by Peter Jenkins. He also has a school, where he trains people to climb.
W: But why trees?
M: Well, Jenkins is a tree surgeon and a former rock climber. He just combined his two loves into a sport. He says tree climbing is safer than mountain climbing, and, well, a lot more convenient.
W: So what do you use for equipment?
M: Ropes to hoist yourself into the tree and a tree surgeon's saddle to sit in when you're in the tree top.
W: And how do you get into the tree? I suppose that you choose really tall trees, don't you?
M: A 75-foot tree is a good climb. And, to do that, you also have to be able to use a throwball. A throwball is a weight used to initially loop the rope over the branches.
W: So what kind of trees are you climbing now?
M: Well, trees are classified by difficulty from one to six. I'm on Class Four trees, but if a tree leans, or if you climb in the rain, the difficulty for that tree can go up.
W: I see here in your brochure that Jenkins himself climbed the fifth largest tree in the world, a 357-foot California redwood, and then spent the night in a hammock suspended in the top boughs! Now that sounds like fun!

46. What is the main topic of the conversation?
47. Why did Peter Jenkins begin the sport of tree climbing?
48. Why did the woman think Sam was going mountain climbing?
49. According to the conversation, what is a throwball used for?
50. What impressed the woman most about Peter Jenkins's latest climb?

# PRACTICE TEST TWO TAPESCRIPT

## SECTION 1
## LISTENING COMPREHENSION

In this section of the test, you will have an opportunity to demonstrate your ability to understand spoken English. There are three parts to this section, with special directions for each part.

### Part A

Directions:    For each question in Part A, you will hear a short sentence. Each sentence will be spoken just one time. The sentences you hear will not be written out for you. Therefore, you must listen carefully to understand what the speaker says.

After you hear a sentence, read the four choices in your test book, marked (A), (B), (C), and (D), and decide which one is closest in meaning to the sentence you heard. Then, on your answer sheet, find the number of the question and fill in the space that corresponds to the letter of the answer you have chosen. Fill in the space so that the letter inside the oval cannot be seen.

### Example I

You will hear:  Greg thought typing was a bother.

You will read:  (A) Greg didn't bother to leave a tip.
 (B) Greg thought about typing a letter to his brother.
 (C) Greg didn't like to type.
 (D) My typing bothered Greg.

The speaker said, "Greg thought typing was a bother." Sentence (C), "Greg didn't like to type," is closest in meaning to the sentence you heard. Therefore, you should choose answer (C).

### Example II

You will hear:  Everyone needs a calculator for this test.

You will read:  (A) Everyone will be able to take this exam later.
 (B) Students should bring a calculator to this exam.
 (C) This test will be part of every student's final grade.
 (D) No one can calculate the grades for this test.

The speaker said, "Everyone needs a calculator for this test." Sentence (B), "Students should bring a calculator to this exam," is closest in meaning to the sentence you heard. Therefore, you should choose answer (B).

1. Even though Frank liked his job, he had to quit.
2. She found him studying in the library.
3. He packed the handouts in his suitcase.
4. Karen needs to go to the dentist's today, so she can't go to the theater.
5. Once I get my office cleaned up, I can start working.
6. Tom always travels first class, doesn't he.
7. Have you ever known anyone as gifted in languages as Jane?
8. The physics professor didn't let us finish our experiments at home.
9. Sandy is feeling out of touch with her family.
10. Both students and parents feel free to drop in on Professor Hartwick whenever they want to.
11. I am forwarding you a copy of the contract.
12. She seems to have been misled about the difficulty of this course.
13. Don't give it a second thought.
14. No matter what, my brother and I get together once a year.
15. I've never heard Arthur play the piano.
16. Professor Clark intends to cover the whole book in one semester.
17. Andrew requested that I share my locker with him.
18. Professor Boyd hardly ever calls on me in class.
19. It's a pity that the library closes early on Saturdays.
20. None of the children who played on the large and noisy playground went home unhappy.

Part B

Directions: In Part B you will hear short conversations between two speakers. At the end of each conversation, a third person will ask a question about what was said. You will hear each conversation and question about it just one time. Therefore, you must listen carefully to understand what each speaker says. After you hear a conversation and the question about it, read the four possible answers in your test book and decide which one is the best answer to the question you heard. Then, on your answer sheet, find the number of the question and fill in the space that corresponds to the letter of the answer you have chosen.

Look at the following example.

You will hear:    **Man:**    What's the weather been like there this winter?
                  **Woman:**  About the same as last.
                  **Question:** What does the woman mean?

You will read: (A) At last winter is almost over.
               (B) She doesn't like winter weather very much.
               (C) This winter's weather is similar to last winter's weather.
               (D) Winter won't last as long this year as it did last year.

From the conversation you learn that the woman thinks the weather this winter is almost the same as the weather last winter. The best answer to the question "What does the woman mean?" is (C), "This winter's weather is similar to last winter's weather." Therefore, you should choose answer (C).

21. W: John and his brother seem to have a lot to talk about.
    M: Well, they haven't seen each other for quite a while.
    Q: What does the man imply about John and his brother?

22. M: I'm tired of sitting at home. How about a movie?
    W: Sure, why not?
    Q: What does the woman mean?

23. M: Is it better to take the bus to Chicago or to go by plane?
    W: The bus is a lot cheaper, but it takes at least twice as long.
    Q: What does the woman mean?

24. M: The red one looks better on you than the striped one does.
    W: But the collar on the red one is too big, and the sleeves are too long.
    Q: Where does this conversation most probably take place?

25. M: I heard Ted ended up in the emergency room this morning. Is everything OK?
    W: He's being kept overnight for observation.
    Q: What does the woman imply?

26. M: Let's practice that dance routine some more, Ann, and see if we can get it right this time.
    W: Again! We've already tried it six times!
    Q: What does Ann mean?

27. W: That seafood restaurant we went to last night is the best in town!
    M: Isn't it, though!
    Q: What does the man think about the restaurant?

28. W: Do you want to go to the party?
    M: Well, it doesn't start until 8:00, and I have to get up early tomorrow.
    Q: What does the man imply?

29. W: Kate wants us to pick her up at the airport at 10:30.
    M: Oh, so she did make her connecting flight in Boston.
    Q: What had the man assumed about Kate?

30. M: I had to wait fifty minutes to see the doctor.
    W: I could have told you that would happen!
    Q: What does the woman mean?

31. W: I have to turn my paper in late. I hope Professor Smith won't be too unhappy.
    M: Well, this is the first time you've ever had to ask for an extension, so I don't expect she'll be too hard on you.
    Q: What does the man think Professor Smith will probably do?

32. W: Ray certainly has been late for class a lot this semester!
    M: That's not like him!
    Q: What do we learn from this conversation?

33. W: My history term paper has to be typed.
    M: Shouldn't you type your English paper, too?
    Q: What does the man suggest?

34. M: Do you mind if I use your phone?
    W: John's calling his mother right now.
    Q: What can be inferred from the woman's response?

35. M: Did you hear Jane's presentation last night?
    W: How she can be so calm in front of such a large audience is beyond me!
    Q: What does the woman imply?

## Part C

Directions: In this part of the test, you will hear short talks and conversations. After each of them, you will be asked some questions. You will hear the talks and conversations and the questions about them just one time. They will not be written out for you. Therefore, you must listen carefully to understand what each speaker says.

After you hear a question, read the four possible answers in your test book and decide which one is the best answer to the question you heard. Then, on your answer sheet, find the number of the question and fill in the space that corresponds to the letter of the answer you have chosen.

Answer all questions on the basis of what is stated or implied in the talk or conversation.

Listen to this sample talk.

You will hear:

The familiar black and yellow bumblebee is often found in fields of red clover. It is the only bee with a tongue long enough to fertilize this plant, so it is impossible to raise red clover where there are no bumblebees.

Like the queen wasp, the queen bee is the only member of her colony that lives through the winter. She starts a new colony in her underground nest every spring by laying from 400 to 1,000 eggs in wax cells, or "combs." Bumblebees also produce honey. Their nests are often dug up and the contents eaten by bears, mice, and other animals.

Now look at the following example.

You will hear:

Why is it impossible to raise red clover where there are no bumblebees?

You will read: (A) Only bumblebees can fertilize red clover plants.
(B) Bumblebees protect red clover from plant eating insects.
(C) Bumblebees bring water to red clover plants on their tongues.
(D) Bumblebees keep mice and other animals away from red clover plants.

The best answer to the question "Why is it impossible to raise red clover where there are no bumblebees?" is (A), "Only bumblebees can fertilize red clover plants." Therefore, you should choose answer (A).

Now look at the next example.

You will hear:

According to the speaker, in what way are the queen wasp and the queen bee similar?

You will read: (A) They both make honey.
(B) They both build combs.
(C) Both of them are found in underground nests.
(D) They both live through the winter.

The best answer to the question "According to the speaker, in what way are the queen wasp and the queen bee similar?" is (D), "They both live through the winter." Therefore, you should choose answer (D).

Questions 36 through 40 refer to the following talk.

Once you have decided to share your life with one of our cats, you must decide whether you want an alley cat or a pedigreed cat. Let me explain what those terms mean. An alley cat is one with no special breeding, or ancestry. It is just a common cat, whose parents are of mixed background. This type of cat, unfortunately, often goes homeless and has to hunt for food in the garbage cans found in alleys—and that's how it got it's name. A pedigreed cat, on the other hand, is a pure-bred feline whose ancestry has been recorded and whose history can be traced back several generations. We sell both kinds of cats here, our pedigreed cats, of course, being the more expensive of the two types. But, both types of cats can turn out to be perfect pets.

36. Where does this talk take place?
37. Who is the speaker probably talking to?
38. According to the speaker, what is an *alley* cat?
39. What does the term *breeding* mean in this talk?
40. According to the speaker, what do the two types of cats have in common?

Questions 41 through 45 refer to the following conversation.

W: Have you chosen your options for interdisciplinary studies yet? I've just turned mine in to the registrar's office, but the deadline is tomorrow by 4:00 P.M.

M: What do you mean? I've already preregistered for that course. We did it together, remember?

W: Yes, but did you select four options? The course is one semester, but you have to take four different mini-courses within that time.

M: That's news to me. But it sounds interesting. Where do I find a list of the choices?

W: I got mine in the mail a week after I preregistered for the course. Why don't you come to the library with me, and I'll make you a copy. There are ten different options and a required reading list.

M: OK, thanks, if it's not too much bother. What are you going to take for the first four weeks?

W: Well, there's really no choice for the first four weeks. Everyone attends the interdisciplinary lecture series Tuesday afternoons, and study-discussion groups on Thursdays. This is to give us all the same basic information. But in the second session I want to take art history, then literature in the last session.

M: Well, I'm really glad you mentioned this. I need to get that list and make some decisions. You've probably started reading already, right?

W: As a matter of fact, that's why I'm on my way to the library.

41. How does the man react when he first hears about the deadline?

42. How did the woman know about the course selection requirement?

43. How will the man find out about the choices?

44. How does the man feel about the course when he learns of the options?

45. What will the two people probably do next?

Questions 46 through 50 refer to the following remarks from a history lecture.

I spoke yesterday about the construction of ancient Viking ships. Today I'd like to discuss the trans-ocean voyages that the Norse made in these open boats—voyages made without compasses or charts. Somehow the Vikings managed to get across the North Atlantic and back home again. Although the shortest distance between the coast of Norway and Greenland is about 900 miles, the Vikings preferred to take a longer route south of Iceland and thereby avoid pack-ice. This was a voyage of well over one thousand miles. How did Norse sailors find land after days of sailing out of sight of land? Well, experienced sailors used the relative position of the stars to help them navigate. The sun's position could also be noted, but it moves across the sky and its position alters a little every day, so it was not easy for the Vikings to use. However, even when out of sight of land, an experienced sailor could find information. As there are landmarks on land, so there are at sea. Whales gathered in large numbers to feed at an area half a day's sail south of Iceland. Migrating birds on their annual flight were also helpful because they always followed the same route. So, geese flying between Britain and Iceland were of particular use to the Vikings. One Icelander also took ravens with him, releasing them until one day they didn't return. He followed their direction and found land. In 900 A.D., ingenuity had to take the place of technology.

46. What is the main topic of the talk?

47. What did the speaker talk about yesterday?

48. Why didn't the Vikings take the shortest route between Norway and Greenland?

49. How were whales helpful to the Vikings?

50. What can be inferred about Vikings from the talk?

# PRACTICE TEST THREE TAPESCRIPT

## SECTION 1
## LISTENING COMPREHENSION

In this section of the test, you will have an opportunity to demonstrate your ability to understand spoken English. There are three parts to this section, with special directions for each part.

### Part A

Directions:   For each question in Part A, you will hear a short sentence. Each sentence will be spoken just one time. The sentences you hear will not be written out for you. Therefore, you must listen carefully to understand what the speaker says.

After you hear a sentence, read the four choices in your test book, marked (A), (B), (C), and (D), and decide which <u>one</u> is closest in meaning to the sentence you heard. Then, on your answer sheet, find the number of the question and fill in the space that corresponds to the letter of the answer you have chosen. Fill in the space so that the letter inside the oval cannot be seen.

### Example I

You will hear:  Greg thought typing was a bother.

You will read:  (A) Greg didn't bother to leave
                    a tip.
                (B) Greg thought about typing a
                    letter to his brother.
                (C) Greg didn't like to type.
                (D) My typing bothered Greg.

The speaker said, "Greg thought typing was a bother." Sentence (C), "Greg didn't like to type," is closest in meaning to the sentence you heard. Therefore, you should choose answer (C).

### Example II

You will hear:  Everyone needs a calculator  for
                this test.

You will read:  (A) Everyone will be able to take
                    this exam later.
                (B) Students should bring a
                    calculator to this exam.
                (C) This test will be part of every
                    student's final grade.
                (D) No one can calculate the
                    grades for this test.

The speaker said, "Everyone needs a calculator for this test." Sentence (B), "Students should bring a calculator to this exam," is closest in meaning to the sentence you heard. Therefore, you should choose answer (B).

1.  What a bright tie you have on!

2.  Brian has to write his thesis by next week.

3.  Elaine had her glasses repaired.

4.  The students have shopped for their books already.

5.  Andrea came by to see me a couple of days ago.

6.  George hurt his heel while running for the bus last week.

7.  Only after the dean approved my application was I accepted into law school.

8.  Turn right at the corner, and you'll see the post office.

9.  There's almost nothing that doesn't upset her these days.

10. How tall you've gotten!

11. Ted's aunt was touched by his kind note.

12. Jane works out several times a week at the gym.

13. Bob lost his passport and had to order a new one.

14. He's studying day and night, trying to make a go of it in graduate school.

15. I spent a quarter of an hour tracking down these three history books.

16. Sounds like a great class, don't you think?

17. Carol expects us to clear up this misunderstanding on our own.

18. You're going to hand in your project today, aren't you?

19. Sandy's really been burning the midnight oil in the lab to finish that experiment.

20. His story isn't entirely incorrect.

## Part B

<u>Directions:</u>  In Part B you will hear short conversations between two speakers. At the end of each conversation, a third person will ask a question about what was said. You will hear each conversation and question about it just one time. Therefore, you must listen carefully to understand what each speaker says. After you hear a conversation and the question about it, read the four possible answers in your test book and decide which <u>one</u> is the best answer to the question you heard. Then, on your answer sheet, find the number of the question and fill in the space that corresponds to the letter of the answer you have chosen.

Look at the following example.

You will hear:  **Man:**  What's the weather been like there this winter?
**Woman:**  About the same as last.
**Question:**  What does the woman mean?

You will read:  (A) At last winter is almost over.
(B) She doesn't like winter weather very much.
(C) This winter's weather is similar to last winter's weather.
(D) Winter won't last as long this year as it did last year.

From the conversation you learn that the woman thinks the weather this winter is almost the same as the weather last winter. The best answer to the question "What does the woman mean?" is (C), "This winter's weather is similar to last winter's weather." Therefore, you should choose answer (C).

21. M:  Shall we try one more physics problem?
W:  I'd rather not. I'm fed up.
Q:  How does the woman feel?

22. M:  Will I need to have this tooth pulled?
W:  I don't think so. Let's try filling it first.
Q:  Where does this conversation most probably take place?

23. W:  John really enjoys old movies.
M:  So does Bill.
Q:  What does the man mean?

24. W:  We'll have to hurry if we want to finish this project on time.
M:  I'll say we will!
Q:  What does the man mean?

25. M:  I should keep working, but I don't feel like it.
W:  Why don't you take a breather?
Q:  What does the woman think the man should do?

26. W:  I take it for granted you're happy with your choice of university.
M:  Well, as it turns out, I'm not, really.
Q:  What do we learn about the man?

27. M:  Excuse me. I'm trying to find the library.
W:  Look no further!
Q:  What does the woman mean?

28. M:  Are you going to be working in the garage long?
W:  Until I can finish fixing this lawn mower.
Q:  What is the woman going to do?

29. W:  Well, what do you think?
M:  You really got a short haircut and a tight curl, didn't you?
Q:  Where has the woman been?

30. W:  Charles still has two more chapters of his thesis to write!
M:  Yes, but they're just summaries of the others, aren't they?
Q:  What does the man imply about Charles' thesis?

31. M:  Can you tell me where I might borrow a typewriter?
W:  The library has some. You can use them there.
Q:  What will the man probably do next?

32. M:  If you don't want to go to the party, you shouldn't feel obligated to.
W:  Oh, well. I don't mind going for a little while.
Q:  What is the woman going to do?

33. W:  Did you get the car you wanted?
M:  No. Someone beat me to it.
Q:  What does the man mean?

34. W:  You wouldn't be interested in two tickets to tonight's concert, would you?
M:  Not much, I wouldn't!
Q:  What does the man mean?

35. M:  I was pretty taken aback at Dan's reaction to our proposal!
W:  Me, too. And I thought some of his comments were really out of line.
Q:  How does the woman feel?

## Part C

<u>Directions</u>: In this part of the test, you will hear short talks and conversations. After each of them, you will be asked some questions. You will hear the talks and conversations and the questions about them just one time. They will not be written out for you. Therefore, you must listen carefully to understand what each speaker says.

After you hear a question, read the four possible answers in your test book and decide which <u>one</u> is the best answer to the question you heard. Then, on your answer sheet, find the number of the question and fill in the space that corresponds to the letter of the answer you have chosen.

Answer all questions on the basis of what is <u>stated</u> or <u>implied</u> in the talk or conversation.

Listen to this sample talk.

You will hear:

The familiar black and yellow bumblebee is often found in fields of red clover. It is the only bee with a tongue long enough to fertilize this plant, so it is impossible to raise red clover where there are no bumblebees.

Like the queen wasp, the queen bee is the only member of her colony that lives through the winter. She starts a new colony in her underground nest every spring by laying from 400 to 1,000 eggs in wax cells, or "combs." Bumblebees also produce honey. Their nests are often dug up and the contents eaten by bears, mice, and other animals.

Now look at the following example.

You will hear:

Why is it impossible to raise red clover where there are no bumblebees?

You will read: (A) Only bumblebees can fertilize red clover plants.
(B) Bumblebees protect red clover from plant eating insects.
(C) Bumblebees bring water to red clover plants on their tongues.
(D) Bumblebees keep mice and other animals away from red clover plants.

The best answer to the question "Why is it impossible to raise red clover where there are no bumblebees?" is (A), "Only bumblebees can fertilize red clover plants." Therefore, you should choose answer (A).

Now look at the next example.

You will hear:

According to the speaker, in what way are the queen wasp and the queen bee similar?

You will read: (A) They both make honey.
(B) They both build combs.
(C) Both of them are found in underground nests.
(D) They both live through the winter.

The best answer to the question "According to the speaker, in what way are the queen wasp and the queen bee similar?" is (D), "They both live through the winter." Therefore, you should choose answer (D).

Questions 36 through 40 refer to the following business lecture.

Well, I guess that's it for today's discussion on advertising as an important aspect of marketing. Next week, I'd like to move away from marketing and into distribution—that is, the chain of movement of goods from their sources, often factories, to their final destinations—us—the consumers. For that discussion, you'll need to read Chapter 5 in your text. Make sure you read it carefully. We may have a short quiz on it at the beginning of our next class. As you are reading Chapter 5, pay careful attention to the differences and similarities between wholesalers and retailers. They are the most important middlemen in the chain of distribution of goods and services, and it's crucial for you to understand the roles they play in getting goods from factories to consumers. Oh, and one last thing. Don't forget to leave today's homework on my desk as you leave the classroom. I'll take a look at it this week and get it back to you at our next class meeting.

36. Who was the speaker?

37. What was the topic of today's earlier discussion?

38. According to the speaker, what is *distribution*?

39. What might happen at the beginning of the next class?

40. What would the speaker like the students to think carefully about when doing their assigned reading?

Questions 41 through 45. Listen to the conversation.

W: I just heard something interesting on the public radio station. Do you know why the leaves on trees turn so many different colors in the fall?

M: I think so. When they die, they dry out and turn brown, or frost and cold turn them other, brighter colors.

W: Well, not exactly. Actually, the autumn leaf color that paints our countryside isn't the result of a *loss* of pigment, but of an uncovering of underlying true colors of the leaves.

M: What do you mean by that?

W: Well, during the summer, tree leaves produce chlorophyll, which is green. But they also actively produce other pigments. Then, in the fall, when chlorophyll production stops, the green color breaks down and the other pigments produced in the leaves are uncovered.

M: Amazing. Well, what causes some trees to have red leaves then, and some to have yellow, or brown, or orange?

W: Different chemical pigments. For example, carotene—the same pigment found in carrots—creates the orange color in some species. Anthocyanins produce the bright red we see in sugar maples, and so on.

M: Hum. So the mystery of autumn leaf color really isn't a mystery at all.

41. What is the main topic of the conversation?
42. What prompted the conversation?
43. What had the man thought about leaf coloration?
44. According to the conversation, what color does carotene produce?
45. What causes the different colors found in autumn leaves?

Questions 46 through 50. Listen to the lecture about a museum.

Good morning, ladies and gentlemen. I'm Sam Connor, and I'll be your guide through the first wing of the exhibits this morning. Before we start out, let me give you some orientation to the museum itself. There are four main exhibit areas located off the central and mezzanine galleries, which are used for displays of special exhibitions that change frequently. To our right is the entrance to the art gallery, which also contains the museum research library. This library is available for extensive research assistance for our patrons by appointment. To our left is the firearms museum, which you can see is still partially under construction and unfortunately not open for our visit this morning. Directly ahead, through the garden area, is the Indian museum, of which we are extremely proud. We are thought to have the most complete collection of Indian art and artifacts in this part of the United States. The youngsters will surely enjoy the tipi hall, a replica of an 1890 Sioux camp. You may enter the tipis, but do not touch the exhibits.

I'm sorry to announce that there will be a brief delay in our tour, due to the many school visits at this time of year. Please visit our gift shop, or stroll through the sculpture garden while we are waiting. The tour should begin in fifteen minutes.

46. Who was the speaker?
47. What can be found in the central gallery?
48. Why can't the tour visit the firearms museum?
49. Which exhibit area is the museum best known for?
50. Why was the tour delayed?

# PRACTICE TEST FOUR TAPESCRIPT

## SECTION 1
## LISTENING COMPREHENSION

In this section of the test, you will have an opportunity to demonstrate your ability to understand spoken English. There are three parts to this section, with special directions for each part.

### Part A

Directions:  For each question in Part A, you will hear a short sentence. Each sentence will be spoken just one time. The sentences you hear will not be written out for you. Therefore, you must listen carefully to understand what the speaker says.

After you hear a sentence, read the four choices in your test book, marked (A), (B), (C), and (D), and decide which one is closest in meaning to the sentence you heard. Then, on your answer sheet, find the number of the question and fill in the space that corresponds to the letter of the answer you have chosen. Fill in the space so that the letter inside the oval cannot be seen.

### Example I

You will hear:  Greg thought typing was a bother.

You will read:  (A) Greg didn't bother to leave a tip.
(B) Greg thought about typing a letter to his brother.
(C) Greg didn't like to type.
(D) My typing bothered Greg.

The speaker said, "Greg thought typing was a bother." Sentence (C), "Greg didn't like to type," is closest in meaning to the sentence you heard. Therefore, you should choose answer (C).

### Example II

You will hear:  Everyone needs a calculator for this test.

You will read:  (A) Everyone will be able to take this exam later.
(B) Students should bring a calculator to this exam.
(C) This test will be part of every student's final grade.
(D) No one can calculate the grades for this test.

The speaker said, "Everyone needs a calculator for this test." Sentence (B), "Students should bring a calculator to this exam," is closest in meaning to the sentence you heard. Therefore, you should choose answer (B).

1. See you later.
2. Why don't we get down to business.
3. Chris went to the butcher's to get some meat.
4. Let me give you a hand with that.
5. I just graduated, but my brother has another semester to go.
6. Larry missed the point of today's quiz.
7. Claire has already finished writing her paper.
8. Paul has stopped to admire the painting.
9. The course was supposed to be difficult, and it was.
10. Pam is running to the store to pick up a few things for the party.
11. This portfolio was presented to me by an art student.
12. Robert asked them to return the books they'd borrowed.
13. You were the one who starred in the play, weren't you.
14. Pat used to write to me once a week.
15. Jessica finished school and got a job in Cleveland.
16. Shouldn't he be getting used to his schedule by now?
17. It's hard to believe you're not a professional musician!
18. No one can claim that he didn't put his best foot forward.
19. I wish my car ran, but I can't seem to get it going.
20. You mean you've only read two of the books that are required for the course?

Part B

Directions: In Part B you will hear short conversations between two speakers. At the end of each conversation, a third person will ask a question about what was said. You will hear each conversation and question about it just one time. Therefore, you must listen carefully to understand what each speaker says. After you hear a conversation and the question about it, read the four possible answers in your test book and decide which one is the best answer to the question you heard. Then, on your answer sheet, find the number of the question and fill in the space that corresponds to the letter of the answer you have chosen.

Look at the following example.

You will hear:   **Man:**   What's the weather been like there this winter?
**Woman:**   About the same as last.
**Question:**   What does the woman mean?

You will read:  (A) At last winter is almost over.
(B) She doesn't like winter weather very much.
(C) This winter's weather is similar to last winter's weather.
(D) Winter won't last as long this year as it did last year.

From the conversation you learn that the woman thinks the weather this winter is almost the same as the weather last winter. The best answer to the question "What does the woman mean?" is (C), "This winter's weather is similar to last winter's weather." Therefore, you should choose answer (C).

21. W: Do you mind if I borrow your vacuum to clean out my car?
   M: No problem.
   Q: What does the man mean?

22. M: Shall we set the tent up?
   W: Yes. Right away. Then we'd better start a fire. It's cold out here.
   Q: Where does this conversation most probably take place?

23. M: This apartment isn't in very good shape.
   W: It's the worst one I've seen!
   Q: What does the woman mean?

24. M: Do you know where I can have my clothes cleaned?
   W: Why not wash them yourself? There's a laundromat on Third Street.
   Q: What does the woman mean?

25. M: Are you going to take six classes again this fall?
   W: Not on your life!
   Q: What does the woman mean?

26. W: Karen says her shoulder doesn't hurt today.
   M: She'd better have it looked at by a doctor, anyway.
   Q: What does the man think Karen should do?

27. M: Both of our rear tires have gone flat!
   W: What! (Incredulous)
   Q: What does the woman mean?

28. W: How did Carol's cake turn out?
   M: I don't know. Why don't we try some and see?
   Q: What does the man say about the cake?

29. W: How about some ice cream?
   M: No, thanks. I'm watching my weight.
   Q: What does the man mean?

30. M: Doctor Olsen, do you think I could take my exam a few days ahead of schedule?
   W: I'm sorry. That's out of the question.
   Q: What does Doctor Olsen mean?

31. M: Did you like the joke Professor Stapp told before class this morning?
   W: I'd heard it a hundred times already!
   Q: What does the woman mean by her response?

32. W: You sing beautifully!
   M: Well, I guess I can carry a tune all right, but I could certainly never be an opera star!
   Q: What does the man say about his musical talent?

33. W: There should be two dozen sandwiches in the picnic basket.
   M: Is that counting the ones I brought, too?
   Q: What is the man asking?

34. M: This heat is really getting to me.
   W: Me, too. What would you say to a swim?
   Q: What does the woman mean?

35. M: Professor Larson doesn't accept late papers.
   W: Neither does Professor Andrews.
   Q: What does the woman mean?

## Part C

<u>Directions:</u>   In this part of the test, you will hear short talks and conversations. After each of them, you will be asked some questions. You will hear the talks and conversations and the questions about them just one time. They will not be written out for you. Therefore, you must listen carefully to understand what each speaker says.

After you hear a question, read the four possible answers in your test book and decide which <u>one</u> is the best answer to the question you heard. Then, on your answer sheet, find the number of the question and fill in the space that corresponds to the letter of the answer you have chosen.

Answer all questions on the basis of what is <u>stated</u> or <u>implied</u> in the talk or conversation.

Listen to this sample talk.

You will hear:

The familiar black and yellow bumblebee is often found in fields of red clover. It is the only bee with a tongue long enough to fertilize this plant, so it is impossible to raise red clover where there are no bumblebees.
Like the queen wasp, the queen bee is the only member of her colony that lives through the winter. She starts a new colony in her underground nest every spring by laying from 400 to 1,000 eggs in wax cells, or "combs." Bumblebees also produce honey. Their nests are often dug up and the contents eaten by bears, mice, and other animals.

Now look at the following example.

You will hear:

Why is it impossible to raise red clover where there are no bumblebees?

You will read:  (A) Only bumblebees can fertilize red clover plants.
(B) Bumblebees protect red clover from plant eating insects.
(C) Bumblebees bring water to red clover plants on their tongues.
(D) Bumblebees keep mice and other animals away from red clover plants.

The best answer to the question "Why is it impossible to raise red clover where there are no bumblebees?" is (A), "Only bumblebees can fertilize red clover plants." Therefore, you should choose answer (A).

Now look at the next example.

You will hear:

According to the speaker, in what way are the queen wasp and the queen bee similar?

You will read:  (A) They both make honey.
(B) They both build combs.
(C) Both of them are found in underground nests.
(D) They both live through the winter.

The best answer to the question "According to the speaker, in what way are the queen wasp and the queen bee similar?" is (D), "They both live through the winter." Therefore, you should choose answer (D).

Questions 36 through 41 refer to the following conversation.

M: Do you have much left to do before you go?
W: Not too much. Right now, I'm cleaning my apartment one last time, trying to get everything in shape.
M: You know, I've been meaning to tell you that I'd be glad to help you with that in any way I can.
W: Thanks. I appreciate that. Actually, I'm almost finished. But, if you have a minute right now, I'd like to ask you to help me move the bed so I can clean under it.
M: Sure. You certainly are doing a thorough job!
W: I don't think anyone should have to move into someone else's mess.
M: I agree. Do you need a hand with anything else?
W: Hum. Well, not for now, I don't think. But, would you mind giving me a ride to the airport tomorrow morning?
M: No problem.

36. Where does this conversation take place?
37. What is the woman getting ready to do?
38. What does the man offer to do?
39. From the conversation, what can be inferred about the woman?
40. What does the man mean when he says, "Do you need a hand with anything else"?
41. How will the woman get to the airport?

Questions 42 through 46 refer to the following talk.

Hi. My name's Tammy Mullen, and I'll be your guide on our campus tour. As we walk through the campus, I'll provide a bit of history about the college, and I'll describe some of our fine academic programs. Right now we're standing in the lobby of the Boyd Memorial Library. This library is named after Alexander Boyd, its first director and greatest benefactor. Thanks to Dr. Boyd's fine efforts, library development got off to a very good start here, and the Boyd Library now houses over 800,000 volumes, including periodicals and newspapers. We also have more than 60,000 maps and 2,000 photographs in our collection. All of the library's collections are arranged for easy student access. There are comfortable study and reading lounges; in addition, more than 500 individual student study desks are located in the library within easy reach of reference materials and library stacks. Are there any questions about the library? Good. Then let's move on to the Cline Biology Building. If we're lucky, the greenhouse will be open and we can take a peek inside.

42. Who is the speaker?
43. Where does this talk take place?
44. Who is the speaker probably talking to?
45. Who was Alexander Boyd?
46. Where will the speaker probably go next?

Questions 47 through 50 refer to the following conversation.

M: I thought you were going to start recycling, but I see you've put all your bottles and cans in the trash again. Did you change your mind?
W: Well, I started saving all the cans and bottles I use, but I found it so time consuming! I mean, clear glass and brown glass and green glass all have to be separated for recycling. Then, as if that's not bad enough, some kinds of plastic containers *can* be recycled while others *can't*, so they have to be very carefully sorted, too, and, well, it just didn't seem worth it.
M: But, it really *is* worth it. Using the same materials over and over again can help save the environment. It can also save you money!
W: OK, OK. I know you're right. I'll start recycling again today. Now, let's take that walk you promised me.

47. What had the man thought at first?
48. From the conversation, what can we assume that recycling means?
49. Why doesn't the woman think recycling is a good idea?
50. What does the woman promise to do?

# PRACTICE TEST FIVE TAPESCRIPT

## SECTION 1
## LISTENING COMPREHENSION

In this section of the test, you will have an opportunity to demonstrate your ability to understand spoken English. There are three parts to this section, with special directions for each part.

### Part A

<u>Directions:</u>  For each question in Part A, you will hear a short sentence. Each sentence will be spoken just one time. The sentences you hear will not be written out for you. Therefore, you must listen carefully to understand what the speaker says.

After you hear a sentence, read the four choices in your test book, marked (A), (B), (C), and (D), and decide which <u>one</u> is closest in meaning to the sentence you heard. Then, on your answer sheet, find the number of the question and fill in the space that corresponds to the letter of the answer you have chosen. Fill in the space so that the letter inside the oval cannot be seen.

### Example I

You will hear:  Greg thought typing was a bother.

You will read:  (A) Greg didn't bother to leave a tip.
(B) Greg thought about typing a letter to his brother.
(C) Greg didn't like to type.
(D) My typing bothered Greg.

The speaker said, "Greg thought typing was a bother." Sentence (C), "Greg didn't like to type," is closest in meaning to the sentence you heard. Therefore, you should choose answer (C).

### Example II

You will hear:  Everyone needs a calculator for this test.

You will read:  (A) Everyone will be able to take this exam later.
(B) Students should bring a calculator to this exam.
(C) This test will be part of every student's final grade.
(D) No one can calculate the grades for this test.

The speaker said, "Everyone needs a calculator for this test." Sentence (B), "Students should bring a calculator to this exam," is closest in meaning to the sentence you heard. Therefore, you should choose answer (B).

1. I think I'll go for a long walk later.
2. My parents just celebrated their 40th anniversary.
3. What a beautiful day it is!
4. I don't think they understood my instructions.
5. As they were entering the room, the band began to play.
6. If we had started this sooner, we wouldn't be so rushed right now.
7. There's almost nobody in town who doesn't know Frank.
8. He listened to the message again because he couldn't believe his ears.
9. I got one of the books I wanted, but the other was already checked out.
10. History 506 will be meeting on Tuesdays at 1:30.
11. Dave's been to the library a couple of times looking for the article.
12. Dormitory food grows on you after a while, doesn't it.
13. He thought he did well on the test, and he did.
14. Doctors are trying to cut back on expenses.
15. Give her your new address, and she'll be in touch with you.
16. To be honest, I don't really care much for athletics.
17. You can't start your project until you get the professor's approval.
18. If Rick felt better, he could join us at the concert tonight.
19. It may rain tomorrow, but we'll play soccer in any case.
20. Both Pat and Chris tried to make light of their disappointment at not being chosen for the scholarship.

## Part B

Directions:    In Part B you will hear short conversations between two speakers. At the end of each conversation, a third person will ask a question about what was said. You will hear each conversation and question about it just one time. Therefore, you must listen carefully to understand what each speaker says. After you hear a conversation and the question about it, read the four possible answers in your test book and decide which one is the best answer to the question you heard. Then, on your answer sheet, find the number of the question and fill in the space that corresponds to the letter of the answer you have chosen.

Look at the following example.

You will hear:    **Man:**   What's the weather been like there this winter?
**Woman:**   About the same as last.
**Question:**   What does the woman mean?

You will read:   (A)  At last winter is almost over.
(B)  She doesn't like winter weather very much.
(C)  This winter's weather is similar to last winter's weather.
(D)  Winter won't last as long this year as it did last year.

From the conversation you learn that the woman thinks the weather this winter is almost the same as the weather last winter. The best answer to the question "What does the woman mean?" is (C), "This winter's weather is similar to last winter's weather." Therefore, you should choose answer (C).

21.  M:  Do you still want to go to the party tonight?
W:  For sure!
Q:  What does the woman mean?

22.  W:  Where can I meet Flight 104?
M:  It will be arriving at Gate 32 in about 10 minutes.
Q:  Where does this conversation probably take place?

23.  W:  We've been working for twelve hours straight. Don't you think we should stop for today?
M:  Good idea. I'm bushed.
Q:  How does the man feel?

24.  W:  How much do I owe you for the dinner?
M:  Oh, don't worry about it.
Q:  What does the man mean?

25.  M:  I assume you've finished all your term papers?
W:  Well, actually, I've fallen a little behind.
Q:  What do we learn about the woman from this conversation?

26.  M:  Sorry. What did you just say?
W:  Never mind.
Q:  What does the woman mean?

27.  W:  Frank, did you mail my letter for me?
M:  I had George do it.
Q:  What does Frank say about the letter?

28.  M:  I understand you missed the calculus problem on today's homework.
W:  Yes, and if I had just used my head, I would have figured it out!
Q:  What does the woman mean?

29.  M:  Your clean shirts are hanging in the closet.
W:  Great! So you *did* get the laundry done after all!
Q:  What had the woman thought before?

30.  W:  Do you know where I can buy a used sociology book?
M:  Why not borrow mine? I'm through with it.
Q:  What is the man suggesting?

31.  W:  When are you going to start writing your book, Larry?
M:  I'm not sure. I'd like to be able to wait until the end of the school year.
Q:  What does Larry mean?

32.  W:  Did you enjoy visiting the museum?
M:  I've been there a hundred times!
Q:  What does the man mean by his response?

33.  W:  Sarah was the most talented singer in the production, wasn't she!
M:  No question about it.
Q:  What does the man say about Sarah?

34.  W:  I hear you're taking the advanced physics class.
M:  Yes, but I'm not sure I can handle it.
Q:  What is the man worried about?

35.  M:  What's this I hear about your receiving a scholarship!
W:  Oh, that. One person from every school gets one, and I was the only one from mine to apply.
Q:  What does the woman mean?

## Part C

**Directions:** In this part of the test, you will hear short talks and conversations. After each of them, you will be asked some questions. You will hear the talks and conversations and the questions about them just one time. They will not be written out for you. Therefore, you must listen carefully to understand what each speaker says.

After you hear a question, read the four possible answers in your test book and decide which <u>one</u> is the best answer to the question you heard. Then, on your answer sheet, find the number of the question and fill in the space that corresponds to the letter of the answer you have chosen.

Answer all questions on the basis of what is <u>stated</u> or <u>implied</u> in the talk or conversation.

Listen to this sample talk.

You will hear:

The familiar black and yellow bumblebee is often found in fields of red clover. It is the only bee with a tongue long enough to fertilize this plant, so it is impossible to raise red clover where there are no bumblebees.

Like the queen wasp, the queen bee is the only member of her colony that lives through the winter. She starts a new colony in her underground nest every spring by laying from 400 to 1,000 eggs in wax cells, or "combs." Bumblebees also produce honey. Their nests are often dug up and the contents eaten by bears, mice, and other animals.

Now look at the following example.

You will hear:

Why is it impossible to raise red clover where there are no bumblebees?

You will read: (A) Only bumblebees can fertilize red clover plants.
(B) Bumblebees protect red clover from plant eating insects.
(C) Bumblebees bring water to red clover plants on their tongues.
(D) Bumblebees keep mice and other animals away from red clover plants.

The best answer to the question "Why is it impossible to raise red clover where there are no bumblebees?" is (A), "Only bumblebees can fertilize red clover plants." Therefore, you should choose answer (A).

Now look at the next example.

You will hear:

According to the speaker, in what way are the queen wasp and the queen bee similar?

You will read: (A) They both make honey.
(B) They both build combs.
(C) Both of them are found in underground nests.
(D) They both live through the winter.

The best answer to the question "According to the speaker, in what way are the queen wasp and the queen bee similar?" is (D), "They both live through the winter." Therefore, you should choose answer (D).

Questions 36 through 39 refer to the following talk.

I'd like to talk to you about a television program that's going to be shown tonight, and that I want you all to watch. It will present work that's currently being done by geologists off the coast of Hawaii. The only active underwater volcano in the U.S. is located there. It's growing and may reach the surface of the ocean in about 50,000 years—not very long from now in geological time. Anyway, geologists are setting up an unmanned observatory at the top of this volcano, which is located about 70 miles southeast of Hawaii and about 3,000 feet below the surface of the ocean. They plan to install seismometers, thermal sensors, chemical detectors, video cameras, and other equipment to monitor the volcano's activities. Then they'll hook up an electric cable between the observatory and the mainland so they can receive information electronically from these instruments. Geologists are pretty excited about this project, and I hope you are too. It ties in very nicely with the work we've been doing in class on volcanoes. Watch the program about it tonight, and be prepared to discuss it tomorrow.

36. Who is the speaker?
37. What is the main purpose of the television program?
38. How will information get from the observatory to the mainland?
39. Why does the speaker recommend watching the program?

Questions 40 through 44 refer to the following conversation.

W: I thought you were going to take anthropology this semester.
M: I am! Why?
W: Well, I didn't see you in class this morning.
M: That's because I decided to take a course in physical anthropology. Yours is in cultural anthropology, isn't it?
W: That's the name of the course all right, but what's the difference?
M: Well, as I understand it, both kinds of anthropology involve the study of human beings, so they are alike in that way. But, cultural anthropology is the study of human cultures, or the ways of life in societies. For instance, a cultural anthropologist might try to understand family structures or marriage customs in different societies, and other culturally related things like that.
W: Yes, we started talking about family organization around the world on the first day of class.
M: Well, in my class, we started talking about the physical characteristics of humans and some of the ways in which different humans are different in size and shape and so on. That's what physical anthropology is all about. Physical anthropologists are required to include a lot more biology in their approach. I'm a biology major, so I'm more interested in the physical anthropology class.
W: Oh, I see. Well, I'm perfectly happy right where I am, too.

40. What is the main subject of this conversation?
41. Why was the woman surprised when she went to class?
42. Which of the following was most likely a topic of discussion on the first day of the woman's class?
43. Why did the man decide to take the physical anthropology class?
44. How does the woman feel about her class?

Questions 45 through 50 are based on the following talk given on a tour of a factory where clothing materials are made.

Manmade fibers have only been used to make clothing for a little over a century, but their use is quite widespread nowadays. Rayon, the first manmade fiber commercially produced in the United States, appeared in 1910. In 1939, nylon, the first chemically synthesized fiber, was first produced in this country on a commercial basis. Since that time, the number of manmade fibers has expanded to include more than 20 types.

Although the list of manmade clothing fibers is long, rayon remains one of the most popular of all time, and that is why we continue to produce it in such great quantities here. Rayon is made of cellulose, a naturally occurring substance found in cotton and in certain vegetables, like celery, of all things. The cellulose in rayon has been recycled and treated to make it a usable fiber for clothing.

One of the reasons rayon is so popular for clothing is that it is soft and comfortable to wear. Most rayon washes well, too, although it does shrink when it is washed in hot water.

The biggest problem with rayon is that it tends to fade in sunlight. It wouldn't be a good idea to leave a red rayon dress to dry in a sunny window. If you did that for very long, you might come back to a pink dress.

If you'll just step this way, I'd like to show you our rayon production room.

45. What is the main topic of this talk?
46. For how long have manmade fibers been used for clothing?
47. According to the speaker, why does this factory continue to produce rayon?
48. What happens to rayon when it is washed in hot water?
49. According to the speaker, what is the biggest problem with rayon?
50. What is the speaker probably going to do next?

# PRACTICE TEST ONE ANSWER KEY

**1 · 1 · 1 · 1 · 1 · 1 · 1**

## SECTION 1
## LISTENING COMPREHENSION

| | | | |
|---|---|---|---|
| 1. A | 14. D | 27. C | 40. C |
| 2. B | 15. D | 28. D | 41. A |
| 3. C | 16. A | 29. B | 42. D |
| 4. A | 17. C | 30. B | 43. B |
| 5. B | 18. C | 31. C | 44. C |
| 6. B | 19. B | 32. D | 45. B |
| 7. B | 20. D | 33. B | 46. B |
| 8. D | 21. D | 34. A | 47. C |
| 9. A | 22. C | 35. A | 48. B |
| 10. D | 23. C | 36. A | 49. D |
| 11. C | 24. D | 37. A | 50. C |
| 12. B | 25. B | 38. D | |
| 13. A | 26. A | 39. B | |

**2 · 2 · 2 · 2 · 2 · 2 · 2**

## SECTION 2
## STRUCTURE AND WRITTEN EXPRESSION

1. D    See G✔2
Only a verb is needed. (A) contains an unnecessary subordinate clause marker *(which)*. (B) contains an extra subject *(it)*. (C) contains an unnecessary direct object *(it)*.

2. A    See G✔14
A relative pronoun is needed to complete an unfinished adjective clause. (B) contains an adverb clause marker *(where)*. (C) and (D) contain unnecessary prepositions.

3. C    See G✔28
A structure parallel to the prepositional phrase *to their parents* is needed. Only (C) contains such a structure.

4. B    See G✔1
A subject is needed. (A) contains an unnecessary preposition before the subject *(Because of)*. (C) contains an unnecessary clause marker *(which)* after the subject. (D) contains an unnecessary clause marker *(That)* before the subject.

5. B    See G✔1, G✔2, and G✔9
An active verb and a direct object are needed. (A) and (D) contain passive constructions. (C) contains a subordinate clause and a verb.

6. A    See G✔14
Negation of an existing prepositional phrase is needed. No further prepositions or clause markers are needed. (B) contains an additional clause marker. (C) contains an unnecessary additional preposition, and (D) contains an incomplete compound preposition *(instead of)*.

7. C    See G✔14
An introductory prepositional phrase is needed. (A) and (B) consist of main clauses. Two main clauses cannot be joined by a comma. (D) consists of a noun clause subject. There is already a subject, *Henry David Thoreau*.

8. A    See G✔2 and G✔7
Only a finite verb is needed. (B) contains an unnecessary clause marker *(which)* before the verb. (C) contains a subject *(it)* and a verb *(stands)*. (D) is composed of a nonfinite verb form.

9. C    See G✔28
A structure parallel to the gerund *building* is needed. Only (C) contains such a structure.

10. A    See G✔2 and G✔25
A subject and a verb are needed. (B) contains no subject. (C) contains an unnecessary *there are* construction. (D) contains incorrect word order.

11. C    See the Grammar Appendix, #34
A conditional subordinate clause is signaled by the verbs *were* and *could*. *If* is needed to start this conditional.

12. B    See G✔25 and G✔27
Inverted word order is needed after the expression *rarely*. Incorrect word order is used in (A), (C), and (D).

13. B    See G✔15
An appositive is needed to rephrase *Water*. (A) contains an unnecessary verb *(is)*. (C) and (D) contain unnecessary clause markers *(of which* and *which)*.

14. A    See G✔17
An *-ed* adjective to complete the phrase modifying *American Sign Language* is needed. (B), (C), and (D) all contain an unnecessary pronoun *(it)*.

15. A    See G✔9 and G✔10
A correctly formed modal passive is needed. (B) and (C) do not contain correctly formed modal passives. The word order in (D) is incorrect.

16. B    See G✔24
A comparative form is used where a superlative form is needed. Correction: tallest

17. C    See G✔20
A noun form is used where a verb form is needed. Correction: acts

18. A    See G✔11
The singular verb *is* doesn't agree in number with the plural subject *Scientists*. Correction: are

19. A    See G✔20
A noun form is used where an adjective form is needed. Correction: frail

20. B    See G✔14
A preposition is used where an adverb clause marker is needed. Correction: while

21. B    See G✔9
A passive is incorrectly formed. A past participle is needed. Correction: found

22. A    See G✔9 and G✔10
A modal passive is incorrectly formed. Correction: can be based

23. A    See G✔22
An incorrect noun form is used. *Architecture* is the profession. *Architect* is the person who practices this profession. Correction: architect

24. B    See G✔6
A singular noun is used where a plural noun is needed. Correction: women

25. B    See G✔6
A plural noun is used where a singular noun is needed. Correction: bee

26. B    See G✔7 and G✔27
Both *did* and *developed* are in the past tense form. Only *did* needs to show the past tense. Correction: develop

27. C    See G✔7
A nonfinite verb form *(having)* is used where a finite form is needed. Correction: has transcended

28. C    See G✔12
An incorrect preposition is used. Correction: of

29. D    See G✔20
An adjective form is used where a noun form is needed. Correction: prestige

30. B    See G✔18
A gerund is used where an infinitive is needed (When the intended meaning is "in order to," an infinitive is needed.) Correction: to identify

31. A    See G✔20
A verb form is used where a noun form is needed. Correction: computation

32. C    See G✔12
A preposition is missing. Correction: out of essential

33. A    See G✔20
A verb form is used where a noun form is needed. Correction: discovery

34. B    See G✔1
There are two objects for the preposition *to*. The second object *(that)* is unnecessary. Correction: of

35. C    See G✔12
A preposition is missing. Correction: roles in the

36. B    See G✔20
An adverb form is used where an adjective form is needed. Correction: national

37. A    See G✔30
*Farther* is incorrectly being used to refer to extent or degree. *Farther* should be used only to refer to physical distance. In this sentence, extent or degree is being discussed. Correction: Further

38. B    See G✔6
Incorrect adjective-noun word order is used. Correction: humorous commentaries

39. D    See G✔6
A compound adjective is incorrectly formed. *Hundred* is functioning as part of a compound adjective, so it should not be made plural. Correction: hundred

40. B    See G✔20
An adjective form is used where a noun form is needed. Correction: reproduction

---

| 3 | • | 3 | • | 3 | • | 3 | • | 3 | • | 3 | • | 3 |

## SECTION 3
## VOCABULARY AND READING COMPREHENSION

| | | | |
|---|---|---|---|
| 1. D | 9. B | 17. C | 24. B |
| 2. C | 10. B | 18. B | 25. C |
| 3. B | 11. C | 19. D | 26. C |
| 4. A | 12. D | 20. A | 27. B |
| 5. C | 13. B | 21. B | 28. C |
| 6. B | 14. C | 22. A | 29. A |
| 7. A | 15. D | 23. A | 30. C |
| 8. C | 16. D | | |

31. A    See R✔3
The key phrase in the answer is *raising a family*. All the paragraphs in the passage are related to raising a family, from mating to sending the young owls away. (B), (C), and (D) are too specific.

32. B    See R✔6
The reference to the answer is found in paragraph one, lines 5–10, where the courtship is described. All verbs used in this description are verbs of action. To understand the incorrect answer choices refer to: line 7 for (A); lines 2–3 for (C); lines 8–10 for (D).

33. C    See R✔5
The choices are all about nests, which are mentioned in paragraph two. The correct answer (C) is found in lines 11–12. (A) is wrong because the passage says that owls are *poor home builders*, which is the opposite of *discriminate nest builders*. (B) is incorrect because line 15 states that *the mother lays two or three . . . eggs*, in contrast to *numerous eggs*. (D) is not correct because lines 11–12 state that owls *prefer to nest in a large hollow in a tree*, not on the tree limb.

34. C    See R✔5
The correct answer (C) is found in lines 15–17: *she . . . settles herself on the nest.* According to paragraph one, the male initiates the courtship ritual. Lines 20–21 tell us that both parents feed the owlets, and in paragraph two the use of the word *owls* implies that both males and females build nests.

35. D    See R✔5
The correct answer (D) is found in lines 20–23; nuts and seeds are not mentioned. *Beetles* are insects. Birds are mentioned and so are *mice, squirrels, and rabbits*, which are small mammals.

36. C    See R✔6
The correct answer (C) is found in lines 24–25: *and drive the young owls away.* (A) is not true because line 24 states *The parent birds weary of family life*, in contrast to being sorry. (B) is wrong because careless feeding is not implied. (D) is not discussed in the passage.

37. B    See R✔5
The correct answer (B) is found in lines 1–2: *of being hypotheses with a minimum of supporting evidence.* The other answer choices are not mentioned in the passage.

38. B    See R✔5
The correct answer (B) is found by skimming the passage and noting the phrases which signal introduction of main points. Line 2 introduces *One viewpoint*, and line 5 states *Following a different vein.* The rest of the passage describes the second theory of aging, concerning cells.

39. A    See R✔5
The correct answer (A) is found in lines 8–9. The statement that human fibroblasts *divide only a limited number of times and then die* is contrasted to *Only cancer cells seem immortal in this respect.* This concept is similar in meaning to the idea *divide infinitely.*

40. A    See R✔6
The correct answer (A) is found in lines 9–10. An embryo is the earliest form of life. The passage states that *cells from an embryo divide more times that those taken from an adult.* This is similar to saying that *cells from an adult* (a later state in life) *divide fewer times.* (B) is not true: fibroblast cells are used as an example of cellular research. (C) is incorrect: lines 7–9. (D) is incorrect because cells and organ systems are discussed as two different theories of aging.

41. B    See R✔5
The correct answer is (B) because the organ system is central to a theory of aging different from the theory which examines the cellular level. (A), (C), and (D) all are mentioned in the passage in lines 10–14 as support for the cellular theory.

42. B    See R✔6
The correct answer (B) is found by reading the first and last sentences of the paragraph. The first sentence of the paragraph states *There are many theories of aging.* The last sentence of the passage states that other theories of aging exist and is a transition to the next part of the larger passage. The first sentence and the last sentence of this paragraph help the reader to predict that the next part of the discussion will further discuss the theories of aging.

43. B    See R✔2
The correct answer (B) is arrived at by skimming the entire passage to find the main ideas. The three paragraphs all describe a different aspect of preparing for the journey to the West. (A), (C), and (D) are mentioned in the passage as details to further describe aspects of the topic, getting started on the trip West.

44. D    See R✔6
The correct answer (D) can be inferred from lines 1–6: *could either* (travel by steamboat) *or— as happened more often—*(travel by wagon). This tells us that travel was NOT usually by steamboat. (A), (B), and (C) all describe travel East of the Missouri: lines 5–6.

45. B    See R✔6
The correct answer (B) is found in line 11. The town of Independence is the river town that is mentioned first in the passage. (C) and (D) are said to be *upriver* (north) of Independence. Line 11 states that St. Joseph was *55 miles to the northwest* (of Independence). Logical reasoning tells us that this point is farther west than Independence. A second clue is found in lines 11–13, which states that four days travel west could be saved by departing from St. Joe (Joseph), implying that St. Joseph was four days farther west than the other river towns.

46. D    See R✔6

The correct answer (D) is found in line 18 (*A family man usually chose the wagon*) and also in lines 23–24 (*most pioneers, with their farm background, were used to wagons*). To understand why other choices are incorrect refer to: (A) lines 14–16; (B) lines 6–7; (C) lines 7–10 and line 14.

47. B    See R✔5

The correct answer is (B) because the riverboat was mentioned only as transportation to reach Missouri from the East. Lines 16–18 describe the choices of transportation from the jump-off points on the Missouri River to the West, (A), (C), and (D).

48. C    See R✔7

The correct answer is (C). Clues to inferring that inexperienced is the best replacement are found in lines 14–15: *the emigrants studied guidebooks and directions, asked questions of others.* Studying guidebooks and directions, and asking questions of other travelers indicate that the emigrants lacked experience and needed information about the trip West. (A), (B), and (C) do not logically fit in this context.

49. C    See R✔5

The correct answer C is found in lines 19–20 (*but it provided space and shelter for children and for a wife*) and also in lines 23–24 (*most pioneers, with their farm background, were used to wagons*). (A), (B), and (D) are all negative features of a wagon for travel to the West; lines 18–19 and 20–22.

50. C    See R✔2

The correct answer is (C) because the passage discusses the issues of economics, not history, finance, or culture. Key terms are *natural resources, capital, capital accumulation, and savings.*

51. B    See R✔6

The correct answer (B) can be predicted by understanding the first sentence in the passage *Our excellent natural resources paved the way for the development of abundant capital to increase our growth.* The rest of the passage discusses capital and growth. We can predict that the previous passage discussed what was necessary for the accumulation of capital and growth—natural resources. (A) and (C) include ideas which are mentioned in the passage only incidentally and would not need to be discussed in the preceding paragraph. (D) is not at all related to the topic of the passage.

52. D    See R✔5

The correct answer (D) is found in lines 3–4, where capital is described as *machines, vehicles, and buildings.* (A) is a building, (B) is a vehicle. (C) is found in line 4, which states *But it also includes the funds*, where "it" is capital. The only choice not mentioned is (D) workers, which is the correct answer.

53. D    See R✔5

The correct answer is found in lines 8–9: *This process of capital accumulation*, where "this process" refers to lines 6–8: *But if a farmer can grow more corn than his family needs to eat, he can use the surplus as seed to increase the next crop.* (A), (B), and (C) do not result in accumulating capital.

54. C    See R✔6

The correct answer (C) is found in lines 9–10: *Saving played an important role in the European tradition.* Something that people are accustomed to plays an important role. (A), (B), and (D) are not mentioned in the passage as things that the European ancestors of early Americans did.

55. A    See R✔2

The correct answer (A) is the most general of the choices and includes the topics of the three paragraphs in the passage. (B), (C), and (D) are too specific and are mentioned as details in the passage.

56. C    See R✔5

The correct answer (C) is found in lines 1–4: *Sometimes it's hard to figure out if you have a food allergy, since it can show up so many different ways.* "It can show up so many different ways" is similar in meaning to (C) *similarity of symptoms of the allergy to other problems.* (A), (B), and (D) are not true according to the passage.

57. B    See R✔6

The correct answer (B) is found in lines 6–8. The passage states *if these foods are not fed to an infant until her or his intestines mature at around seven months*, which is similar in meaning to (B) *have a carefully restricted diet as infants.* (A), (C), and (D) are not true according to the passage.

58. C    See R✔5

The correct answer (C) is found in lines 6–8. The clause *until her or his intestines mature* is similar in meaning to (C) *underdeveloped intestinal tract.* The other choices are not true according to the passage.

59. D    See R✔5

The correct answer (D) is found in lines 12–14. The other answer choices are not mentioned in the passage as a treatment for migraines.

60. A    See R✔5

The correct answer (A) is found in line 19. *Other researchers have had mixed results when testing whether the diet is effective* is similar in meaning to (A) *NOT verified by researchers as being consistently effective.* (B), (C), and (D) are true for the Feingold diet according to lines 15–19.

# PRACTICE TEST TWO ANSWER KEY

**1 • 1 • 1 • 1 • 1 • 1 • 1**

## SECTION 1
### LISTENING COMPREHENSION

| | | | |
|---|---|---|---|
| 1.  A | 14.  B | 27.  B | 40.  B |
| 2.  D | 15.  C | 28.  D | 41.  D |
| 3.  B | 16.  B | 29.  B | 42.  B |
| 4.  C | 17.  D | 30.  B | 43.  C |
| 5.  D | 18.  A | 31.  A | 44.  A |
| 6.  A | 19.  B | 32.  C | 45.  D |
| 7.  B | 20.  C | 33.  C | 46.  C |
| 8.  B | 21.  A | 34.  D | 47.  A |
| 9.  C | 22.  A | 35.  B | 48.  B |
| 10.  A | 23.  C | 36.  C | 49.  A |
| 11.  D | 24.  D | 37.  C | 50.  D |
| 12.  C | 25.  C | 38.  A | |
| 13.  C | 26.  A | 39.  B | |

**2 • 2 • 2 • 2 • 2 • 2 • 2**

## SECTION 2
### STRUCTURE AND WRITTEN EXPRESSION

1. **B**    See G✔13 and G✔14
An adjective clause using a relative pronoun that refers to *man* is needed. (A) and (C) contain prepositions only. (D) contains a relative pronoun *(which)* that cannot refer to a human noun.

2. **B**    See G✔4 and G✔12
A correctly formed prepositional phrase showing location is needed. The indefinite article is needed before *small midwestern town*. (A), (C), and (D) are missing the preposition, the article, or both.

3. **C**    See G✔12 and G✔14
A preposition is needed to begin the modifying phrase. (A) would change the modifying phrase to a main clause. Two main clauses cannot be joined by a comma. (B) contains an adverb clause marker that cannot be used as a preposition. (D) contains a preposition that doesn't fit the meaning of the sentence.

4. **A**    See G✔1
An article is needed in this sentence to complete the subject. (B) and (D) contain unnecessary clause markers before the article and would change the sentence to a subordinate clause. Subordinate clauses cannot stand alone as sentences. (C) contains an unnecessary preposition before the article and would embed the subject in a prepositional phrase.

5. **C**    See G✔26
Standard subject-verb word order is needed when a question word begins a subordinate clause that is not a direct question. (A), (B), and (D) contain incorrect word order.

6. **D**    See G✔27
Inverted subject-verb word order is needed after the introductory expression of location, *Just off the Massachusetts coast*. Both a subject and a verb are needed to complete the sentence. Incorrect word order is used in (A). (B) contains an unnecessary clause marker *(where)* before the subject. (C) is missing a verb.

7. **B**    See G✔14
(A) would be correct only if *owners* were followed by a period (.) or a semicolon (;). (C) contains a preposition. There is no noun object to complete a prepositional phrase in this sentence. (D) creates a main clause. Two main clauses cannot stand next to each other with no punctuation mark between them.

8. **D**    See G✔25
A main clause using standard subject-verb word order is needed. Incorrect word order is used in (A), (B), and (C).

9. **C**    See G✔15
An appositive noun phrase or noun clause structure is needed to rename *John Updike*. (A) contains an unnecessary verb before the appositive noun phrase. (B) contains an unnecessary relative pronoun before the appositive noun phrase. (D) contains a complete sentence, which cannot function as an appositive.

10. **C**    See G✔13 and G✔14
An adverb clause marker is needed to begin the subordinate clause. (A) and (D) contain prepositions, which cannot be used as adverb clause markers. (B) contains a noun clause marker and would create a noun clause with no place to function as a subject, object, or complement in this sentence.

11. **B**    See G✔1
A subject is needed to complete the main clause of this sentence. (A) contains a relative pronoun, which would change the main clause to an adjective clause. (C) contains a conjunction, which would leave the main clause without a subject. (D) contains a determiner, which cannot function as a subject in this sentence.

12. **C**    See G✔28
A noun structure parallel to the phrases *true empathy* and *commitment to a principle* is needed. Only (C) contains such a structure.

13. D    See G✔13
A preposition is needed to complete the modifying phrase. (A), (B), and (C) contain clause markers.

14. A    See G✔27
Inverted subject-verb word order is needed after the special expression *not only*. Incorrect word order is used in (B), (C), and (D).

15. B    See G✔17
An *-ing* modifying phrase is needed. (A) and (D) would create main clauses. Two main clauses cannot be joined only by a comma. (C) contains a prepositional phrase that does not fit the meaning of the sentence.

16. A    See G✔18
An infinitive is incorrectly formed. Correction: To make

17. C    See G✔20
A verb form is used where a noun form is needed. Correction: shapes

18. B    See G✔6
A singular noun is used where a plural noun is needed. Correction: millions

19. B    See G✔20
A noun form is used where a verb form is needed. Correction: fails

20. A    See G✔18
A gerund is used where a regular noun is needed. Correction: preference

21. D    See G✔5
A masculine pronoun adjective is used where a feminine one is needed to refer to *Mary Rowlandson*. Correction: her

22. C    See G✔20
An adjective form is used where an adverb form is needed. Correction: strategically

23. B    See G✔24
The equative form *so . . . as* is incorrectly formed. Correction: as are

24. C    See G✔30
*On the contrary* is not parallel in meaning to *on the one hand*. Correction: on the other hand

25. A    See G✔7
A nonfinite verb form is used where a finite verb form is needed. Correction: provides

26. B    See G✔10
An infinitive is used after a modal. Modals are not followed by infinitives. Correction: be

27. B    See G✔11
The plural subject, *cabinets and furniture,* doesn't agree in number with the verb *is*. Correction: are

28. A    See G✔18
A gerund is used where a regular noun form is needed. Correction: recommendations

29. B    See G✔6
A singular noun is used where a plural noun is needed. Correction: 100 feet long

30. A    See G✔29
The second half of a paired expression *(neither . . . nor)* is incorrect. Correction: nor

31. D    See G✔30
The pronoun *none* is used where an adjective is needed. Correction: no

32. C    See G✔20
A verb form is used where a noun form is needed. Correction: design

33. D    See G✔12
There are two objects (*it* and *increasing*) for the preposition *for*. Correction: for

34. D    See G✔30
*Similar* is confused with *the same*. Correction: same

35. B    See G✔12
An incorrect preposition is used. Correction: to

36. B    See G✔18
An infinitive is incorrectly formed. Correction: to split

37. A    See G✔30
The first half of the expression *so . . . that* is incorrect. Correction: so

38. C    See G✔26
Inverted word order is used after *how* when it is not needed. Correction: her work would be

39. A    See G✔29
The second half of the expression *from . . . to* is incorrectly formed. Correction: to

40. B    See G✔7 and G✔9
The present perfect passive is incorrectly formed. A form of the verb *have* is needed. Correction: has been given

## SECTION 3
## VOCABULARY AND READING
## COMPREHENSION

| | | | |
|---|---|---|---|
| 1. D | 9. C | 17. B | 24. A |
| 2. D | 10. C | 18. A | 25. D |
| 3. B | 11. A | 19. B | 26. A |
| 4. A | 12. B | 20. B | 27. C |
| 5. C | 13. B | 21. C | 28. A |
| 6. A | 14. C | 22. A | 29. A |
| 7. D | 15. A | 23. C | 30. B |
| 8. B | 16. B | | |

31. A    See R✔2

The correct answer is (A) because this idea is central to the complete passage. Key words and phrases that carry this idea in the passage are found in lines 4–5 (*One of the most remarkable adjustments . . . the tiny kangaroo rat*) and in lines 8–9 (*But it is notable for the parsimony*. (B) and (C) are too general, and (D) is too detailed to be the main idea of this passage.

32. D    See R✔5

The correct answer is (D) because it is the only choice which is not mentioned in the passage. All other choices are found in the passage: (A) in line 4, (B) in lines 7–8, and (C) in lines 3–4.

33. D    See R✔4

The noun *water*, (D), is the referent immediately preceding the pronoun *it*. In addition, water is logically what herbivores find in plants, based on the meaning in the previous sentences.

34. C    See R✔5

The correct answer (C) is the only choice which is NOT mentioned in relation to the kangaroo rat. (A), (B), and (D) are mentioned in lines 5–9.

35. B    See R✔7

In the part of the passage preceding the word *slake*, the concepts discussed are the desert animals and their need for water to live. The immediate context of the word *slake* is *slake their thirst*; thirst is the need for water, and the logical inference is that this need must be satisfied, (B).

36. D    See R✔2

The correct answer (D) is found by quickly reading the passage and noting that the key concepts that are repeated throughout the passage are women who open businesses of their own, and the change in the type of work women have engaged in over the past twenty years. (D) is the only choice that paraphrases these concepts. (A) is a supporting detail in the passage; (B) and (C) are not mentioned in the passage.

37. B    See R✔5

The correct answer (B) can be arrived at by eliminating the answer choices that are mentioned in the passage as detriments to women in the business world. (A), (C), and (D) are mentioned in lines 1–3. (B) is not mentioned in the passage and therefore is the correct answer.

38. A    See R✔5

The correct answer (A) is found by quickly scanning the passage to find the name Charlotte Taylor and then reading carefully lines 12–14, which contain her quotation. The best paraphrase of her point of view—*In the 1970s women believed if . . . Now they've found out that isn't going to happen*— is (A) *unrealistic about their opportunities*. The other answer choices are incorrect according to the passage.

39. C    See R✔3

The correct answer (C) is found in lines 18–21. The discussion of Sandra Kurtzig in the passage points out that she had little money at the beginning of her business venture, in contrast to her later success. Key words in the passage to suggest lack of financial resources are: *housewife* (not a paid occupation), *her office was a bedroom at home* (computer business offices are not usually bedrooms), and *shoebox under the bed to hold the company's cash* (rather than a bank). A shoebox is for shoes, not money. The author uses this comparison to add specific emphasis to the main point about women in business—that their position is improving. (A) and (D) are not true according to the passage, and although (B) is true, it is not related to the shoebox under the bed.

40. B    See R✔7

Lines 26–27 mention a negative concept— women failing in business. The immediate context of the word *hurdles—They still face hurdles in the business world . . . problems . . . is still dominated by men*—contains other negative concepts. (B) is the answer choice that also contains a negative connotation.

41. C    See R✔6

Line 25 in the passage states that *Most businesses owned by women are still quite small*. Lines 27–29 explain the problems women have in business, *especially problems in raising money; the banking and finance world is still dominated by men, and old attitudes die hard*. The implication of the sequencing of this information is that there is a cause and effect relationship—raising money is hard because banks don't lend money, so businesses owned by women are small rather than large. (A), (B), and (D) are not true according to the passage.

42. B   See R✔8
The last lines, 30–31, indicate the author's attitude. From the negative tone of lines 26–29 the author states *But the situation is changing.* Sandra Kurtzig is an example of a successful businesswoman, and the author ends by stating *there are likely to be many more Sandra Kurtzigs in the years ahead.* The attitude conveyed by the author is optimistic.

43. A   See R✔2
The correct answer (A) is arrived at by quickly reading the passage and noting the recurring key concepts which are set out in contrast: the new American literature and the change from traditional to more liberal authors, characters, settings, literary forms, and readers. The conclusion of the passage, in lines 15–19, restates the main idea: *In sum, American literature in these years . . . expands . . . and includes the world. . . connecting an American citizen with the citizens of all nations.* This concept is a change from the earlier, more traditional, and conservative local views implying that the new literature is less provincial than the old.

44. B   See R✔6
The correct answer (B) is found in lines 1–2 —*This transcontinental settlement and these new urban industrial circumstances* which is paraphrased in (B) as *industrialization* and *population shifts. This* and *these* indicate that the concepts of population shifts and industrialization were discussed in the passage immediately preceding.

45. A   See R✔3
The point that the author is making in lines 3-15 is the contrast of the old literature to the new literature. The repetition of the phrase *no longer* introduces each supporting detail; the use of *indeed* adds emphasis to one example—the contrast of the literary forms of the past and the new American literature.

46. C   See R✔6
Lines 3–15 contain many examples of comparison of the new American literature and the old. The phrase of contrast, *no longer,* is repeated to introduce examples of the old tradition in literature and suggest that the new literature was quite different. This is best restated as *the new literature broke with many literary traditions of the past.* (A) is incorrect according to the passage; (B) and (D) are not discussed in the passage.

47. C   See R✔6
The correct answer (C) can be inferred by using the clues in lines 15–19: *the condition Walt Whitman called for in 1867 in describing* Leaves of Grass: *it treats, he said of his own major work.* The passage states that Walt Whitman's description of *Leaves of Grass* is a description of his own major work (his own book). (A) and (D) cannot be inferred from the passage. (B) is untrue according to the passage—Whitman called for the condition which the new literature fulfilled, implying that he approved of it.

48. B   See R✔6
The topic of the passage is literature, specifically American literature. Therefore, (B) is the logical academic course in which the passage would be read.

49. A   See R✔3
The correct answer (A) is found in lines 3–4: *But Boone already exemplified the pioneer at his best.* The rest of the passage describes the character and exploits of Boone. This is restated in (A) as *. . . chronicle the life of a model pioneer.* (B) is not true according to the passage, which tries to present Boone's positive and negative characteristics. Neither (C) nor (D) is the main purpose of the passage. Parts of the passage related to (C) and (D) are an elaboration of specific aspects of Boone's life.

50. C   See R✔6
The correct answer (C) can be inferred by noting the examples of Boone's dealings in land given throughout the passage and the key words used in describing these dealings: in lines 10–21 (*Boone was recruited . . . to undertake a scheme . . . He arranged a deal . . . the scheme . . . was declared illegal and Boone lost his land*) and in lines 22–23 (*he staked out more claims—and lost them because he impatiently neglected to register his deeds*). He was successful in politics, (A), lines 17–19; in hunting and trapping, (B), lines 26–27; and in the military, (D), lines 19–20.

51. B   See R✔6
The correct answer (B) can be inferred from paragraph three. Paragraph two states that Boone lost all his land in Kentucky, which would be a reason for unhappiness. However, in paragraph three, very positive words are used to describe Boone's later life: *Undaunted; Ever hopeful; Old and broke, Boone cheerfully continued hunting and trapping ; Shortly before he died, he was talking knowledgeably . . . about the joys to be experienced in settling California.* (A), (C), and (D) are not true according to the passage.

52. C    See R✔5

The correct answer (C) is found in lines 10–11, *Kentucky;* and in lines 13–17, *Boonesboro.*

53. A    See R✔5

The correct answer (A) is found in lines 10–11 *(There Boone was recruited at age 40 to undertake a scheme designed to open up Kentucky to settlers and establish it as a 14th colony)* and in line 13: *(to Boone's employers, the Transylvania Company).* (B) and (C) are incorrect because they were Boone's own ideas. (D) is incorrect because the Spanish invited Boone to come to Missouri.

54. B    See R✔5

The correct answer (B) is found in lines 25–26, which state *But the Louisiana Purchase, which embraced Missouri, again left him. . . . landless.* The land previously given to Boone was taken away by the Louisiana Purchase. (A) is incorrect—Boone's claim was revoked, not legitimized. (C) is not mentioned in the passage. (D) is incorrect: Missouri was included, not excluded, from the jurisdiction of the Louisiana Purchase.

55. A    See R✔6

The correct answer (A) can be inferred from lines 1–2, which state that Boone's son Nathan had an *elegant stone Missouri farmhouse,* and line 26, which states that Boone, *but not his children,* was left *landless.* Boone ended up *Old and broke* while his son lived in an elegant house and owned land, both of which imply wealth, a good financial condition.

56. A    See R✔8

The correct answer is (A) because the author describes Boone in positive terms throughout the passage. In the first paragraph, the author states that Boone was an example of the *pioneer at his best* and gives examples to support this view. In the last paragraph, Boone is portrayed as *undaunted; hopeful;* and acting *cheerfully*—all positive attributes. This description of Boone reflects an admiring attitude on the part of the author.

57. C    See R✔2

The correct answer is (C) because the words *sweets* and *cavities* are the key concepts developed in the passage. (A) reflects only a part of the passage; (B) is a supporting detail; (D) is too general for the passage.

58. B    See R✔6

The correct answer is (B) because the passage discusses the relation of sweets to cavities and suggests how to reduce the risk of cavities if sweets are eaten. Lines 9–10 state *if these rules are followed when eating sweets.* Following rules implies being careful when eating sweets. (A) is too strong based on the information in the passage; (C) is incorrect according to lines 3–4; (D) is incorrect according to lines 5–6.

59. C    See R✔5

The correct answer (C) is found in lines 8–9. *That scrape off plaque, acting as a toothbrush* is similar in meaning to (C) *remove the plaque from your teeth.* (A), (B), and (D) are not mentioned in the passage.

60. B    See R✔5

The correct answer (B) is found in lines 3–4, which state *The number of times you eat sweets rather than the total amount determines how much harmful acid the bacteria in your saliva produces.* (A) is incorrect because the amount of sweets influences the quality of your saliva, not the amount of acid. (C) and (D) are incorrect because they are not mentioned in the passage as related to acid production.

# PRACTICE TEST THREE ANSWER KEY

## SECTION 1
## LISTENING COMPREHENSION

| | | | |
|---|---|---|---|
| 1. C | 14. B | 27. C | 40. B |
| 2. B | 15. A | 28. B | 41. D |
| 3. B | 16. C | 29. A | 42. B |
| 4. D | 17. B | 30. B | 43. A |
| 5. A | 18. C | 31. D | 44. D |
| 6. C | 19. B | 32. C | 45. C |
| 7. A | 20. A | 33. B | 46. B |
| 8. C | 21. B | 34. C | 47. A |
| 9. D | 22. A | 35. A | 48. D |
| 10. B | 23. C | 36. B | 49. D |
| 11. C | 24. C | 37. D | 50. A |
| 12. D | 25. D | 38. A | |
| 13. D | 26. D | 39. C | |

## SECTION 2
## STRUCTURE AND WRITTEN EXPRESSION

1. C   See G✔1
Only a subject is needed. (A) contains an unnecessary structure (*There are*) before the subject. (B) and (D) contain unnecessary clause markers (*that* and *after*).

2. C   See G✔15
An appositive is needed to rename *anorexia nervosa*. (A) contains an unnecessary finite verb before the appositive. (B) and (D) contain unnecessary clause markers (*which* and *for which*).

3. D   See G✔7 and G✔8
A finite verb in the past tense is needed. (A) and (B) contain nonfinite verbs. (C) contains a verb in the present perfect tense, which doesn't match the meaning of the time marker *In the 1960s.*

4. C   See G✔16 and G✔17
An *-ing* participle is needed to complete the modifying phrase. (A) and (D) contain finite verbs. (B) contains an *-ed* participle.

5. D   See G✔24 and G✔25
A correctly worded comparative structure is needed. (A), (B), and (C) contain incorrect word order.

6. C   See G✔16 and G✔17
An *-ed* adjective phrase is needed. (A) contains a noun phrase. (B) contains a passive verb phrase. (D) contains a prepositional phrase and a main clause.

7. D   See G✔7
Only an active finite verb is needed. (A) and (C) contain nonfinite verb forms. (B) contains a passive verb phrase.

8. D   See G✔24
The comparative degree of *large* needs to be completed. (A) contains an unnecessary verb (*does*). (B) is missing the word *than*, which is needed in comparative degree forms. (C) contains the word *of* instead of *than*.

9. B   See G✔10
A modal passive is needed. Only (B) contains such a structure.

10. D   See G✔30
The adverb *not* is needed to negate the verb *is*.

11. D   See G✔19 and G✔2
(A), (B), and (C) all create subordinate clauses. Subordinate clauses cannot stand alone as sentences. Only (D) creates a main and subordinate clause combination.

12. B   See G✔14
A subordinate clause marker is needed to create a subordinate clause. (A) and (C) create main clauses. Two main clauses cannot be joined by a comma. (D) contains a subordinate clause marker, but the word order is incorrect.

13. B   See G✔2
A subject and a finite verb are needed. (A) contains a subject but no verb. (C) contains an unnecessary clause marker before the verb. (D) contains a nonfinite verb.

14. A   See G✔25
A finite verb followed by a direct object is needed. Incorrect word order is used in (B), (C), and (D).

15. A   See G✔27
Inverted subject-verb word order is needed after the introductory expression of location, *Nestled along the shoreline of Hudson Bay.* Incorrect word order is used in (B), (C), and (D).

16. B   See G✔20
A noun form is used where an adjective form is needed. Correction: injurious

17. C   See G✔11
The verb *are* doesn't agree in number with the singular subject *thing*. Correction: is

18. A   See G✔7 and G✔17.
The past participle of *write* is incorrectly formed. It is needed to begin an *-ed* modifying phrase. Correction: written

19. C    See G✔20 and G✔28
An adjective form is used where a noun form parallel to *ions, minerals,* and *gases* is needed. Correction: of elements

20. B    See G✔7 and Grammar Appendix #15
*Have* is not followed by a past participle. This results in an incorrectly formed present perfect verb. Correction: have been perfecting

21. C    See G✔28
An adjective is used where a noun parallel to *agility* and *ability* is needed. Correction: timidity

22. A    See G✔4
The indefinite article is needed in front of this singular count noun. Correction: a hand tool

23. D    See G✔20
An adverb form is used where an adjective form is needed. Correction: historical

24. A    See G✔11
The singular subject *government* doesn't agree in number with the verb. Correction: uses

25. C    See G✔20 and G✔28
An adjective is used where a noun parallel to *exercise* and *diet* is needed. Correction: heredity

26. C    See G✔13
An incorrect relative pronoun is used to refer to *method. Who* is used to refer to people. Correction: that/which

27. B    See G✔30 and the Grammar Appendix #35
The adjective *alike* is used where a similar-sounding preposition is needed. Correction: like

28. C    See G✔7
A nonfinite verb form is used where a finite verb is needed. Correction: builds on

29. B    See G✔20
A verb form is used where a noun form is needed. Correction: sale

30. A    See G✔17
A noun form is used where a nonfinite verb form is needed. Correction: attempting

31. B    See G✔25
Incorrect verb-complement word order is used. Correction: is unstable

32. C    See G✔5
A reflexive pronoun is incorrectly formed. Correction: themselves

33. A    See G✔11
The plural subject *scholars* doesn't agree in number with the verb. Correction: feel

34. C    See G✔12
An incorrect preposition is used. Correction: to talk about

35. D    See G✔17 and G✔25
Incorrect word order has been used. The adverb should come before the adjective. Correction: strictly controlled

36. C    See G✔4
The indefinite article is spelled incorrectly before a word beginning with a vowel sound. Correction: an interest

37. D    See G✔24
The equative degree of *popular* is incorrectly formed. Correction: as he

38. C    See G✔5
The pronoun *its* doesn't agree in number with the noun it refers to (*birds*). Correction: their

39. B    See G✔7
A nonfinite verb form is used where a finite form is needed. Correction: made it

40. C    See G✔11
The verb *chronicle* does not agree in number with its subject, *(who)*, which refers to a pronoun (*someone*) that takes a singular verb. Correction: chronicles

**3 • 3 • 3 • 3 • 3 • 3 • 3**

SECTION 3
VOCABULARY AND READING
COMPREHENSION

| 1. C | 9. A | 17. C | 24. C |
|---|---|---|---|
| 2. B | 10. C | 18. C | 25. A |
| 3. B | 11. C | 19. B | 26. A |
| 4. B | 12. C | 20. D | 27. A |
| 5. A | 13. A | 21. A | 28. D |
| 6. A | 14. D | 22. C | 29. D |
| 7. D | 15. C | 23. D | 30. C |
| 8. B | 16. D | | |

31. D    See R✔2
The correct answer (D) is arrived at by quickly reading the passage and noting the key words and repeated concepts in paragraph one (*photographer, pioneer era, farm photos, Butcher's Pioneer History*) and in paragraph two (*photographer, portraits, pioneers*). (D) is the only answer choice that contains all the key concepts.

**32. D   See R✔5**

The correct answer (D) is found by scanning the passage to find the jobs that Butcher had. In line 5 *newspaper* is mentioned, but not as a job that Butcher held. (A) is found in line 1 (*sodbuster* is another word for *farmer*) and line 7; (B) in lines 2–3 (*an album of his fellow settlers* means that he was also a settler); and (C) in line 2 and implied throughout the passage.

**33. C   See R✔5**

The correct answer (C) is found in lines 8–9: *But his genius as a photographer lay in allowing them to pose as they wished, against scenes of their own choosing*. The rest of paragraph two states that *The portraits that resulted convey the dignity of pioneers . . . and they remain a classic record of a resolute breed*. These positive statements imply that Butcher was famous for this aspect of his photography.

**34. A   See R✔6**

The correct answer (A) is found in lines 7–11. The phrases *pose as they wished, against scenes of their own choosing*; and *in challenging circumstances* suggest that (A) realistic is the best answer. Answer choices (B), (C), and (D) are not implied in the passage.

**35. C   See R✔4**

In the context of the clause *they remain a classic record of a resolute breed*, logical reasoning tells us that what is a record is not the pioneers but the portraits of the pioneers. Therefore, (C) is the correct answer.

**36. A   See R✔3**

The correct answer (A) is arrived at by quickly reading the whole passage to find key points and relationships. Lines 1–5 introduce the concept of the row house; lines 5–7 describe the row house in New York; and lines 7–18 describe the row house of California. The phrases *In contrast* (line 7) and *which were as important to sun-loving San Franciscans as brownstone fronts were to New Yorkers* (lines 14–16) indicate that contrast is made between the two forms. (B) and (C) are not correct according to the passage, and (D) is too general to be the purpose of the passage.

**37. A   See R✔5**

The correct answer is (A) is found in lines 1–5. In lines 1–2 we note that *speculative builders discovered a bonanza in the form of the row house*; a bonanza implies a profit. Lines 3–5 tell us why: *these dwellings cost relatively little to build because . . .* (B) is only part of the reason; (C) and (D) are not related in the passage to the low cost or profit.

**38. B   See R✔6**

The correct answer is (B) because the other answer choices are all mentioned as true in the passage: (A) in lines 2–5 (*shared common walls with their neighbors; many could be erected side by side*) and in line 6 (*rose block after block of row houses*); (C) in line 2 (*discovered a bonanza in the form of the row house*); and (D) in lines 4–5 (*could be erected side by side on a narrow street frontage* which implies no space between the street and the building for a yard).

**39. A   See R✔6**

The correct answer (A) can be inferred by noting the features of New York row houses and California row houses in the passage. Lines 6–7 mention that New York row houses were *faced with brownstone*, which means these exterior walls were made of brownstone—a material lacking in color. Line 7 states that *In contrast, California houses had coats of bright paint* (lines 7–8). Logical reasoning tells us the brownstone of New York is less colorful than the bright paint of California.

**40. B   See R✔5**

The correct answer is (B) because of the relation in meaning of ostentatious decoration (particularly showy, highly decorated or attention getting) and the critics' comparison of the California row houses to the *puffing, paint and powder of our female friends*. Both statements have negative connotations.

**41. C   See R✔6**

The correct answer (C) is inferred from lines 14–18 (*windows, which were as important to sun-loving San Franciscans as brownstone fronts were to New Yorkers*) and later in the conclusion (*California architecture . . . should rightly be called the "bay-window order"*). This labeling of the architecture according to the feature of windows indicates the great importance of windows in California row houses.

**42. C   See R✔2**

The correct answer (C) is found by quickly reading the passage to note the key words and central concept. In paragraph one, we find *desert, creatures of the desert*, and *water*; in paragraph two, *desert, large animals*, and *creatures*. In paragraph three, the pronouns refer to desert animals, and lines 16–19 describe animal behavior in the desert. (A) is not mentioned in the passage; (B) is a supporting detail; and (D) is mentioned only briefly in paragraph one.

43. A    See R✔7
The correct answer (A) can be inferred by
understanding the sentences before and after
line 7. Lines 2–3 tell us there is little water in the
desert (*crucial problem ; survive . . . . sources of
flowing water are rare*). Line 5 state that some
creatures pass their entire lives without a single
drop, implying a dry environment. Lines 7–8
tell us *no moist skinned, water-loving animal can
exist there*, again implying the drying effect of
the desert. (B) contradicts the information in the
passage; (C) is too extreme, since we know that
life exists in the desert; and (D) is too general.

44. C    See R✔5
The correct answer is (C) because it is not mentioned in the passage. (A) and (B) are found in
lines 16–19: *pass the burning hours asleep in cool,
humid burrows (underground homes of animals)* and
*but 18 inches down the temperature is only 60 degrees*.
(D) is found in lines 11–12: *Its population are . . .
silent, filled with reticence, and ruled by stealth*.

45. A    See R✔5
The correct answer (A) is found in lines 8–11.
Key phrases are *Few large animals are found* and
*it holds more swift-footed, running, leaping
creatures*. Words of similar meaning in answer
choice (A) are *smaller and fleeter*. (B), (C), and
(D) are not true according to the passage.

46. B    See R✔7
The correct answer is (B) because *they* refers
to *Its population*, which means the desert
population. The previous context and logical
reasoning tell us that (A), (C), and (D) are not
possible referents for *they*.

47. B    See R✔6
The correct answer (B) is found by logically
deciding which generalizations are too general.
Lines 5–15 support (B). In this part of the
passage, it is established that humans need water
to live, that water is rare in the desert, and that
desert animals adjust to these conditions. (A) and
(C) are too broad to be concluded from the
passage. (D) is not supported in the passage.

48. A    See R✔2
The correct answer (A) is arrived at by quickly
reading the passage and noting key words and
concepts, especially in the topic sentences of the
passage, lines 1–4, and the concluding sentence.
In lines 1–4 we find *Oregon, dispute, argument,
originated in the fact that the boundaries of Oregon
had never been clearly fixed*. In lines 24–25, we find
*So they quietly settled for the 49th parallel, the
boundary that the United States had proposed in the
first place*. The other answer choices are incorrect
according to the passage: (B) is implied as
incorrect in lines 7–9; (C) is a supporting detail;
and (D) is not true according to the passage.

49. D    See R✔7
In the context of line 6, *clearly fixed* is used in
relation to the boundaries of Oregon. Lines 5–7
go on to explain the lack of precision of the
boundaries: *The name vaguely embraced the
territory*. In the context of lines 3–7, logical
reasoning leads us to answer choice (D). (A)
and (C) are not appropriate replacements for
the context of the passage, and (B) is logically
incorrect.

50. C    See R✔4
The correct answer is (C) because the main idea
of paragraph one is the dispute between the
United States and Great Britain over Oregon's
boundaries. *The issue* in line 12 refers to this
concept, which was established in the previous
paragraph. (A) is not mentioned in paragraph
one; (B) is incorrect because Alaska was not
claimed by the United States according to the
passage; and (D) is not correct because going to
war was one proposed solution to the problem.

51. C    See R✔5
The correct answer (C) is found by checking the
passage for the facts: (A) is found in lines 1–3; (B)
in lines 15–21, which link Polk, the president-
elect, with expansionist views; (D) in lines 12 –
13. (C) is NOT true according to lines 13–15:
*Though many eastern Americans considered Oregon
country too remote to become excited about, demands
for its occupation were shouted with almost religious
fervor*, which implies two different views existed.

52. B    See R✔6
The correct answer (B) is found in lines 15–17:
*Senator Thomas Hart Benton, for one, (for example)
urged Congress . . . to muster rifles* to settle the issue
of the Oregon boundary. Use of rifles is similar in
meaning to *by force*. The other answer choices are
not possible according to the passage. (A) is
incorrect because a temperate man would not
advocate the use of rifles; (C) is not correct
because using rifles precludes negotiation; and
(D) is not true according to the passage.

53. D    See R✔5
The correct answer is (D) because lines 20–25
mention (A), (B), and (C) as conditions which
led to the peaceful settlement of the dispute. In
addition, logical reasoning tells us that a desire
for a good fight would NOT have led to the
peaceful settlement of the dispute which the
passage describes.

54. A    See R✔6

The correct answer (A) is found in lines 7–10 (*In 1818 when America proposed a boundary at the 49th parallel—an extension of the border with Canada that already existed east of the Rockies—and the British suggested a line farther south*) and in lines 24–25 (*So they quietly settled for the 49th parallel, the boundary that the United States had proposed in the first place*). The conclusion is that the United States got only what it originally asked for.

55. B    See R✔2

The correct answer is (B) because after the general introduction to glaciers in paragraph one, paragraphs two, three, and four of the passage describe how glaciers are formed. The topic sentence of each of these paragraphs supports (B). Lines 8–9 state the conditions for formation of glaciers. Lines 17–18 tell about *the time required for the creation of glacier ice*, and lines 23–26 describe the *critical thickness* necessary for ice to become a true glacier in order for it to begin to move. (A) and (D) are mentioned only in paragraph one, and (C) is mentioned in paragraph 4.

56. C    See R✔3

The correct answer (C) is found in paragraph one, which gives a general definition and classification of glaciers, pointing out the age of glaciers. Lines 5–6 state that *most glaciers are remnants of great shrouds of ice that covered the earth eons ago*. In lines 6–7, the author becomes more specific (*In a few of these glaciers the oldest ice*), and in line 7, the author uses Antarctica as an example of an extremely old glacier.

57. A    See R✔5

The correct answer is (A) because an analogy is a comparison of one process to a similar, perhaps more familiar, process. In line 8 we find: *Glaciers are born in rocky wombs above the snow line*. Lines 9–11 state *The long gestation period of the glacier begins*. Lines 16–17 state that the process *continues throughout the life of the glacier*. *Born, womb,* and *gestation* (a term of pregnancy leading to birth) are used by the author to establish the lengthy process of the formation of a glacier as similar to that leading to birth. (B) and (C) are used as descriptive details in the formation of the glacier, not as analogies. (D) is mentioned in a separate paragraph and is not related to the analogy.

58. B    See R✔5

The correct answer (B) is found by checking the facts in the passage. (B) is found in lines 2–5. (A), (C), and (D) are not mentioned in the passage.

59. B    See R✔4

The correct answer is (B) because the context of the sentence describes the formation of a glacier from ice; when the ice moves under its own weight, the ice has become a glacier.

60. C    See R✔5

The item asks what characteristic identifies a glacier. The correct answer (C) is stated in lines 23–24: *The ice does not become a glacier until it moves under its own weight.* (A), (B), and (D) are factors which contribute to causing the ice to move.

# PRACTICE TEST FOUR ANSWER KEY

## SECTION 1
## LISTENING COMPREHENSION

| | | | |
|---|---|---|---|
| 1. C | 14. A | 27. B | 40. C |
| 2. C | 15. A | 28. C | 41. A |
| 3. B | 16. A | 29. D | 42. B |
| 4. D | 17. A | 30. D | 43. A |
| 5. B | 18. C | 31. A | 44. B |
| 6. C | 19. D | 32. C | 45. C |
| 7. D | 20. C | 33. C | 46. A |
| 8. D | 21. D | 34. A | 47. D |
| 9. B | 22. C | 35. A | 48. B |
| 10. B | 23. D | 36. B | 49. B |
| 11. D | 24. B | 37. D | 50. C |
| 12. C | 25. C | 38. A | |
| 13. C | 26. B | 39. D | |

## SECTION 2
## STRUCTURE AND WRITTEN EXPRESSION

1. A    See G✔14

   The adverb clause needs to be completed. A clause marker, subject, and verb are needed to do so. (B) contains a compound preposition, which cannot be followed by an adjective (in this case, *noncorrosive*). (C) contains a subject and a verb, but no clause marker. (D) contains a clause marker, but no subject or verb.

2. D    See G✔15

   A noun subject is needed to come before the appositive *cultural diffusion*. (A) and (B) contain nonfinite verb forms which cannot be subjects in this sentence. (C) contains an unnecessary preposition (*To*) before the subject.

3. D    See G✔14

   The adverb clause needs to be completed. A clause marker, subject, and verb are needed to do so. (A) contains a subject and verb, but no clause marker. (B) and (C) contain question word order, which is not needed.

4. C    See G✔18

   A gerund subject is needed. (A) contains the *-ing* verb form, but it is being used as a participle, not a gerund. The subject of (B) is *Those*, which does not agree with the verb *promotes*. (D) contains an unnecessary preposition (*for*) before the gerund.

5. D    See G✔25, G✔1, and G✔2

   A verb followed by its complement is needed. (A) contains incorrect word order. (B) and (C) contain the unnecessary pronoun *it*.

6. B    See G✔19, G✔11, and G✔1

   A verb and direct object are needed. (A) contains a verb only. (C) contains a verb and object, but the verb does not agree with the subject *Spectrographs*. (D) contains a passive construction.

7. A    See G✔24

   A correctly formed equative structure is needed. (B) contains a superlative structure. Incorrect word order is used in (C). (D) includes no structures of comparison.

8. B    See G✔2

   Only a finite verb is needed. (A) contains an unnecessary subject (*they*) before the verb. (C) contains an unnecessary clause marker (*which*) before the verb. (D) contains a nonfinite verb form.

9. B    See G✔2

   A subject and a verb are needed. (A) contains a subject, *potassium*, which does not fit the meaning of the sentence. (C) and (D) contain the unnecessary clause marker *Since*.

10. B    See G✔7

   Only an active finite verb is needed. (A) contains both a subject and a verb. (C) contains a nonfinite verb. (D) contains a passive verb form.

11. B    See G✔17

   A main clause is needed that has a subject that can be modified by the adjective phrase *Declared an endangered species in the United States*. In (A), *people* is the subject. It is not people who have been declared an endangered species, so (A) is incorrect. (C) and (D) also contain subjects (*extinction*) and (*gathering*) which cannot be endangered species. Only (B) contains a subject (*ginseng root*) which could be an endangered species.

12. D    See G✔15.

   A direct object followed by its appositive phrase is needed. (A) contains an entire main clause. (B) contains an unnecessary verb. (C) contains an unnecessary clause marker.

13. A    See G✔18 and G✔25.

   An appropriate object for the preposition *by* is needed. (B) contains a past participle, which cannot be the object of a preposition. (C) contains a main clause, which also cannot be the object of a preposition. (D) contains incorrect word order. The gerund in (A) can be the direct object of a preposition.

14. C    See G✔15
A subject is needed to be renamed by the appositive *ceiling joists*. (A) contains a prepositional phrase. (B) contains a passive verb form. (D) contains an infinitive, which cannot be renamed by the appositive.

15. B    See G✔12
The correct preposition is needed to begin the prepositional phrase. The prepositions in (A), (C), and (D) are incorrect.

16. B    See G✔20
A verb form is used where a noun form is needed. Correction: accumulation

17. D    See G✔28
A gerund is used where a noun parallel in structure to *society* and *culture* is needed. Correction: behavior

18. B    See G✔14 and G✔19
The noun clause following *it* is incorrectly formed. An adverb clause marker has been used where a noun clause marker is needed. Correction: that

19. B    See G✔20
An adjective form is used where an adverb form is needed. Correction: innately

20. D    See G✔20
An adjective form is used where a verb form is needed. Correction: save

21. D    See G✔30
*Either* is used to refer to one out of two things. In this sentence, two things (*metal* and *glass*) are both being referred to. Correction: for both

22. A    See G✔12
An incorrect preposition is used. Correction: for

23. B    See G✔13
An unnecessary preposition precedes the relative pronoun. Correction: that

24. B    See G✔12
An incorrect preposition is used. Correction: in/into

25. A    See G✔20
An adverb form is used where an adjective form is needed. Correction: poor

26. A    See G✔7
The past participle form of *see* is used where the past form is needed. Correction: saw

27. A    See G✔30
The expression *so . . . that* is incorrectly formed. Correction: so

28. B    See G✔5
The pronoun *they* does not agree in number with the noun (*writing*) that it refers to. Correction: it

29. A    See G✔6
Incorrect adjective-noun word order is used. Correction: Metropolitan newspapers

30. C    See G✔5
An object pronoun is used where a possessive adjective is needed. Correction: for his

31. A    See G✔14
A subordinate clause marker is used where a preposition is needed. Correction: During

32. A    See G✔20
A verb form is used where an adjective form is needed. Correction: promotional

33. B    See G✔18
An infinitive is incorrectly formed. Correction: to open

34. C    See G✔6
A singular noun is used where a plural noun is needed. Correction: years

35. B    See G✔24
The superlative degree of *little* is incorrectly formed. Correction: at least

36. C    See G✔6
A singular noun is used where a plural noun is needed. Correction: feet

37. D    See G✔28
An infinitive is used where a noun parallel to *intelligence* is needed. Correction: experience

38. B    See G✔4
The indefinite article is used in an expression that does not need it. Correction: night

39. B    See G✔3
*Much*, an expression of quantity, should be used only with uncountable nouns. In this sentence, *much* is being used with a plural countable noun (*amino acids*). Correction: many

40. B    See G✔30
The adverb *also* is used where a conjunction is needed. Correction: and

## SECTION 3
## VOCABULARY AND READING COMPREHENSION

| | | | |
|---|---|---|---|
| 1. A | 9. D | 17. B | 24. D |
| 2. B | 10. C | 18. B | 25. D |
| 3. C | 11. B | 19. B | 26. B |
| 4. A | 12. C | 20. A | 27. B |
| 5. A | 13. D | 21. B | 28. B |
| 6. A | 14. D | 22. A | 29. A |
| 7. C | 15. B | 23. A | 30. C |
| 8. B | 16. D | | |

31. D    See R✔3

The correct answer (D) is found by reading the passage quickly to note the key concepts and relationships of swans, mute swans, and the problem they are causing. Paragraph one gives general information on North American swans; paragraph two introduces mute swans and the problem: *increasing by an alarming 30 to 40 percent annually; destroy a pond's plant life and drive away native waterfowl*. The third paragraph adds more facts about the danger of mute swans to the environment: *which can burden delicate and environmentally essential brackish ponds*. (A) is too general for the purpose of this passage; (B) is incorrect because the passage goes beyond description; (C) is not correct according to this passage.

32. C    See R✔5

The correct answer (C) is found in lines 9–11: (*increasing by an alarming 30 to 40 percent*) and in lines 17–19 (*can nest in pairs of as many as three or four on one small coastal pond, which can burden . . .*). (A) is a fact that is not related to the environmental problem. (B) and (D) are facts about swans that are of concern only when there are too many mute swans.

33. C    See R✔5

The correct answer (C) is stated in lines 15–16: *uninhabited summer ground for nesting and feeding* is best restated *unpopulated areas*. (A) is incorrect because it is the opposite of uninhabited. (B) is not mentioned in the passage, and (D) is untrue according to lines 13–17.

34. A    See R✔5

The correct answer is (A) because the other answer choices are mentioned as features of swans in the passage: (B) in lines 15–19; (C) in paragraphs one and two; and (D) in lines 3–10.

35. C    See R✔5

The correct answer is (C) according to lines 3–6, which describe the trumpeter swan. The phrase *was nearly wiped out* is similar in meaning to *was close to extinction*.

36. B    See R✔6

The correct answer is (B) according to lines 12–14 (*with their tendency to destroy a pond's plant life and drive away native waterfowl, might create havoc*) and lines 18–19 (*which can burden . . . ponds*). (A) is incorrect because the passage states that numbers of mute swans are increasing and does not compare them to other types of swans; (C) is implied as not true because of the problems the mute swans pose for coastal ponds and waterfowl; (D) is implied as untrue in line 12: *the majestic white creatures*. Majestic implies an attractive appearance.

37. B    See R✔6

The correct answer (B) can be inferred because the tone of the article is one of concern. Key words are *alarming, create havoc, burden delicate ponds*. The issue the author writes about is the problem that the mute swans create.

38. A    See R✔2

The correct answer (A) is found by reading the passage quickly for key concepts and relationships. Both paragraph one and paragraph two describe the Uruk writing system. (B) is incorrect because the passage mentions the Summerians as originators of the writing system, but then uses the example of the Uruk to describe the writing system at length. (C) and (D) are details used in the description of the Uruk writing system.

39. B    See R✔4

*There* refers to the most recently mentioned place. In lines 1–2, the phrase *Summerians of Mesopotamia* establishes the place as Mesopotamia.

40. B    See R✔5

The correct answer is (B) because the other answer choices are mentioned in the passage as things on which early writing was inscribed: (A) in lines 3–4; (C) and (D) in lines 5–6. According to line 7, *characters* were what were inscribed on a surface.

41. A    See R✔5

The correct answer (A) is found in lines 10–11. *Incised* is similar in meaning to *cut into*. In the context of the passage, *incised with the pointed end of the stylus* is a clue to the meaning of *incised*. (B) and (D) are not mentioned in the passage, and (C) refers to numerical signs, according to line 9.

42. B    See R✔6

The correct answer is (B) because the whole passage refers in a fairly technical way to fats and the function of fats in the body, which is in the field of nutrition. Lines 15–16 conclude with a reference to nutrients and nutritionists. (A) and (C) are incorrect because the passage gives more information about fats than would be of use to a reader of a diet book or of a cookbook. (D) is incorrect because the information on fats is too formal and specific to be found in a popular women's magazine.

43. C    See R✔5

The correct answer is (C) because all other answer choices are mentioned in lines 2–3.

44. D    See R✔5
The correct answer is (D), which is not mentioned in the passage. Other answer choices are mentioned in the passage as functions that fats serve; (A) in lines 4–6; (B) in lines 7–8; and (C) in line 1.

45. A    See R✔5
The correct answer (A) is found in lines 10–11: *When rats are fed a fat-free diet, their growth eventually ceases.* The other answer choices are not mentioned in the passage.

46. A    See R✔5
The correct answer (A) is found in lines 15–16: *Most nutritionists consider linoleic fatty acid an essential nutrient for humans.* The other answer choices are not true according to the passage.

47. B    See R✔5
The correct answer (B) is found in lines 10–11: *Whether a certain amount of fat in the diet is essential to human health is not definitely known.* This is best restated as *not yet a proven fact.* (A) and (C) are not mentioned in the passage; (D) is not correct according to lines 14–15.

48. B    See R✔3
The correct answer is (B) because paragraph one of the passage describes technique, and paragraph two describes style. The relation of the two aspects of dance in the passage is stated in lines 1–2 (*In our discussion of dance, it might be valuable to contrast style with another word often employed by dancers: technique*) and in lines 10–11 (*If technique . . . (then) style*).

49. C    See R✔6
The correct answer (C) is found in lines 1–2: *In our discussion of dance, it might be valuable to contrast style with another word.* The use of *In our discussion* implies the passage is a continuation of a previous discussion of dance. The phrase *contrast style with another word* also suggests style in dance had been discussed earlier. (A) and (B) are mentioned in the passage as details in the discussion of technique in dance. (D) is not mentioned in the passage.

50. A    See R✔6
The correct answer (A) can be inferred from these passages in lines 4–8: *Some dances may contain only the most elementary steps; the experimental Judson Dance Theater . . . that consist of nothing but such basic actions as walking or running.*

51. A    See R✔5
The correct answer is (A) because (B), (C), and (D) are mentioned in the passage: (B) in lines 16–19; (C) in lines 14–16 (*predilections* is similar in meaning to *preference* (s)); and (D) in lines 12–14.

52. D    See R✔4
The correct answer (D) can be arrived at checking the context in which the word *work* is used. In the sentences *Many things can affect the style of a work: for instance* and *The style of an abstract dance may also be determined*, we can

infer from context that a *work* has style and that style is being discussed in relation to dance. The main point in this paragraph is that dances are organized and choreographed. (A), (B), and (C) are not logical replacements in this context.

53. A    See R✔2
The correct answer is (A) because the "white plague" is used in line 1 to describe destructive hailstorms. The other answer choices do not reflect the topic or the main ideas of the passage.

54. C    See R✔7
The meaning of *it wipes you out* can be found by checking the context of the phrase in paragraph one. Lines 1–2 state that sudden destruction of crops can be caused by hail, which is what *wipes you out*. Line 4 state that this loss of crops ready to harvest leaves you without a penny—in financial ruin. We can infer that *wipes you out* means financial disaster.

55. D    See R✔6
The correct answer (D) can be inferred from lines 5–6: *Thousands of hailstorms occur each year, especially in the moist, temperate climates of the middle latitudes.* Of the answer choices, only (D) is similar in meaning to the moist, temperate climates of the middle latitudes. Logical reasoning also tells us that the middle latitudes have moderate climates, not dry, tropical, or arctic climates.

56. B    See R✔5
The correct answer (B) can be found in lines 10–12: *the air is at first so pure that water droplets can exist at temperatures well below the freezing point without turning to ice.*

57. B    See R✔6
The correct answer (B) can be inferred from lines 16–19, which describe the formation of a hailstone: *Buffeted about by a series of updrafts and downdrafts, the hailstone gathers layer upon layer of ice. When it has grown so heavy that even the strongest updraft.* This description can best be restated as cumulative.

58. C    See R✔5
The correct answer (C) is found in lines 17–19: *When it has grown so heavy that even the strongest updraft cannot sustain it, the mature hailstone plummets to earth.*

59. B    See R✔6
The correct answer (B) is found in line 20: *While weak storms produce small stones that melt before reaching the ground.* Because the stones are small (in size), they melt quickly.

60. C    See R✔4
The correct answer is (C) is found by checking the context of the sentence: *When the amazing specimen was sent to Colorado's National Center for Atmospheric Research, meteorologists confirmed that it set a new record for size . . .* Logical reasoning tells us that the new record for size was set by the specimen stone, not the storm or the National Center for Atmospheric Research.

# PRACTICE TEST FIVE ANSWER KEY

## SECTION 1
## LISTENING COMPREHENSION

| | | | |
|---|---|---|---|
| 1. B | 14. C | 27. D | 40. C |
| 2. C | 15. C | 28. C | 41. A |
| 3. A | 16. B | 29. B | 42. B |
| 4. C | 17. A | 30. A | 43. C |
| 5. B | 18. D | 31. B | 44. D |
| 6. D | 19. A | 32. B | 45. B |
| 7. C | 20. D | 33. D | 46. B |
| 8. D | 21. D | 34. C | 47. C |
| 9. A | 22. B | 35. A | 48. A |
| 10. B | 23. C | 36. C | 49. C |
| 11. A | 24. D | 37. B | 50. D |
| 12. A | 25. B | 38. B | |
| 13. D | 26. B | 39. A | |

## SECTION 2
## STRUCTURE AND WRITTEN EXPRESSION

1. **D** See G✔14
A preposition is needed to complete an unfinished prepositional phrase. (A) contains an article. (B) and (C) contain clause markers (*Because* and *When*) rather than prepositions.

2. **C** See G✔2
A subject and the *be* part of a passive are needed. Only (C) contains both of these elements.

3. **D** See G✔28
A structure parallel to the gerunds *influencing*, *maintaining*, and *changing* is needed. Only (D) contains such a structure.

4. **B** See G✔4 and G✔1
Only an article is needed to complete the subject of this sentence. (A) embeds the subject in a prepositional phrase. (C) embeds the subject in a subordinate clause. (D) does not contain an article.

5. **B** See G✔14
A relative pronoun is needed to complete an unfinished relative clause. (A) contains a conjunction. (C) contains a subject pronoun. There is already a subject, *Depressant drugs*. (D) contains an unnecessary preposition before the relative pronoun.

6. **D** See G✔12, G✔14, and G✔26
A subordinate clause needs to be completed. The word order in (A) is incorrect, because it creates a question. (B) and (C) create main clauses. Two main clauses cannot be joined by a comma.

7. **C** See G✔14
A completed modifier is needed to describe *organic compounds*. (A) creates a noun clause, and (B) creates a main clause. These clause types do not act as modifiers. (D) contains an unnecessary object *(them)*. Only (C) creates a relative clause which can modify *organic compounds*.

8. **D** See G✔14
A correctly formed subordinate clause or a modifying phrase is needed. (A) and (B) create main clauses. Two main clauses cannot be joined by only a comma. (C) contains only part of a subordinate clause. Only (D) contains a correctly formed modifying prepositional phrase.

9. **B** See G✔14
An object is needed for the preposition *because of*. (A) contains a main clause, which cannot be the object of a preposition. (C) contains an incorrect *of* phrase. (D) contains an adjective phrase, which cannot be the object of a preposition.

10. **A** See G✔9
Only a correctly formed passive verb is needed. (B) and (C) contain nonfinite verb forms. (D) contains an unnecessary subject *(they)* before the passive verb.

11. **C** See G✔6 and G✔24
A singular word is needed to describe the singular *instinct*. (A), (B), and (D) contain words that describe plurals.

12. **C** See G✔17
A main clause is needed that contains *llamas* as its subject, to be modified by the phrase *considered unique and exotic*. (A) and (B) contain the subject *over 4,000 American households*. (D) is not a complete main clause. It is missing the verb *is*, which is necessary to complete the passive verb construction *is kept*.

13. **B** See G✔18 and G✔1
A simple direct object for the infinitive *to cause* is needed. (A) contains another infinitive, which would need to be preceded by an indirect object (e.g., to cause people to sleep fitfully). (C) does not contain a direct object noun structure. It contains an adjective and a prepositional phrase. In (D), *sleep* is a noun direct object followed by the adverb *fitfully*. Adverbs do not modify nouns.

14. C    See G✔15
An appositive to rename *One of the most influential Virginians of colonial times* and a verb are needed. Only (C) contains these two structures together.

15. D    See G✔14 and G✔28
Two parallel structures, *merge* and *produce*, need to be joined together. Only (D) contains a structure (a coordinating conjunction) that can be used to join these two structures.

16. C    See G✔6
Incorrect adjective-noun word order is used. Correction: powerful forces

17. C    See G✔9
A passive is incorrectly formed. Correction: are

18. A    See G✔18
A gerund is used where a regular noun is needed. Correction: discovery

19. C    See G✔20 and G✔30
An incorrect adjective form is used. *Four* does not show order or sequence. Correction: fourth

20. C    See G✔28
A structure parallel to the subject-verb combination *which is* is needed to form the equative. The subject is missing in the second half of this equative comparison. Correction: as it is

21. A    See G✔14
A noun clause marker is needed to start the noun clause that is the object of the preposition *of*. An adjective clause marker (a relative pronoun) has been used instead. Correction: of what

22. A    See G✔5
An object pronoun is used where a reflexive pronoun is needed. Correction: himself

23. B    See G✔18
An infinitive is incorrectly formed. Correction: to provide

24. A    See G✔29
The second part of the paired expression *neither . . . nor* is incorrectly formed. Correction: nor

25. B    See G✔30
The adverb *also* is used where a conjunction is needed. Correction: and

26. B    See G✔13 and G✔14
A relative pronoun is needed to begin the adjective clause that modifies *liquids*. A noun clause marker has been used instead. Correction: that/which

27. C    See G✔7
A nonfinite verb form is used where a finite

verb form is needed. Correction: encourage

28. C    See G✔11
The verb *increase* doesn't agree in number with its singular subject, *specialization*. Correction: increases

29. D    See G✔6
A plural noun is used with the indefinite article *a*. This article is used only with singular countable nouns. Correction: location

30. A    See G✔12
Part of a compound preposition is missing. Correction: In accordance with the

31. C    See G✔20
An adverb form is used where an adjective form is needed. Correction: successive

32. A    See G✔24
The comparative degree of *low* is formed incorrectly. Correction: lower

33. D    See G✔20 and G✔30
An incorrect noun form is used. *Percentage* is not used to indicate specific amounts (in this case, *nine*). Correction: percent

34. D    See G✔20
A noun form is used where an adjective form is needed. Correction: rough

35. C    See G✔30
An intensifier is incorrectly used. *Such* is an intensifier which is used before nouns. *Similar* is an adjective, not a noun. Correction: so

36. B    See G✔18
A finite verb form is used where a gerund is needed. Correction: expecting

37. D    See G✔14
A clause marker (*as soon as*) is used but is not followed by a clause. Correction: as soon as they arrive

38. D    See G✔30
The adjective *another* is used with singular countable nouns. *Sources* is a plural noun. Correction: other

39. A    See G✔13
A compound adverb clause marker is incorrectly formed. Correction: though

40. C    See G✔12
An incorrect preposition is used. Correction: on

## SECTION 3
## VOCABULARY AND READING
## COMPREHENSION

| | | | |
|---|---|---|---|
| 1. C | 9. B | 17. B | 24. A |
| 2. D | 10. A | 18. C | 25. D |
| 3. B | 11. B | 19. B | 26. D |
| 4. B | 12. C | 20. B | 27. B |
| 5. C | 13. B | 21. B | 28. A |
| 6. A | 14. C | 22. C | 29. B |
| 7. B | 15. C | 23. B | 30. C |
| 8. D | 16. C | | |

**31. B    See R✔2**
The correct answer (B) is found by quickly reading the passage to find key words and main ideas. Paragraph one discusses prehistoric man and his first use of plants and animals. Lines 6–7 connect the ideas in paragraph one and the main idea of the passage: *humans began to organize their knowledge of nature into the broad field of natural history.* (A) and (D) are too specific to be the title. (C) is too general to be the title.

**32. A    See R✔5**
The correct answer is (A) because lines 1–3 state: *Long ago prehistoric man began to domesticate a number of wild plants and animals for his own use. This not only provided more abundant food but also* . . . (B), (C), and (D) are not mentioned as reasons for domestication of plants and animals in the passage.

**33. C    See R✔6**
The correct answer (C) can be inferred from lines 8–10. Lines 8–9 tell us: *One aspect of early natural history concerned the use of plants for drugs and medicine.* This sentence establishes the specific topic of *plants for drugs and medicine.* The next sentence introduces "The early herbalists." The sequencing of information in the passage implies a direct relationship between plants and medicine and the early herbalists. This inference is supported by the details in the rest of the passage about how herbalists used plants as medicine.

**34. D    See R✔6**
The correct answer (D) can be inferred from lines 9–15. Lines 9–10 state that the early herbalists *sometimes overworked their imaginations in this respect* (plants for drugs and medicine). This information is followed by an example of "overworked imaginations": *it was widely believed that a plant or part of a plant that resembled an internal organ would cure ailments of that organ.* The inference that this belief is not well founded is further supported by the contrast word *Nevertheless* in line 14 of the conclusion.

**35. B    See R✔6**
The correct answer (B) can be concluded by noting that the topic and key concepts (natural history, use of plants for drugs and medicine) are in the area of (B) (biology) rather than (A), (C), or (D).

**36. A    See R✔3**
The correct answer is (A) because each of the other answer choices is too specific to be the purpose of the whole passage. The three paragraphs give different information about interpreting: paragraph one gives an explanation of what it is not, and a definition; paragraph two gives an example to illustrate the complexity of interpreting; and paragraph three discusses two kinds of interpreters. This is a broad range of information and is best stated as an explanation of the scope of interpreting.

**37. A    See R✔6**
The correct answer (A) can be inferred from lines 1–3: *Simply being bilingual does not qualify someone to interpret. Interpreting is not merely a mechanical process of converting one sentence in language A into the same sentence in language B. Rather, it's a complex art.* The tone of this information implies that the author is not just stating information but is developing a persuasive argument to convince someone that interpreting is complex, not simple.

**38. C    See R✔3**
The correct answer is (C) in lines 3–6. Lines 5–6 state that interpreting must be done *in such a way that the message is clearly and accurately expressed to the listener.* In this context, "the message" is similar to "the meaning" in (C). Lines 7–10 give an example of an idiom whose correct interpretation depended on *an idiom that the Spanish understood and that conveyed the same idea.* "The same idea" in this context is similar to "the meaning."

**39. B    See R✔6**
The correct answer (B) can be inferred from line 1: *Simply being bilingual does not qualify someone to interpret.* This statement implies that being bilingual is a basic qualification, but not the only qualification. (C) is incorrect according to lines 15–17, which state that consecutive interpreters do not need *high-tech gear.* (A) and (D) are not discussed in the passage.

40. A    See R✔6
The correct answer (A) can be inferred from lines 15–20. Lines 16–17 state that consecutive interpreters are *mainly employed for smaller meetings*. Line 18 state that *consecutive interpretation requires two-person teams*. Lines 18–20 describe the transaction between two people using a consecutive interpreter.

41. C    See R✔6
The correct answer (C) can be inferred from lines 11–15, which describe the work of a simultaneous interpreter. Lines 12–13 state: *The former*, (referring to a simultaneous translator) *sitting in an isolated booth . . . Speaks to listeners who wear headphones*.

42. B    See R✔5
The correct answer (B) is found by comparing lines 12–13, which describe a simultaneous interpreter as *usually at a large multilingual conference*, with lines 16–17, which describe a consecutive interpreter as *mainly employed for smaller meetings*.

43. A    See R✔2
The correct answer (A) is found by quickly reading the passage for key concepts. Each paragraph of the passage contains the ideas of forest soil and life in the soil—line 1: *Watching for wildlife in the forest*; lines 2–3: *overlooking the living world in the soil beneath our feet*; line 5: *But life bustles down below*; line 11: *leaving more organic matter to fuel the folks downstairs*; line 12: *the soil protects its tenants*; line 17: *Earthworms and ants are the champion earth-movers*. (B) is too specific. (C) and (D) are not specific enough to be the topic of this passage.

44. A    See R✔6
The correct answer (A) can be inferred from lines 5–6: *But life bustles down below: a cubic inch of topsoil may contain billions of creatures*. Logical reasoning tells us that a cubic inch of topsoil containing billions of creatures is very densely inhabited.

45. B    See R✔5
The correct answer (B) is found in lines 8–10: *Soil-dwelling bacteria and fungi break down dead organic matter into molecules that aboveground plants use for food*. This is best restated in (B) as "provide food for plant life."

46. C    See R✔5
The correct answer is (C) because all of the other answer choices are mentioned in the passage as things the soil protects creatures against. (A) in lines 13–14 (*predators* is similar in meaning to *enemies*); (B) and (D) in lines 12–13.

47. B    See R✔6
The correct answer is (B) because lines 18–19 tells us that *While ants travel relatively far from their nests, earthworms work small areas*. This is best restated in (B) as (ants) are more mobile than earthworms."

48. D    See R✔6
The correct answer (D) is found throughout the passage in the use of parts of a building to designate parts of the forest or forest soil—line 2: *ground floor, rafters*; line 4: *basement*; lines 7–8: *forest floor, upstairs, downstairs*; line 12: *a well-insulated house*.

49. C    See R✔2
The correct answer (C) is found by quickly reading the passage to establish the key concepts. Paragraph one is a very short introduction to two house types in the same historical period; paragraph two develops one of these in length—the Cape Cod house. For this reason, (A) is incorrect. (B) is not discussed for both house types. (D) is a supporting detail in the discussion of the Cape Cod house.

50. B    See R✔6
The correct answer (B) is found in lines 4–5: *both varieties enjoyed widespread popularity, and their derivatives are still with us today*. "Their derivatives" refers to the same housing form as it appears today. (A) and (C) are not true according to the passage. (D) is incorrect according to the description in the passage of Cape Cod houses as modest and unpretentious.

51. B    See R✔5
The correct answer is (B) because of the description of the Cape Cod house in paragraph one as modest and unpretentious, which is similar in meaning to free from affectation. This is supported later in the passage in line 12 (*In Cape communities where pretension was abhorred*) and in the description of the Cape Cod house by a Bostonian, lines 14–19.

52. C    See R✔7
The correct answer (C) can be arrived at by the context of the passage in lines 12–19. Lines 12–14 state: *In Cape communities, where pretension was abhorred, and where the homes of captain and crewman were undifferentiated, even painted clapboards were considered "showy."* We can conclude that *showy* must be similar in meaning to what Cape communities disliked—pretension.

53. B    See R✔6

The correct answer (B) is a restatement of the view expressed in lines 15–19: *seem of an unsuitable inferiority of style to those who live in them; a remarkable republican simplicity in the style; little distinction that betokens wealth; equality that extends to everything.* (A), (C), and (D) are not mentioned or implied in the passage.

54. D    See R✔6

The correct answer (D) is correct according to paragraph one of the passage. The introduction in paragraph one introduces two house types—the log cabin and the Cape Cod house; paragraph two discusses the Cape Cod house, and it is logical to predict that the next paragraph will discuss the log cabin.

55. B    See R✔5

The correct answer is (B) is found in lines 2–4: *Aaron Copland succeeded so well in assimilating the materials of American folk song into his own highly personal style that, in the eyes of the world, he came to be regarded as "the" American composer of his time.* (A), (B), and (C) are facts about Copland that are less important than his work with American themes in his music.

56. D    See R✔5

The correct answer (D) can be arrived at by noting that the other answer choices are mentioned in the passage. (A) in lines 21–22; (B) in line 22; and (C) in line 21.

57. B    See R✔5

The correct answer (B) is found in lines 14–16 in which we learn that the most productive phase of Copland's career is due to the fact that *He realized that a new public for modern music was being created by the new media of radio, phonograph, and film scores.*

58. D    See R✔5

The correct answer (D) is found in lines 16–18: *Copland was therefore led to what became a most significant development after the 1930s; the attempt to simplify the new music in order that it would have meaning for a large public.*

59. B    See R✔4

The correct answer is (B) because *these*, in line 21, means *three ballets; an orchestral piece;* and *a series of film scores.* In the preceding sentence, *scores* is the only possible referent.

60. C    See R✔6

The correct answer (C) is found in Copland's quotation in lines 26–28: *Because we live here and work here, we can be certain that when our music is mature it will also be American in quality.* This is best restated in (C).

# SCORE CONVERSION TABLES

Use TOEFL Score Conversion Table 1 below to estimate your TOEFL scores for each section of each of the practice tests in this book.

## Score Conversion Table 1

| Number Correct (Cs) | Converted Score Section 1 | Converted Score Section 2 | Converted Score Section 3 |
|---|---|---|---|
| 60 | _____ | _____ | 67 |
| 59 | _____ | _____ | 67 |
| 58 | _____ | _____ | 66 |
| 57 | _____ | _____ | 66 |
| 56 | _____ | _____ | 65 |
| 55 | _____ | _____ | 64 |
| 54 | _____ | _____ | 63 |
| 53 | _____ | _____ | 62 |
| 52 | _____ | _____ | 61 |
| 51 | _____ | _____ | 61 |
| 50 | 68 | _____ | 60 |
| 49 | 66 | _____ | 59 |
| 48 | 64 | _____ | 58 |
| 47 | 63 | _____ | 58 |
| 46 | 61 | _____ | 57 |
| 45 | 61 | _____ | 56 |
| 44 | 60 | _____ | 56 |
| 43 | 59 | _____ | 55 |
| 42 | 58 | _____ | 54 |
| 41 | 57 | _____ | 54 |
| 40 | 56 | 68 | 53 |
| 39 | 55 | 67 | 53 |
| 38 | 55 | 66 | 52 |
| 37 | 54 | 64 | 51 |
| 36 | 53 | 62 | 51 |
| 35 | 52 | 60 | 50 |
| 34 | 51 | 59 | 50 |
| 33 | 51 | 58 | 49 |
| 32 | 50 | 56 | 49 |
| 31 | 49 | 55 | 48 |
| 30 | 49 | 54 | 47 |
| 29 | 48 | 54 | 46 |
| 28 | 48 | 52 | 45 |
| 27 | 47 | 51 | 45 |
| 26 | 47 | 50 | 44 |
| 25 | 46 | 49 | 43 |
| 24 | 46 | 48 | 42 |
| 23 | 45 | 47 | 41 |
| 22 | 44 | 46 | 41 |
| 21 | 44 | 45 | 40 |
| 20 | 43 | 44 | 39 |
| 19 | 43 | 43 | 38 |
| 18 | 42 | 42 | 37 |
| 17 | 41 | 41 | 36 |
| 16 | 40 | 40 | 35 |
| 15 | 40 | 39 | 34 |
| 14 | 39 | 38 | 33 |
| 13 | 37 | 37 | 32 |
| 12 | 36 | 36 | 31 |
| 11 | 35 | 34 | 30 |
| 10 | 34 | 34 | 29 |
| 9 | 33 | 32 | 28 |
| 8 | 32 | 30 | 27 |
| 7 | 31 | 29 | 26 |
| 6 | 30 | 28 | 25 |
| 5 | 29 | 26 | 214 |
| 4 | 28 | 25 | 24 |
| 3 | 27 | 24 | 23 |
| 2 | 25 | 22 | 22 |
| 1 | 24 | 21 | 21 |
| 0 | 20 | 20 | 20 |

Use TOEFL Score conversion Table 2 below to estimate your Total TOEFL score for each of the practice tests in this book.

| Score Conversion Table 2 |
| --- |

Your total score is equal to:

$$\frac{\text{Section 1 Converted Score} + \text{Section 2 Converted Score} + \text{Section 3 Converted Score}}{3} \times 10 = \textbf{Your Score}$$

Following is an example of how the Score Conversion Tables work.

Sample Score Conversion

Mika, a student who has just finished taking Practice Test One, had the following section scores:

Section 1
Number Correct = 27          Converted Score = 47
Using Score Conversion Table 1, she finds that her converted Section 1 score is 47.

Section 2
Number Correct = 29          Converted Score = 54
Using Score Conversion Table 1, she finds that her converted Section 2 score is 54.

Section 3
Number Correct = 40          Converted Score = 53
Using Score Conversion Table 1, she finds that her converted Section 3 score is 53.

Using Score Conversion Table 2, Mika can estimate her total TOEFL score for Practice Test One.

$$\frac{47 + 54 + 53}{3} = 51.3 \times 10 = 513$$

Mika's estimated TOEFL score is 513.

**Special Note About the Meaning of Converted TOEFL Scores**
Converted TOEFL scores are only estimates of scores you would actually receive on a TOEFL. If your converted score goes down from one test to the next, it may mean that the second test was slightly more difficult than the first or that you were not concentrating quite as well during the second test. Use converted scores only to judge approximately how well you would do on an official TOEFL. Do not be overly concerned about differences in estimated TOEFL scores.

# Complete Practice TOEFL Test Answer Sheet

**Name** (print)_____

Choose only one answer for each question. Carefully fill in the oval corresponding to the answer you choose so that the letter inside the oval cannot be seen. Completely erase any other marks you may have made. Choose only one answer for each question.

| CORRECT | WRONG | WRONG | WRONG | WRONG |
|---|---|---|---|---|
| Ⓐ Ⓑ ● Ⓓ | Ⓐ Ⓑ ⊗ Ⓓ | Ⓐ Ⓑ Ⓒ Ⓓ | Ⓐ Ⓑ ⊖ Ⓓ | Ⓐ Ⓑ ⊘ Ⓓ |

## SECTION 1

1 Ⓐ Ⓑ Ⓒ Ⓓ
2 Ⓐ Ⓑ Ⓒ Ⓓ
3 Ⓐ Ⓑ Ⓒ Ⓓ
4 Ⓐ Ⓑ Ⓒ Ⓓ
5 Ⓐ Ⓑ Ⓒ Ⓓ
6 Ⓐ Ⓑ Ⓒ Ⓓ
7 Ⓐ Ⓑ Ⓒ Ⓓ
8 Ⓐ Ⓑ Ⓒ Ⓓ
9 Ⓐ Ⓑ Ⓒ Ⓓ
10 Ⓐ Ⓑ Ⓒ Ⓓ
11 Ⓐ Ⓑ Ⓒ Ⓓ
12 Ⓐ Ⓑ Ⓒ Ⓓ
13 Ⓐ Ⓑ Ⓒ Ⓓ
14 Ⓐ Ⓑ Ⓒ Ⓓ
15 Ⓐ Ⓑ Ⓒ Ⓓ
16 Ⓐ Ⓑ Ⓒ Ⓓ
17 Ⓐ Ⓑ Ⓒ Ⓓ
18 Ⓐ Ⓑ Ⓒ Ⓓ
19 Ⓐ Ⓑ Ⓒ Ⓓ
20 Ⓐ Ⓑ Ⓒ Ⓓ
21 Ⓐ Ⓑ Ⓒ Ⓓ
22 Ⓐ Ⓑ Ⓒ Ⓓ
23 Ⓐ Ⓑ Ⓒ Ⓓ
24 Ⓐ Ⓑ Ⓒ Ⓓ
25 Ⓐ Ⓑ Ⓒ Ⓓ
26 Ⓐ Ⓑ Ⓒ Ⓓ
27 Ⓐ Ⓑ Ⓒ Ⓓ
28 Ⓐ Ⓑ Ⓒ Ⓓ
29 Ⓐ Ⓑ Ⓒ Ⓓ
30 Ⓐ Ⓑ Ⓒ Ⓓ
31 Ⓐ Ⓑ Ⓒ Ⓓ
32 Ⓐ Ⓑ Ⓒ Ⓓ
33 Ⓐ Ⓑ Ⓒ Ⓓ
34 Ⓐ Ⓑ Ⓒ Ⓓ
35 Ⓐ Ⓑ Ⓒ Ⓓ
36 Ⓐ Ⓑ Ⓒ Ⓓ
37 Ⓐ Ⓑ Ⓒ Ⓓ
38 Ⓐ Ⓑ Ⓒ Ⓓ
39 Ⓐ Ⓑ Ⓒ Ⓓ
40 Ⓐ Ⓑ Ⓒ Ⓓ
41 Ⓐ Ⓑ Ⓒ Ⓓ
42 Ⓐ Ⓑ Ⓒ Ⓓ
43 Ⓐ Ⓑ Ⓒ Ⓓ
44 Ⓐ Ⓑ Ⓒ Ⓓ
45 Ⓐ Ⓑ Ⓒ Ⓓ
46 Ⓐ Ⓑ Ⓒ Ⓓ
47 Ⓐ Ⓑ Ⓒ Ⓓ
48 Ⓐ Ⓑ Ⓒ Ⓓ
49 Ⓐ Ⓑ Ⓒ Ⓓ
50 Ⓐ Ⓑ Ⓒ Ⓓ

## SECTION 2

1 Ⓐ Ⓑ Ⓒ Ⓓ
2 Ⓐ Ⓑ Ⓒ Ⓓ
3 Ⓐ Ⓑ Ⓒ Ⓓ
4 Ⓐ Ⓑ Ⓒ Ⓓ
5 Ⓐ Ⓑ Ⓒ Ⓓ
6 Ⓐ Ⓑ Ⓒ Ⓓ
7 Ⓐ Ⓑ Ⓒ Ⓓ
8 Ⓐ Ⓑ Ⓒ Ⓓ
9 Ⓐ Ⓑ Ⓒ Ⓓ
10 Ⓐ Ⓑ Ⓒ Ⓓ
11 Ⓐ Ⓑ Ⓒ Ⓓ
12 Ⓐ Ⓑ Ⓒ Ⓓ
13 Ⓐ Ⓑ Ⓒ Ⓓ
14 Ⓐ Ⓑ Ⓒ Ⓓ
15 Ⓐ Ⓑ Ⓒ Ⓓ
16 Ⓐ Ⓑ Ⓒ Ⓓ
17 Ⓐ Ⓑ Ⓒ Ⓓ
18 Ⓐ Ⓑ Ⓒ Ⓓ
19 Ⓐ Ⓑ Ⓒ Ⓓ
20 Ⓐ Ⓑ Ⓒ Ⓓ
21 Ⓐ Ⓑ Ⓒ Ⓓ
22 Ⓐ Ⓑ Ⓒ Ⓓ
23 Ⓐ Ⓑ Ⓒ Ⓓ
24 Ⓐ Ⓑ Ⓒ Ⓓ
25 Ⓐ Ⓑ Ⓒ Ⓓ
26 Ⓐ Ⓑ Ⓒ Ⓓ
27 Ⓐ Ⓑ Ⓒ Ⓓ
28 Ⓐ Ⓑ Ⓒ Ⓓ
29 Ⓐ Ⓑ Ⓒ Ⓓ
30 Ⓐ Ⓑ Ⓒ Ⓓ
31 Ⓐ Ⓑ Ⓒ Ⓓ
32 Ⓐ Ⓑ Ⓒ Ⓓ
33 Ⓐ Ⓑ Ⓒ Ⓓ
34 Ⓐ Ⓑ Ⓒ Ⓓ
35 Ⓐ Ⓑ Ⓒ Ⓓ
36 Ⓐ Ⓑ Ⓒ Ⓓ
37 Ⓐ Ⓑ Ⓒ Ⓓ
38 Ⓐ Ⓑ Ⓒ Ⓓ
39 Ⓐ Ⓑ Ⓒ Ⓓ
40 Ⓐ Ⓑ Ⓒ Ⓓ

## SECTION 3

1 Ⓐ Ⓑ Ⓒ Ⓓ         31 Ⓐ Ⓑ Ⓒ Ⓓ
2 Ⓐ Ⓑ Ⓒ Ⓓ         32 Ⓐ Ⓑ Ⓒ Ⓓ
3 Ⓐ Ⓑ Ⓒ Ⓓ         33 Ⓐ Ⓑ Ⓒ Ⓓ
4 Ⓐ Ⓑ Ⓒ Ⓓ         34 Ⓐ Ⓑ Ⓒ Ⓓ
5 Ⓐ Ⓑ Ⓒ Ⓓ         35 Ⓐ Ⓑ Ⓒ Ⓓ
6 Ⓐ Ⓑ Ⓒ Ⓓ         36 Ⓐ Ⓑ Ⓒ Ⓓ
7 Ⓐ Ⓑ Ⓒ Ⓓ         37 Ⓐ Ⓑ Ⓒ Ⓓ
8 Ⓐ Ⓑ Ⓒ Ⓓ         38 Ⓐ Ⓑ Ⓒ Ⓓ
9 Ⓐ Ⓑ Ⓒ Ⓓ         39 Ⓐ Ⓑ Ⓒ Ⓓ
10 Ⓐ Ⓑ Ⓒ Ⓓ        40 Ⓐ Ⓑ Ⓒ Ⓓ
11 Ⓐ Ⓑ Ⓒ Ⓓ        41 Ⓐ Ⓑ Ⓒ Ⓓ
12 Ⓐ Ⓑ Ⓒ Ⓓ        42 Ⓐ Ⓑ Ⓒ Ⓓ
13 Ⓐ Ⓑ Ⓒ Ⓓ        43 Ⓐ Ⓑ Ⓒ Ⓓ
14 Ⓐ Ⓑ Ⓒ Ⓓ        44 Ⓐ Ⓑ Ⓒ Ⓓ
15 Ⓐ Ⓑ Ⓒ Ⓓ        45 Ⓐ Ⓑ Ⓒ Ⓓ
16 Ⓐ Ⓑ Ⓒ Ⓓ        46 Ⓐ Ⓑ Ⓒ Ⓓ
17 Ⓐ Ⓑ Ⓒ Ⓓ        47 Ⓐ Ⓑ Ⓒ Ⓓ
18 Ⓐ Ⓑ Ⓒ Ⓓ        48 Ⓐ Ⓑ Ⓒ Ⓓ
19 Ⓐ Ⓑ Ⓒ Ⓓ        49 Ⓐ Ⓑ Ⓒ Ⓓ
20 Ⓐ Ⓑ Ⓒ Ⓓ        50 Ⓐ Ⓑ Ⓒ Ⓓ
21 Ⓐ Ⓑ Ⓒ Ⓓ        51 Ⓐ Ⓑ Ⓒ Ⓓ
22 Ⓐ Ⓑ Ⓒ Ⓓ        52 Ⓐ Ⓑ Ⓒ Ⓓ
23 Ⓐ Ⓑ Ⓒ Ⓓ        53 Ⓐ Ⓑ Ⓒ Ⓓ
24 Ⓐ Ⓑ Ⓒ Ⓓ        54 Ⓐ Ⓑ Ⓒ Ⓓ
25 Ⓐ Ⓑ Ⓒ Ⓓ        55 Ⓐ Ⓑ Ⓒ Ⓓ
26 Ⓐ Ⓑ Ⓒ Ⓓ        56 Ⓐ Ⓑ Ⓒ Ⓓ
27 Ⓐ Ⓑ Ⓒ Ⓓ        57 Ⓐ Ⓑ Ⓒ Ⓓ
28 Ⓐ Ⓑ Ⓒ Ⓓ        58 Ⓐ Ⓑ Ⓒ Ⓓ
29 Ⓐ Ⓑ Ⓒ Ⓓ        59 Ⓐ Ⓑ Ⓒ Ⓓ
30 Ⓐ Ⓑ Ⓒ Ⓓ        60 Ⓐ Ⓑ Ⓒ Ⓓ

# Complete Practice TOEFL Test Answer Sheet

**Name** (print)_____

Choose only one answer for each question. Carefully fill in the oval corresponding to the answer you choose so that the letter inside the oval cannot be seen. Completely erase any other marks you may have made. Choose only one answer for each question.

| CORRECT | WRONG | WRONG | WRONG | WRONG |
|---|---|---|---|---|
| Ⓐ Ⓑ ● Ⓓ | Ⓐ Ⓑ Ⓧ Ⓓ | Ⓐ Ⓑ Ⓒ Ⓓ | Ⓐ Ⓑ ⊖ Ⓓ | Ⓐ Ⓑ ⊘ Ⓓ |

## SECTION 1

1 Ⓐ Ⓑ Ⓒ Ⓓ
2 Ⓐ Ⓑ Ⓒ Ⓓ
3 Ⓐ Ⓑ Ⓒ Ⓓ
4 Ⓐ Ⓑ Ⓒ Ⓓ
5 Ⓐ Ⓑ Ⓒ Ⓓ
6 Ⓐ Ⓑ Ⓒ Ⓓ
7 Ⓐ Ⓑ Ⓒ Ⓓ
8 Ⓐ Ⓑ Ⓒ Ⓓ
9 Ⓐ Ⓑ Ⓒ Ⓓ
10 Ⓐ Ⓑ Ⓒ Ⓓ
11 Ⓐ Ⓑ Ⓒ Ⓓ
12 Ⓐ Ⓑ Ⓒ Ⓓ
13 Ⓐ Ⓑ Ⓒ Ⓓ
14 Ⓐ Ⓑ Ⓒ Ⓓ
15 Ⓐ Ⓑ Ⓒ Ⓓ
16 Ⓐ Ⓑ Ⓒ Ⓓ
17 Ⓐ Ⓑ Ⓒ Ⓓ
18 Ⓐ Ⓑ Ⓒ Ⓓ
19 Ⓐ Ⓑ Ⓒ Ⓓ
20 Ⓐ Ⓑ Ⓒ Ⓓ
21 Ⓐ Ⓑ Ⓒ Ⓓ
22 Ⓐ Ⓑ Ⓒ Ⓓ
23 Ⓐ Ⓑ Ⓒ Ⓓ
24 Ⓐ Ⓑ Ⓒ Ⓓ
25 Ⓐ Ⓑ Ⓒ Ⓓ
26 Ⓐ Ⓑ Ⓒ Ⓓ
27 Ⓐ Ⓑ Ⓒ Ⓓ
28 Ⓐ Ⓑ Ⓒ Ⓓ
29 Ⓐ Ⓑ Ⓒ Ⓓ
30 Ⓐ Ⓑ Ⓒ Ⓓ
31 Ⓐ Ⓑ Ⓒ Ⓓ
32 Ⓐ Ⓑ Ⓒ Ⓓ
33 Ⓐ Ⓑ Ⓒ Ⓓ
34 Ⓐ Ⓑ Ⓒ Ⓓ
35 Ⓐ Ⓑ Ⓒ Ⓓ
36 Ⓐ Ⓑ Ⓒ Ⓓ
37 Ⓐ Ⓑ Ⓒ Ⓓ
38 Ⓐ Ⓑ Ⓒ Ⓓ
39 Ⓐ Ⓑ Ⓒ Ⓓ
40 Ⓐ Ⓑ Ⓒ Ⓓ
41 Ⓐ Ⓑ Ⓒ Ⓓ
42 Ⓐ Ⓑ Ⓒ Ⓓ
43 Ⓐ Ⓑ Ⓒ Ⓓ
44 Ⓐ Ⓑ Ⓒ Ⓓ
45 Ⓐ Ⓑ Ⓒ Ⓓ
46 Ⓐ Ⓑ Ⓒ Ⓓ
47 Ⓐ Ⓑ Ⓒ Ⓓ
48 Ⓐ Ⓑ Ⓒ Ⓓ
49 Ⓐ Ⓑ Ⓒ Ⓓ
50 Ⓐ Ⓑ Ⓒ Ⓓ

## SECTION 2

1 Ⓐ Ⓑ Ⓒ Ⓓ
2 Ⓐ Ⓑ Ⓒ Ⓓ
3 Ⓐ Ⓑ Ⓒ Ⓓ
4 Ⓐ Ⓑ Ⓒ Ⓓ
5 Ⓐ Ⓑ Ⓒ Ⓓ
6 Ⓐ Ⓑ Ⓒ Ⓓ
7 Ⓐ Ⓑ Ⓒ Ⓓ
8 Ⓐ Ⓑ Ⓒ Ⓓ
9 Ⓐ Ⓑ Ⓒ Ⓓ
10 Ⓐ Ⓑ Ⓒ Ⓓ
11 Ⓐ Ⓑ Ⓒ Ⓓ
12 Ⓐ Ⓑ Ⓒ Ⓓ
13 Ⓐ Ⓑ Ⓒ Ⓓ
14 Ⓐ Ⓑ Ⓒ Ⓓ
15 Ⓐ Ⓑ Ⓒ Ⓓ
16 Ⓐ Ⓑ Ⓒ Ⓓ
17 Ⓐ Ⓑ Ⓒ Ⓓ
18 Ⓐ Ⓑ Ⓒ Ⓓ
19 Ⓐ Ⓑ Ⓒ Ⓓ
20 Ⓐ Ⓑ Ⓒ Ⓓ
21 Ⓐ Ⓑ Ⓒ Ⓓ
22 Ⓐ Ⓑ Ⓒ Ⓓ
23 Ⓐ Ⓑ Ⓒ Ⓓ
24 Ⓐ Ⓑ Ⓒ Ⓓ
25 Ⓐ Ⓑ Ⓒ Ⓓ
26 Ⓐ Ⓑ Ⓒ Ⓓ
27 Ⓐ Ⓑ Ⓒ Ⓓ
28 Ⓐ Ⓑ Ⓒ Ⓓ
29 Ⓐ Ⓑ Ⓒ Ⓓ
30 Ⓐ Ⓑ Ⓒ Ⓓ
31 Ⓐ Ⓑ Ⓒ Ⓓ
32 Ⓐ Ⓑ Ⓒ Ⓓ
33 Ⓐ Ⓑ Ⓒ Ⓓ
34 Ⓐ Ⓑ Ⓒ Ⓓ
35 Ⓐ Ⓑ Ⓒ Ⓓ
36 Ⓐ Ⓑ Ⓒ Ⓓ
37 Ⓐ Ⓑ Ⓒ Ⓓ
38 Ⓐ Ⓑ Ⓒ Ⓓ
39 Ⓐ Ⓑ Ⓒ Ⓓ
40 Ⓐ Ⓑ Ⓒ Ⓓ

## SECTION 3

1 Ⓐ Ⓑ Ⓒ Ⓓ        31 Ⓐ Ⓑ Ⓒ Ⓓ
2 Ⓐ Ⓑ Ⓒ Ⓓ        32 Ⓐ Ⓑ Ⓒ Ⓓ
3 Ⓐ Ⓑ Ⓒ Ⓓ        33 Ⓐ Ⓑ Ⓒ Ⓓ
4 Ⓐ Ⓑ Ⓒ Ⓓ        34 Ⓐ Ⓑ Ⓒ Ⓓ
5 Ⓐ Ⓑ Ⓒ Ⓓ        35 Ⓐ Ⓑ Ⓒ Ⓓ
6 Ⓐ Ⓑ Ⓒ Ⓓ        36 Ⓐ Ⓑ Ⓒ Ⓓ
7 Ⓐ Ⓑ Ⓒ Ⓓ        37 Ⓐ Ⓑ Ⓒ Ⓓ
8 Ⓐ Ⓑ Ⓒ Ⓓ        38 Ⓐ Ⓑ Ⓒ Ⓓ
9 Ⓐ Ⓑ Ⓒ Ⓓ        39 Ⓐ Ⓑ Ⓒ Ⓓ
10 Ⓐ Ⓑ Ⓒ Ⓓ       40 Ⓐ Ⓑ Ⓒ Ⓓ
11 Ⓐ Ⓑ Ⓒ Ⓓ       41 Ⓐ Ⓑ Ⓒ Ⓓ
12 Ⓐ Ⓑ Ⓒ Ⓓ       42 Ⓐ Ⓑ Ⓒ Ⓓ
13 Ⓐ Ⓑ Ⓒ Ⓓ       43 Ⓐ Ⓑ Ⓒ Ⓓ
14 Ⓐ Ⓑ Ⓒ Ⓓ       44 Ⓐ Ⓑ Ⓒ Ⓓ
15 Ⓐ Ⓑ Ⓒ Ⓓ       45 Ⓐ Ⓑ Ⓒ Ⓓ
16 Ⓐ Ⓑ Ⓒ Ⓓ       46 Ⓐ Ⓑ Ⓒ Ⓓ
17 Ⓐ Ⓑ Ⓒ Ⓓ       47 Ⓐ Ⓑ Ⓒ Ⓓ
18 Ⓐ Ⓑ Ⓒ Ⓓ       48 Ⓐ Ⓑ Ⓒ Ⓓ
19 Ⓐ Ⓑ Ⓒ Ⓓ       49 Ⓐ Ⓑ Ⓒ Ⓓ
20 Ⓐ Ⓑ Ⓒ Ⓓ       50 Ⓐ Ⓑ Ⓒ Ⓓ
21 Ⓐ Ⓑ Ⓒ Ⓓ       51 Ⓐ Ⓑ Ⓒ Ⓓ
22 Ⓐ Ⓑ Ⓒ Ⓓ       52 Ⓐ Ⓑ Ⓒ Ⓓ
23 Ⓐ Ⓑ Ⓒ Ⓓ       53 Ⓐ Ⓑ Ⓒ Ⓓ
24 Ⓐ Ⓑ Ⓒ Ⓓ       54 Ⓐ Ⓑ Ⓒ Ⓓ
25 Ⓐ Ⓑ Ⓒ Ⓓ       55 Ⓐ Ⓑ Ⓒ Ⓓ
26 Ⓐ Ⓑ Ⓒ Ⓓ       56 Ⓐ Ⓑ Ⓒ Ⓓ
27 Ⓐ Ⓑ Ⓒ Ⓓ       57 Ⓐ Ⓑ Ⓒ Ⓓ
28 Ⓐ Ⓑ Ⓒ Ⓓ       58 Ⓐ Ⓑ Ⓒ Ⓓ
29 Ⓐ Ⓑ Ⓒ Ⓓ       59 Ⓐ Ⓑ Ⓒ Ⓓ
30 Ⓐ Ⓑ Ⓒ Ⓓ       60 Ⓐ Ⓑ Ⓒ Ⓓ

# Complete Practice TOEFL Test Answer Sheet

**Name** (print) _____

Choose only one answer for each question. Carefully fill in the oval corresponding to the answer you choose so that the letter inside the oval cannot be seen. Completely erase any other marks you may have made. Choose only one answer for each question.

| CORRECT | WRONG | WRONG | WRONG | WRONG |
|---|---|---|---|---|
| Ⓐ Ⓑ ⬛ Ⓓ | Ⓐ Ⓑ Ⓧ Ⓓ | Ⓐ Ⓑ Ⓒ Ⓓ | Ⓐ Ⓑ ⊖ Ⓓ | Ⓐ Ⓑ Ⓓ |

## SECTION 1

1 Ⓐ Ⓑ Ⓒ Ⓓ
2 Ⓐ Ⓑ Ⓒ Ⓓ
3 Ⓐ Ⓑ Ⓒ Ⓓ
4 Ⓐ Ⓑ Ⓒ Ⓓ
5 Ⓐ Ⓑ Ⓒ Ⓓ
6 Ⓐ Ⓑ Ⓒ Ⓓ
7 Ⓐ Ⓑ Ⓒ Ⓓ
8 Ⓐ Ⓑ Ⓒ Ⓓ
9 Ⓐ Ⓑ Ⓒ Ⓓ
10 Ⓐ Ⓑ Ⓒ Ⓓ
11 Ⓐ Ⓑ Ⓒ Ⓓ
12 Ⓐ Ⓑ Ⓒ Ⓓ
13 Ⓐ Ⓑ Ⓒ Ⓓ
14 Ⓐ Ⓑ Ⓒ Ⓓ
15 Ⓐ Ⓑ Ⓒ Ⓓ
16 Ⓐ Ⓑ Ⓒ Ⓓ
17 Ⓐ Ⓑ Ⓒ Ⓓ
18 Ⓐ Ⓑ Ⓒ Ⓓ
19 Ⓐ Ⓑ Ⓒ Ⓓ
20 Ⓐ Ⓑ Ⓒ Ⓓ
21 Ⓐ Ⓑ Ⓒ Ⓓ
22 Ⓐ Ⓑ Ⓒ Ⓓ
23 Ⓐ Ⓑ Ⓒ Ⓓ
24 Ⓐ Ⓑ Ⓒ Ⓓ
25 Ⓐ Ⓑ Ⓒ Ⓓ
26 Ⓐ Ⓑ Ⓒ Ⓓ
27 Ⓐ Ⓑ Ⓒ Ⓓ
28 Ⓐ Ⓑ Ⓒ Ⓓ
29 Ⓐ Ⓑ Ⓒ Ⓓ
30 Ⓐ Ⓑ Ⓒ Ⓓ
31 Ⓐ Ⓑ Ⓒ Ⓓ
32 Ⓐ Ⓑ Ⓒ Ⓓ
33 Ⓐ Ⓑ Ⓒ Ⓓ
34 Ⓐ Ⓑ Ⓒ Ⓓ
35 Ⓐ Ⓑ Ⓒ Ⓓ
36 Ⓐ Ⓑ Ⓒ Ⓓ
37 Ⓐ Ⓑ Ⓒ Ⓓ
38 Ⓐ Ⓑ Ⓒ Ⓓ
39 Ⓐ Ⓑ Ⓒ Ⓓ
40 Ⓐ Ⓑ Ⓒ Ⓓ
41 Ⓐ Ⓑ Ⓒ Ⓓ
42 Ⓐ Ⓑ Ⓒ Ⓓ
43 Ⓐ Ⓑ Ⓒ Ⓓ
44 Ⓐ Ⓑ Ⓒ Ⓓ
45 Ⓐ Ⓑ Ⓒ Ⓓ
46 Ⓐ Ⓑ Ⓒ Ⓓ
47 Ⓐ Ⓑ Ⓒ Ⓓ
48 Ⓐ Ⓑ Ⓒ Ⓓ
49 Ⓐ Ⓑ Ⓒ Ⓓ
50 Ⓐ Ⓑ Ⓒ Ⓓ

## SECTION 2

1 Ⓐ Ⓑ Ⓒ Ⓓ
2 Ⓐ Ⓑ Ⓒ Ⓓ
3 Ⓐ Ⓑ Ⓒ Ⓓ
4 Ⓐ Ⓑ Ⓒ Ⓓ
5 Ⓐ Ⓑ Ⓒ Ⓓ
6 Ⓐ Ⓑ Ⓒ Ⓓ
7 Ⓐ Ⓑ Ⓒ Ⓓ
8 Ⓐ Ⓑ Ⓒ Ⓓ
9 Ⓐ Ⓑ Ⓒ Ⓓ
10 Ⓐ Ⓑ Ⓒ Ⓓ
11 Ⓐ Ⓑ Ⓒ Ⓓ
12 Ⓐ Ⓑ Ⓒ Ⓓ
13 Ⓐ Ⓑ Ⓒ Ⓓ
14 Ⓐ Ⓑ Ⓒ Ⓓ
15 Ⓐ Ⓑ Ⓒ Ⓓ
16 Ⓐ Ⓑ Ⓒ Ⓓ
17 Ⓐ Ⓑ Ⓒ Ⓓ
18 Ⓐ Ⓑ Ⓒ Ⓓ
19 Ⓐ Ⓑ Ⓒ Ⓓ
20 Ⓐ Ⓑ Ⓒ Ⓓ
21 Ⓐ Ⓑ Ⓒ Ⓓ
22 Ⓐ Ⓑ Ⓒ Ⓓ
23 Ⓐ Ⓑ Ⓒ Ⓓ
24 Ⓐ Ⓑ Ⓒ Ⓓ
25 Ⓐ Ⓑ Ⓒ Ⓓ
26 Ⓐ Ⓑ Ⓒ Ⓓ
27 Ⓐ Ⓑ Ⓒ Ⓓ
28 Ⓐ Ⓑ Ⓒ Ⓓ
29 Ⓐ Ⓑ Ⓒ Ⓓ
30 Ⓐ Ⓑ Ⓒ Ⓓ
31 Ⓐ Ⓑ Ⓒ Ⓓ
32 Ⓐ Ⓑ Ⓒ Ⓓ
33 Ⓐ Ⓑ Ⓒ Ⓓ
34 Ⓐ Ⓑ Ⓒ Ⓓ
35 Ⓐ Ⓑ Ⓒ Ⓓ
36 Ⓐ Ⓑ Ⓒ Ⓓ
37 Ⓐ Ⓑ Ⓒ Ⓓ
38 Ⓐ Ⓑ Ⓒ Ⓓ
39 Ⓐ Ⓑ Ⓒ Ⓓ
40 Ⓐ Ⓑ Ⓒ Ⓓ

## SECTION 3

1 Ⓐ Ⓑ Ⓒ Ⓓ
2 Ⓐ Ⓑ Ⓒ Ⓓ
3 Ⓐ Ⓑ Ⓒ Ⓓ
4 Ⓐ Ⓑ Ⓒ Ⓓ
5 Ⓐ Ⓑ Ⓒ Ⓓ
6 Ⓐ Ⓑ Ⓒ Ⓓ
7 Ⓐ Ⓑ Ⓒ Ⓓ
8 Ⓐ Ⓑ Ⓒ Ⓓ
9 Ⓐ Ⓑ Ⓒ Ⓓ
10 Ⓐ Ⓑ Ⓒ Ⓓ
11 Ⓐ Ⓑ Ⓒ Ⓓ
12 Ⓐ Ⓑ Ⓒ Ⓓ
13 Ⓐ Ⓑ Ⓒ Ⓓ
14 Ⓐ Ⓑ Ⓒ Ⓓ
15 Ⓐ Ⓑ Ⓒ Ⓓ
16 Ⓐ Ⓑ Ⓒ Ⓓ
17 Ⓐ Ⓑ Ⓒ Ⓓ
18 Ⓐ Ⓑ Ⓒ Ⓓ
19 Ⓐ Ⓑ Ⓒ Ⓓ
20 Ⓐ Ⓑ Ⓒ Ⓓ
21 Ⓐ Ⓑ Ⓒ Ⓓ
22 Ⓐ Ⓑ Ⓒ Ⓓ
23 Ⓐ Ⓑ Ⓒ Ⓓ
24 Ⓐ Ⓑ Ⓒ Ⓓ
25 Ⓐ Ⓑ Ⓒ Ⓓ
26 Ⓐ Ⓑ Ⓒ Ⓓ
27 Ⓐ Ⓑ Ⓒ Ⓓ
28 Ⓐ Ⓑ Ⓒ Ⓓ
29 Ⓐ Ⓑ Ⓒ Ⓓ
30 Ⓐ Ⓑ Ⓒ Ⓓ
31 Ⓐ Ⓑ Ⓒ Ⓓ
32 Ⓐ Ⓑ Ⓒ Ⓓ
33 Ⓐ Ⓑ Ⓒ Ⓓ
34 Ⓐ Ⓑ Ⓒ Ⓓ
35 Ⓐ Ⓑ Ⓒ Ⓓ
36 Ⓐ Ⓑ Ⓒ Ⓓ
37 Ⓐ Ⓑ Ⓒ Ⓓ
38 Ⓐ Ⓑ Ⓒ Ⓓ
39 Ⓐ Ⓑ Ⓒ Ⓓ
40 Ⓐ Ⓑ Ⓒ Ⓓ
41 Ⓐ Ⓑ Ⓒ Ⓓ
42 Ⓐ Ⓑ Ⓒ Ⓓ
43 Ⓐ Ⓑ Ⓒ Ⓓ
44 Ⓐ Ⓑ Ⓒ Ⓓ
45 Ⓐ Ⓑ Ⓒ Ⓓ
46 Ⓐ Ⓑ Ⓒ Ⓓ
47 Ⓐ Ⓑ Ⓒ Ⓓ
48 Ⓐ Ⓑ Ⓒ Ⓓ
49 Ⓐ Ⓑ Ⓒ Ⓓ
50 Ⓐ Ⓑ Ⓒ Ⓓ
51 Ⓐ Ⓑ Ⓒ Ⓓ
52 Ⓐ Ⓑ Ⓒ Ⓓ
53 Ⓐ Ⓑ Ⓒ Ⓓ
54 Ⓐ Ⓑ Ⓒ Ⓓ
55 Ⓐ Ⓑ Ⓒ Ⓓ
56 Ⓐ Ⓑ Ⓒ Ⓓ
57 Ⓐ Ⓑ Ⓒ Ⓓ
58 Ⓐ Ⓑ Ⓒ Ⓓ
59 Ⓐ Ⓑ Ⓒ Ⓓ
60 Ⓐ Ⓑ Ⓒ Ⓓ

# Complete Practice TOEFL Test Answer Sheet

**Name** (print) _____

Choose only one answer for each question. Carefully fill in the oval corresponding to the answer you choose so that the letter inside the oval cannot be seen. Completely erase any other marks you may have made. Choose only one answer for each question.

| CORRECT | WRONG | WRONG | WRONG | WRONG |
|---------|-------|-------|-------|-------|
| Ⓐ Ⓑ ● Ⓓ | Ⓐ Ⓑ Ⓧ Ⓓ | Ⓐ Ⓑ Ⓒ Ⓓ | Ⓐ Ⓑ ⊖ Ⓓ | Ⓐ Ⓑ Ⓒ Ⓓ |

## SECTION 1

1 Ⓐ Ⓑ Ⓒ Ⓓ
2 Ⓐ Ⓑ Ⓒ Ⓓ
3 Ⓐ Ⓑ Ⓒ Ⓓ
4 Ⓐ Ⓑ Ⓒ Ⓓ
5 Ⓐ Ⓑ Ⓒ Ⓓ
6 Ⓐ Ⓑ Ⓒ Ⓓ
7 Ⓐ Ⓑ Ⓒ Ⓓ
8 Ⓐ Ⓑ Ⓒ Ⓓ
9 Ⓐ Ⓑ Ⓒ Ⓓ
10 Ⓐ Ⓑ Ⓒ Ⓓ
11 Ⓐ Ⓑ Ⓒ Ⓓ
12 Ⓐ Ⓑ Ⓒ Ⓓ
13 Ⓐ Ⓑ Ⓒ Ⓓ
14 Ⓐ Ⓑ Ⓒ Ⓓ
15 Ⓐ Ⓑ Ⓒ Ⓓ
16 Ⓐ Ⓑ Ⓒ Ⓓ
17 Ⓐ Ⓑ Ⓒ Ⓓ
18 Ⓐ Ⓑ Ⓒ Ⓓ
19 Ⓐ Ⓑ Ⓒ Ⓓ
20 Ⓐ Ⓑ Ⓒ Ⓓ
21 Ⓐ Ⓑ Ⓒ Ⓓ
22 Ⓐ Ⓑ Ⓒ Ⓓ
23 Ⓐ Ⓑ Ⓒ Ⓓ
24 Ⓐ Ⓑ Ⓒ Ⓓ
25 Ⓐ Ⓑ Ⓒ Ⓓ
26 Ⓐ Ⓑ Ⓒ Ⓓ
27 Ⓐ Ⓑ Ⓒ Ⓓ
28 Ⓐ Ⓑ Ⓒ Ⓓ
29 Ⓐ Ⓑ Ⓒ Ⓓ
30 Ⓐ Ⓑ Ⓒ Ⓓ
31 Ⓐ Ⓑ Ⓒ Ⓓ
32 Ⓐ Ⓑ Ⓒ Ⓓ
33 Ⓐ Ⓑ Ⓒ Ⓓ
34 Ⓐ Ⓑ Ⓒ Ⓓ
35 Ⓐ Ⓑ Ⓒ Ⓓ
36 Ⓐ Ⓑ Ⓒ Ⓓ
37 Ⓐ Ⓑ Ⓒ Ⓓ
38 Ⓐ Ⓑ Ⓒ Ⓓ
39 Ⓐ Ⓑ Ⓒ Ⓓ
40 Ⓐ Ⓑ Ⓒ Ⓓ
41 Ⓐ Ⓑ Ⓒ Ⓓ
42 Ⓐ Ⓑ Ⓒ Ⓓ
43 Ⓐ Ⓑ Ⓒ Ⓓ
44 Ⓐ Ⓑ Ⓒ Ⓓ
45 Ⓐ Ⓑ Ⓒ Ⓓ
46 Ⓐ Ⓑ Ⓒ Ⓓ
47 Ⓐ Ⓑ Ⓒ Ⓓ
48 Ⓐ Ⓑ Ⓒ Ⓓ
49 Ⓐ Ⓑ Ⓒ Ⓓ
50 Ⓐ Ⓑ Ⓒ Ⓓ

## SECTION 2

1 Ⓐ Ⓑ Ⓒ Ⓓ
2 Ⓐ Ⓑ Ⓒ Ⓓ
3 Ⓐ Ⓑ Ⓒ Ⓓ
4 Ⓐ Ⓑ Ⓒ Ⓓ
5 Ⓐ Ⓑ Ⓒ Ⓓ
6 Ⓐ Ⓑ Ⓒ Ⓓ
7 Ⓐ Ⓑ Ⓒ Ⓓ
8 Ⓐ Ⓑ Ⓒ Ⓓ
9 Ⓐ Ⓑ Ⓒ Ⓓ
10 Ⓐ Ⓑ Ⓒ Ⓓ
11 Ⓐ Ⓑ Ⓒ Ⓓ
12 Ⓐ Ⓑ Ⓒ Ⓓ
13 Ⓐ Ⓑ Ⓒ Ⓓ
14 Ⓐ Ⓑ Ⓒ Ⓓ
15 Ⓐ Ⓑ Ⓒ Ⓓ
16 Ⓐ Ⓑ Ⓒ Ⓓ
17 Ⓐ Ⓑ Ⓒ Ⓓ
18 Ⓐ Ⓑ Ⓒ Ⓓ
19 Ⓐ Ⓑ Ⓒ Ⓓ
20 Ⓐ Ⓑ Ⓒ Ⓓ
21 Ⓐ Ⓑ Ⓒ Ⓓ
22 Ⓐ Ⓑ Ⓒ Ⓓ
23 Ⓐ Ⓑ Ⓒ Ⓓ
24 Ⓐ Ⓑ Ⓒ Ⓓ
25 Ⓐ Ⓑ Ⓒ Ⓓ
26 Ⓐ Ⓑ Ⓒ Ⓓ
27 Ⓐ Ⓑ Ⓒ Ⓓ
28 Ⓐ Ⓑ Ⓒ Ⓓ
29 Ⓐ Ⓑ Ⓒ Ⓓ
30 Ⓐ Ⓑ Ⓒ Ⓓ
31 Ⓐ Ⓑ Ⓒ Ⓓ
32 Ⓐ Ⓑ Ⓒ Ⓓ
33 Ⓐ Ⓑ Ⓒ Ⓓ
34 Ⓐ Ⓑ Ⓒ Ⓓ
35 Ⓐ Ⓑ Ⓒ Ⓓ
36 Ⓐ Ⓑ Ⓒ Ⓓ
37 Ⓐ Ⓑ Ⓒ Ⓓ
38 Ⓐ Ⓑ Ⓒ Ⓓ
39 Ⓐ Ⓑ Ⓒ Ⓓ
40 Ⓐ Ⓑ Ⓒ Ⓓ

## SECTION 3

1 Ⓐ Ⓑ Ⓒ Ⓓ
2 Ⓐ Ⓑ Ⓒ Ⓓ
3 Ⓐ Ⓑ Ⓒ Ⓓ
4 Ⓐ Ⓑ Ⓒ Ⓓ
5 Ⓐ Ⓑ Ⓒ Ⓓ
6 Ⓐ Ⓑ Ⓒ Ⓓ
7 Ⓐ Ⓑ Ⓒ Ⓓ
8 Ⓐ Ⓑ Ⓒ Ⓓ
9 Ⓐ Ⓑ Ⓒ Ⓓ
10 Ⓐ Ⓑ Ⓒ Ⓓ
11 Ⓐ Ⓑ Ⓒ Ⓓ
12 Ⓐ Ⓑ Ⓒ Ⓓ
13 Ⓐ Ⓑ Ⓒ Ⓓ
14 Ⓐ Ⓑ Ⓒ Ⓓ
15 Ⓐ Ⓑ Ⓒ Ⓓ
16 Ⓐ Ⓑ Ⓒ Ⓓ
17 Ⓐ Ⓑ Ⓒ Ⓓ
18 Ⓐ Ⓑ Ⓒ Ⓓ
19 Ⓐ Ⓑ Ⓒ Ⓓ
20 Ⓐ Ⓑ Ⓒ Ⓓ
21 Ⓐ Ⓑ Ⓒ Ⓓ
22 Ⓐ Ⓑ Ⓒ Ⓓ
23 Ⓐ Ⓑ Ⓒ Ⓓ
24 Ⓐ Ⓑ Ⓒ Ⓓ
25 Ⓐ Ⓑ Ⓒ Ⓓ
26 Ⓐ Ⓑ Ⓒ Ⓓ
27 Ⓐ Ⓑ Ⓒ Ⓓ
28 Ⓐ Ⓑ Ⓒ Ⓓ
29 Ⓐ Ⓑ Ⓒ Ⓓ
30 Ⓐ Ⓑ Ⓒ Ⓓ

31 Ⓐ Ⓑ Ⓒ Ⓓ
32 Ⓐ Ⓑ Ⓒ Ⓓ
33 Ⓐ Ⓑ Ⓒ Ⓓ
34 Ⓐ Ⓑ Ⓒ Ⓓ
35 Ⓐ Ⓑ Ⓒ Ⓓ
36 Ⓐ Ⓑ Ⓒ Ⓓ
37 Ⓐ Ⓑ Ⓒ Ⓓ
38 Ⓐ Ⓑ Ⓒ Ⓓ
39 Ⓐ Ⓑ Ⓒ Ⓓ
40 Ⓐ Ⓑ Ⓒ Ⓓ
41 Ⓐ Ⓑ Ⓒ Ⓓ
42 Ⓐ Ⓑ Ⓒ Ⓓ
43 Ⓐ Ⓑ Ⓒ Ⓓ
44 Ⓐ Ⓑ Ⓒ Ⓓ
45 Ⓐ Ⓑ Ⓒ Ⓓ
46 Ⓐ Ⓑ Ⓒ Ⓓ
47 Ⓐ Ⓑ Ⓒ Ⓓ
48 Ⓐ Ⓑ Ⓒ Ⓓ
49 Ⓐ Ⓑ Ⓒ Ⓓ
50 Ⓐ Ⓑ Ⓒ Ⓓ
51 Ⓐ Ⓑ Ⓒ Ⓓ
52 Ⓐ Ⓑ Ⓒ Ⓓ
53 Ⓐ Ⓑ Ⓒ Ⓓ
54 Ⓐ Ⓑ Ⓒ Ⓓ
55 Ⓐ Ⓑ Ⓒ Ⓓ
56 Ⓐ Ⓑ Ⓒ Ⓓ
57 Ⓐ Ⓑ Ⓒ Ⓓ
58 Ⓐ Ⓑ Ⓒ Ⓓ
59 Ⓐ Ⓑ Ⓒ Ⓓ
60 Ⓐ Ⓑ Ⓒ Ⓓ

# Complete Practice TOEFL Test Answer Sheet

**Name** (print)_____

Choose only one answer for each question. Carefully fill in the oval corresponding to the answer you choose so that the letter inside the oval cannot be seen. Completely erase any other marks you may have made. Choose only one answer for each question.

| CORRECT | WRONG | WRONG | WRONG | WRONG |
|---|---|---|---|---|
| Ⓐ Ⓑ ⬤ Ⓓ | Ⓐ Ⓑ Ⓧ Ⓓ | Ⓐ Ⓑ Ⓒ Ⓓ | Ⓐ Ⓑ ⊖ Ⓓ | Ⓐ Ⓑ Ⓒ Ⓓ |

## SECTION 1

1  Ⓐ Ⓑ Ⓒ Ⓓ
2  Ⓐ Ⓑ Ⓒ Ⓓ
3  Ⓐ Ⓑ Ⓒ Ⓓ
4  Ⓐ Ⓑ Ⓒ Ⓓ
5  Ⓐ Ⓑ Ⓒ Ⓓ
6  Ⓐ Ⓑ Ⓒ Ⓓ
7  Ⓐ Ⓑ Ⓒ Ⓓ
8  Ⓐ Ⓑ Ⓒ Ⓓ
9  Ⓐ Ⓑ Ⓒ Ⓓ
10 Ⓐ Ⓑ Ⓒ Ⓓ
11 Ⓐ Ⓑ Ⓒ Ⓓ
12 Ⓐ Ⓑ Ⓒ Ⓓ
13 Ⓐ Ⓑ Ⓒ Ⓓ
14 Ⓐ Ⓑ Ⓒ Ⓓ
15 Ⓐ Ⓑ Ⓒ Ⓓ
16 Ⓐ Ⓑ Ⓒ Ⓓ
17 Ⓐ Ⓑ Ⓒ Ⓓ
18 Ⓐ Ⓑ Ⓒ Ⓓ
19 Ⓐ Ⓑ Ⓒ Ⓓ
20 Ⓐ Ⓑ Ⓒ Ⓓ
21 Ⓐ Ⓑ Ⓒ Ⓓ
22 Ⓐ Ⓑ Ⓒ Ⓓ
23 Ⓐ Ⓑ Ⓒ Ⓓ
24 Ⓐ Ⓑ Ⓒ Ⓓ
25 Ⓐ Ⓑ Ⓒ Ⓓ
26 Ⓐ Ⓑ Ⓒ Ⓓ
27 Ⓐ Ⓑ Ⓒ Ⓓ
28 Ⓐ Ⓑ Ⓒ Ⓓ
29 Ⓐ Ⓑ Ⓒ Ⓓ
30 Ⓐ Ⓑ Ⓒ Ⓓ
31 Ⓐ Ⓑ Ⓒ Ⓓ
32 Ⓐ Ⓑ Ⓒ Ⓓ
33 Ⓐ Ⓑ Ⓒ Ⓓ
34 Ⓐ Ⓑ Ⓒ Ⓓ
35 Ⓐ Ⓑ Ⓒ Ⓓ
36 Ⓐ Ⓑ Ⓒ Ⓓ
37 Ⓐ Ⓑ Ⓒ Ⓓ
38 Ⓐ Ⓑ Ⓒ Ⓓ
39 Ⓐ Ⓑ Ⓒ Ⓓ
40 Ⓐ Ⓑ Ⓒ Ⓓ
41 Ⓐ Ⓑ Ⓒ Ⓓ
42 Ⓐ Ⓑ Ⓒ Ⓓ
43 Ⓐ Ⓑ Ⓒ Ⓓ
44 Ⓐ Ⓑ Ⓒ Ⓓ
45 Ⓐ Ⓑ Ⓒ Ⓓ
46 Ⓐ Ⓑ Ⓒ Ⓓ
47 Ⓐ Ⓑ Ⓒ Ⓓ
48 Ⓐ Ⓑ Ⓒ Ⓓ
49 Ⓐ Ⓑ Ⓒ Ⓓ
50 Ⓐ Ⓑ Ⓒ Ⓓ

## SECTION 2

1  Ⓐ Ⓑ Ⓒ Ⓓ
2  Ⓐ Ⓑ Ⓒ Ⓓ
3  Ⓐ Ⓑ Ⓒ Ⓓ
4  Ⓐ Ⓑ Ⓒ Ⓓ
5  Ⓐ Ⓑ Ⓒ Ⓓ
6  Ⓐ Ⓑ Ⓒ Ⓓ
7  Ⓐ Ⓑ Ⓒ Ⓓ
8  Ⓐ Ⓑ Ⓒ Ⓓ
9  Ⓐ Ⓑ Ⓒ Ⓓ
10 Ⓐ Ⓑ Ⓒ Ⓓ
11 Ⓐ Ⓑ Ⓒ Ⓓ
12 Ⓐ Ⓑ Ⓒ Ⓓ
13 Ⓐ Ⓑ Ⓒ Ⓓ
14 Ⓐ Ⓑ Ⓒ Ⓓ
15 Ⓐ Ⓑ Ⓒ Ⓓ
16 Ⓐ Ⓑ Ⓒ Ⓓ
17 Ⓐ Ⓑ Ⓒ Ⓓ
18 Ⓐ Ⓑ Ⓒ Ⓓ
19 Ⓐ Ⓑ Ⓒ Ⓓ
20 Ⓐ Ⓑ Ⓒ Ⓓ
21 Ⓐ Ⓑ Ⓒ Ⓓ
22 Ⓐ Ⓑ Ⓒ Ⓓ
23 Ⓐ Ⓑ Ⓒ Ⓓ
24 Ⓐ Ⓑ Ⓒ Ⓓ
25 Ⓐ Ⓑ Ⓒ Ⓓ
26 Ⓐ Ⓑ Ⓒ Ⓓ
27 Ⓐ Ⓑ Ⓒ Ⓓ
28 Ⓐ Ⓑ Ⓒ Ⓓ
29 Ⓐ Ⓑ Ⓒ Ⓓ
30 Ⓐ Ⓑ Ⓒ Ⓓ
31 Ⓐ Ⓑ Ⓒ Ⓓ
32 Ⓐ Ⓑ Ⓒ Ⓓ
33 Ⓐ Ⓑ Ⓒ Ⓓ
34 Ⓐ Ⓑ Ⓒ Ⓓ
35 Ⓐ Ⓑ Ⓒ Ⓓ
36 Ⓐ Ⓑ Ⓒ Ⓓ
37 Ⓐ Ⓑ Ⓒ Ⓓ
38 Ⓐ Ⓑ Ⓒ Ⓓ
39 Ⓐ Ⓑ Ⓒ Ⓓ
40 Ⓐ Ⓑ Ⓒ Ⓓ

## SECTION 3

1  Ⓐ Ⓑ Ⓒ Ⓓ
2  Ⓐ Ⓑ Ⓒ Ⓓ
3  Ⓐ Ⓑ Ⓒ Ⓓ
4  Ⓐ Ⓑ Ⓒ Ⓓ
5  Ⓐ Ⓑ Ⓒ Ⓓ
6  Ⓐ Ⓑ Ⓒ Ⓓ
7  Ⓐ Ⓑ Ⓒ Ⓓ
8  Ⓐ Ⓑ Ⓒ Ⓓ
9  Ⓐ Ⓑ Ⓒ Ⓓ
10 Ⓐ Ⓑ Ⓒ Ⓓ
11 Ⓐ Ⓑ Ⓒ Ⓓ
12 Ⓐ Ⓑ Ⓒ Ⓓ
13 Ⓐ Ⓑ Ⓒ Ⓓ
14 Ⓐ Ⓑ Ⓒ Ⓓ
15 Ⓐ Ⓑ Ⓒ Ⓓ
16 Ⓐ Ⓑ Ⓒ Ⓓ
17 Ⓐ Ⓑ Ⓒ Ⓓ
18 Ⓐ Ⓑ Ⓒ Ⓓ
19 Ⓐ Ⓑ Ⓒ Ⓓ
20 Ⓐ Ⓑ Ⓒ Ⓓ
21 Ⓐ Ⓑ Ⓒ Ⓓ
22 Ⓐ Ⓑ Ⓒ Ⓓ
23 Ⓐ Ⓑ Ⓒ Ⓓ
24 Ⓐ Ⓑ Ⓒ Ⓓ
25 Ⓐ Ⓑ Ⓒ Ⓓ
26 Ⓐ Ⓑ Ⓒ Ⓓ
27 Ⓐ Ⓑ Ⓒ Ⓓ
28 Ⓐ Ⓑ Ⓒ Ⓓ
29 Ⓐ Ⓑ Ⓒ Ⓓ
30 Ⓐ Ⓑ Ⓒ Ⓓ
31 Ⓐ Ⓑ Ⓒ Ⓓ
32 Ⓐ Ⓑ Ⓒ Ⓓ
33 Ⓐ Ⓑ Ⓒ Ⓓ
34 Ⓐ Ⓑ Ⓒ Ⓓ
35 Ⓐ Ⓑ Ⓒ Ⓓ
36 Ⓐ Ⓑ Ⓒ Ⓓ
37 Ⓐ Ⓑ Ⓒ Ⓓ
38 Ⓐ Ⓑ Ⓒ Ⓓ
39 Ⓐ Ⓑ Ⓒ Ⓓ
40 Ⓐ Ⓑ Ⓒ Ⓓ
41 Ⓐ Ⓑ Ⓒ Ⓓ
42 Ⓐ Ⓑ Ⓒ Ⓓ
43 Ⓐ Ⓑ Ⓒ Ⓓ
44 Ⓐ Ⓑ Ⓒ Ⓓ
45 Ⓐ Ⓑ Ⓒ Ⓓ
46 Ⓐ Ⓑ Ⓒ Ⓓ
47 Ⓐ Ⓑ Ⓒ Ⓓ
48 Ⓐ Ⓑ Ⓒ Ⓓ
49 Ⓐ Ⓑ Ⓒ Ⓓ
50 Ⓐ Ⓑ Ⓒ Ⓓ
51 Ⓐ Ⓑ Ⓒ Ⓓ
52 Ⓐ Ⓑ Ⓒ Ⓓ
53 Ⓐ Ⓑ Ⓒ Ⓓ
54 Ⓐ Ⓑ Ⓒ Ⓓ
55 Ⓐ Ⓑ Ⓒ Ⓓ
56 Ⓐ Ⓑ Ⓒ Ⓓ
57 Ⓐ Ⓑ Ⓒ Ⓓ
58 Ⓐ Ⓑ Ⓒ Ⓓ
59 Ⓐ Ⓑ Ⓒ Ⓓ
60 Ⓐ Ⓑ Ⓒ Ⓓ

# SAMPLE TWE ANSWER SHEET

Note: This answer sheet shows the amount of writing space provided in the TOEFL Test.

Name _____     Topic _____

_____
_____
_____
_____
_____
_____
_____
_____
_____
_____
_____
_____
_____
_____
_____
_____
_____
_____
_____
_____
_____
_____
_____
_____
_____
_____
_____
_____